D1237100

From Taiwan to the World and Back

A Memoir of Ambassador Fu-chen Lo

榮町少年走天下：
羅福全回憶錄

陳柔縉執筆

Rou-jin Chen

Translated by
Yew Leong Lee

Proofread by
Lanny T. Chen

From Taiwan to the World and Back
A Memoir of Ambassador Fu-chen Lo

by **Rou-jin Chen**
Translated by **Yew Leong Lee**
Proofread by **Lanny T. Chen**

Distributor
Avanguard Publishing House
4F-3, No.153, Nong-an St., Jhongshan Dist., Taipei 104, Taiwan.
Tel: (886-2)2586-5708
Fax: (886-2)2586-3758
http://www.avanguard.com.tw
e-mail: a4791@ms15.hinet.net

Printed in Taiwan
ISBN 978-957-801-766-5

CONTENTS

Introduction

A few years ago, I began to write a novel that was triggered by the narrative of my great-uncle, the youngest brother of my paternal grandfather, whom I met for the first time when I was in my twenties. His life experiences would exercise considerable influence over the subject of my book. I only came to know him as an adult because for many decades he and his wife were blacklisted by Taiwan's KMT, Chiang Kai-shek's Chinese Nationalist party, and were forced into exile. He wandered the world, working for the UN as an advisor and teaching at universities, always thinking about the homeland he left behind. Much later, when we were finally able to sit down together to a long overdue family dinner, he told us anecdotes from his past, like the time he gathered with Kim Dae-jung and "Ninoy" Aquino. Kim had been banished from Korea, Aquino from the Philippines, and my great-uncle from Taiwan of course. The three exiled men all happened to be scattered across Massachusetts, taking refuge in different universities. Over heavy glasses of amber-colored drinks they would tell each other: whoever returned from exile to their homeland first would play host to the other two.

My great-uncle, like most Taiwanese activists, was blacklisted because he was outspoken about the KMT's corruptions and the crimes the party committed against the Taiwanese people. He was too young in 1947 to be a direct victim of the 2-2-8 incident that killed thousands of Taiwanese, but he would belong to that generation that came of age in the vicious climate of the White Terror. My great-uncle devoted his life to the cause of Taiwanese independence and that made him an eyesore to the KMT party. Although KMT first fled to Taiwan because they were defeated by their communist rival in the fight for control of China, they would eventually side with their former enemy's view that Taiwan was a renegade province of China. This was because they did not consider Taiwan their real home and they still harbored nationalistic feelings about being Chinese. This mentality was the cause for many crimes they committed in Taiwan. Taiwan's greatest tragedy is that until recently, it has never been ruled by people who considered it their home. One colonizer after another — the Portuguese, the Dutch, the Spanish, the French, Imperial China — each had a hand in this little island that was so strategically located, at the intersection of the continental and maritime frontiers. Then came the Japanese who, though it couldn't be denied that they were also self-serving as all colonizers were, at least unified and modernized the island. With the defeat of Japan in WWII came the KMT — and this perhaps was the most biting betrayal of all, for the KMT had posed themselves as liberators not colonizers, fellow blood brothers who planned to incorporate Taiwan into the new Democratic China, but instead would place the island under the longest Martial Law in history.

I did not know of my great-uncle's existence and I did not know this history. I was born on this island and lived there until I was thirteen and every year after I visited at least biannually. How was it possible for me to be so ignorant? But it was possible, very possible under the circumstances in which we lived. The KMT had effectively brutalized and censored the Taiwanese people in the 1940s and 50s. Almost all the native intellectuals and dissidents were either murdered or jailed. The following generation of dissidents such as my great-uncle would be forced into exiled if they wanted to avoid a similar fate. People who had lived through that history were too scarred and too scared to speak of it. Meanwhile, in school they taught us an entirely different history. My parents' generation were fined during classes if they slipped and spoke in Taiwanese instead of Mandarin. Chiang Kai-shek was heralded a hero and a founding father in history textbooks. People bowed their heads and worked hard to make their lives better in more "practical" ways. It was thus that Taiwan became the economic miracle of Asia and by the time I was born, the island enjoyed a booming economy and a high standard of living.

In 1988, Chiang Ching-kuo, Chiang Kai-shek's son, died. Between the father and son they had "elected" themselves to seven presidential terms that lasted more than forty years all in the name of democracy. Then a most miraculous thing happened. A native son — born and raised in Taiwan, had managed to rise through the ranks of KMT, gained the party's support, and was named president. Lee Teng-hui would gradually steer the direction of Taiwan's governance so that opposition parties were allowed to thrive, and when he stepped down in 2000, a candidate from the Democratic Progressive Party was elected president by the people in a real, open election. The peaceful transfer of power from one opposition party to another was at last a sign of democracy in practice rather than in name, and Taiwan became the democratic success story in the world. Life for people such as my great-uncle came full circle. He came home and was awarded the post of Ambassador to Japan.

When I finally sat down with my great-uncle at a family dinner in Taipei, I asked him for recommendations for books on Taiwanese history. He gave me several, including a battered copy of Formosa Betrayed, a book chronicling the 2-2-8 incident by an American attaché stationed in Taiwan who witnessed the massacre. The original version in English is now hard to come by because after its first printing, the KMT bought the copyright and halted the distribution. Before my great-uncle gave me his only copy which had traveled with him all these years, I had tried to obtain the only one listed in the system at Columbia University, where I was studying at the time. But it was permanently checked-out.

It is an incredible change of events, but this is not the happy ending. Taiwan will always live under the menace of nearby China. Although Taiwan is a de facto independent nation — we have our own passport, own government, own president, and have never been ruled by the People's Republic of China, the PRC continues to insist that Taiwan is a renegade province of China. Perhaps it is an example of how the world works that while heralding Taiwan as the Democratic success story, most nations are careful not to overstep China's constraints when it comes to Taiwan, calling our ambassadors "Cultural Representatives," our athletes at the Olympics representatives of "Chinese Taipei" (to get a sense of how ridiculous this sounds, try calling the U.S.A. "English Washington").

The drama and nuances of this history make this memoir an indispensable read for the English-speaking world. But what makes it so engrossing is the unique perspective of the man through which we can witness these events. He is an idealist who has the wisdom and patience to allow for the practical to catch up to the ideal, a perpetual optimistic who inspires rather than embitters, a worldly man without pretension, literary, humorous, and most of all, a fantastic story-teller.

Eva Lou

Eva Lou is a writer with a BA from Brown University and a MFA from Columbia University. Her short stories and poems have been anthologized in America and France. Her first book, *Rapture/d'extases*, was published by Editions Lanore in France in a bilingual edition. Her novel-in-progress is a finalist of the James Jones First Novel Award.

Preface

I am a Taiwanese through and through. I left Taiwan shortly after completing my university studies, not expecting to stay abroad for 45 years before coming home for good.

My initial reason for leaving the country was to evade the oppressive atmosphere of Taiwan under martial law. I went to the United States to study at the University of Pennsylvania in the 1960s. Then, determined to be a free man, I gave up my R.O.C. passport, thereby crossing the point of no return. The founder of the University of Pennsylvania, Benjamin Franklin, was also one of the co-signers of the United States Declaration of Independence. Although people from the United States and England share a same language and racial background, Americans nevertheless wanted to establish their own sovereignty as a country; this was their God-given right. When the United States was declared independent, the first modern nation state was born. Living in exile in the 1960s at that time, Chin-fun and I drew comfort from this Declaration. This time was also the beginning of a new life for me.

In the 1970s, after I presented a paper at the World Geographical Union's annual conference, an official from the United Nations approached me asking me if I would be willing to work for the UN Center for Regional Development (UNCRD) that they had recently set up in Japan. This would be another turning point in my life. I would spend cumulatively 25 years in Japan over the course of my life. The time spent in both pre-war and post-war Japan led me to developing quite a deep personal history with the country. As a young child, I had lived in Japan for five years before the War, and three years as a graduate student for my Master's degree. From 1990 to 2000, I spent another ten years in Tokyo working for the United Nations University, which was followed by four years from 2000 to 2004 as Taiwan's top representative to Japan, I helped to foster bilateral relations between Taiwan and Japan — a most meaningful opportunity of a lifetime.

In the 1970s when I first started my work at the United Nations, East Asian countries one after another entered a period of high economic growth. Japan was first, followed by the four East Asian "dragons": Taiwan, Korea, Hong Kong, and Singapore. The 1990s saw the rise of China and, with it, the Southeastern Asian countries. In the past decade, India's economy has also begun to soar. As economic development advisor to these countries, I experienced a firsthand account of this boom that has been hailed as the "East Asia Miracle" by the World Bank.

It wasn't only an economic shift that these countries experienced but also a deeply societal one; every country inexorably entered the era of modernization. It was a great blessing for me to have witnessed and contributed to it all firsthand. Such historical events include the assassination of South Korean President Park Chung-hee in the 1980s followed by the Gwangju Uprising; the People Power Revolution in 1986 that overturned the Marcos government in the Philippines; the democratization of Indonesia sparked by the transition from pro-Communist Sukarno to pro-US Suharto. I've also seen the chaos before the collapse of Iran's monarchy in 1978; and the change in Pakistan's government. In November of 1980, I visited Beijing for the first time and saw how China put the Gang of Four on trial. On the first anniversary of the Tiananmen Square incident, I happened to be giving a lecture at Peking University, so I had the opportunity to talk with the students while their university's main gate was blockaded by soldiers from the People's Liberation Army. When the Cold War ended, I personally witnessed the upheaval that each Eastern European country went through. I saw how my friends, my students, as well as the general public faced up to the change. All these historical moments contributed to my precious life experience.

During the ten years from 1990 to 2000 that I spent at the United Nations University, the United Nations held its first ever Earth Summit in Rio de Janerio, Brazil. This UN summit announced that the new challenge facing mankind was Earth's sustainable development — this would become one of my core research subjects at the university. My other main research topic was a problem faced by the world's "mega cities," i.e. the problem of a great influx of rural populations into these large cities, partly due to the population explosion in third world countries. On the other hand, due to the maturation of an international economic integration that saw the formation of "world cities" and network of cities controlling major internationalized economies. For both these research topics, I collaborated with scholars and organizations from both developed and developing countries; as such, I traveled all over the world.

For a time, I felt great regret that I could not be by Chin-fun's side as she raised our children in the United States, thousands of miles away. This was the period that Tse-hsin (Ted) and Tse-yen (David) were attending high school and university which is, without a doubt, a period of adolescence where one is most impressionable and when one is most in need of his father's guidance and the warmth of family life. At the end of 1984, after I decided to go back to Asia, I received an offer for a full-time professorship from the University of Pennsylvania's Regional Science Department. Even so, my heart was still pointing me towards helping developing countries, so I flew across the ocean alone to pursue my calling.

Long-distance calls each weekend and postcards from Paris and Argentina cannot make up for my being an absent father to my children. Fortunately for me, Chin-fun was and is a strong woman, who ably took up her wifely duties of looking after the household and the children in my absence.

My children finished their studies smoothly and found jobs in

American companies. One after the other, they were sent to Tokyo for work. During my time at the United Nations University and my four years as Taiwan's top representative to Japan, our family was finally reunited in Tokyo. It was also during this time that my children both got married and our family of four grew to six. Our family gatherings then were the happiest moments of our lives. Ten years later, my grandchildren are now using many different languages to talk to us. After leaving Taiwanese soil for over forty years, my family has become an international one.

In the summer of 2004, I finally came back to Taiwan to stay for good. From my tenth-story apartment, I have a grand view of Tatun Mountain, Yangming Mountain, as well as the undulating peaks of many mountains. The sunset view is especially touching. Protesters bearing blue or green colors represent KMT or opposite parties fill the streets down below from time to time. Evidently, modern society, like the society I grew up with, is still inherently unjust. Nevertheless as a democracy, Taiwan has made leaps and bounds. The era of military rule is over, replaced by that of a new democracy. Like many other Asian countries, Taiwan is now well on its way to becoming a true modern democracy.

Over the last twenty years, the economic growth of China, just across the Taiwan Strait from us, has been a cause for joy. To think that the May Fourth Movement of students in Peking back in 1919 had proclaimed that science and democracy could save China. Today, only Science has prevailed. The Chinese still have quite a long way to go as far as democracy is concerned. Compared to China, Taiwan is truly fortunate in this respect. The Taiwan that I've returned to after forty years of being abroad is a brand-new Taiwan.

Chin-fun loves the opening of Martin Luther King's "I Have a Dream" speech. The word 'dream' can also be interpreted as an ideal, the road striving towards that ideal, a road sign. This book represents that road we've walked together, but it's also a record of our everyday lives.

I'm very grateful to Chen Rou-jin for her professionalism and her dedication in completing this book. For their attentiveness, I want to thank my editors at Commonwealth Publishing, Hsu Yao-yun, Chou Su-yun and Lu Yi-sui. Finally, I'm grateful to Asymptote's editor-in-chief Lee Yew-leong for translating this book into English.

Lo Fu-chen
1 July, 2013

01

A Three-Year Old Giving Away the Bride

ONE DAY, when I was just three years old, I was dressed as a miniature grownup. I became what people back then, in 1938, called "a princely young heir": dressed from head to toe in a Western-style suit with a gold-buttoned double breasted vest. Attached to one of these buttons was a gold chain that led elegantly into a fold of my vest where a pocket watch lay hidden.

That day was my cousin Hsu Shou-luan's (許秀鑾) big wedding day. She was the eldest daughter of my Fourth Aunt — on my father's side. According to tradition, it should have been from the Hsu household that the wedding procession, in all its splendor, should

Born into an affluent family, little Lo Fu-chen dressed in trendy sailor suit, belt and all, even more than 70 years ago.

have started. But Fourth Aunt's husband, a doctor, had died early, leaving Fourth Aunt widowed at the tender age of well within her twenties. Because she had been closest to my father, it was decided that she and her dependents would move in with us. Since Shou-luan had more or less been brought up under our roof, she naturally wanted to be "married out" of the Lo household.

In the 1930s, the Taiwanese still set a great emphasis on marrying within the same class of people. My cousin Shou-luan, who had studied Medicine at a university in Tokyo, should thereby naturally be matched with someone with an exceptional background. The bridegroom was Lai Shun-chang (賴巽章), a gifted student who had studied law at Chūō University — also in Tokyo. His father, Lai Yu-ruo (賴雨若), was a bigger deal than even us in Chiayi city. Since he was the first lawyer to ever come out of these parts, he was very well known here.

Lai Yu-ruo had been born to a wealthy family. In fact his father, Lai Shi-guan (賴世觀), was a xiucai [1] (certified first degree scholar) under Qing dynasty [2], which was by no means an easy feat. When Taiwan came under Japanese rule in 1895, Lai Yu-ruo was already 17 or 18 years old. Normally, someone like him who had studied Confucian teachings and knew nothing but poetry and the old

---

1 The imperial examination was a civil service examination system in Imperial China to select candidates for the state bureaucracy. It was divided into three tiers, from county to provincial to court exams. Xiucai is one who passed the imperial examination at the county level.

2 The Qing dynasty (1644-1911) was the last of the Imperial dynasties of China.

Chinese classics, would have idled at home in the new era, living off of rental income. Lai Yu-ruo, however, decided to pursue a different fate altogether.

At the age when one enters university today, Lai Yu-ruo enrolled into the National Language Institute of Learning set up by the Japanese — to study their language. He quickly picked it up and, upon graduation, became a court interpreter.

Once you found a stable job in the government, you usually slowed down your learning or stopped altogether. Lai Yu-ruo had more ambition than that. When the Japanese Governor-General Office in Taiwan opened its civil service exams to Taiwanese people for the first time in 1905, he signed up to take the exam and passed. He was appointed as the Secretary in the Courts. But he was still not satisfied. He wanted to be able to defend his fellow countrymen in a court of law — to become a lawyer. To pursue his dream, he left to study law at a Japanese university. This took him three years. The first two times

In this wedding picture, sitting to the sides of the newly-weds are wedding hosts representing each families. On the groom's side is the tall, high-position attorney Lai Yu-ruo. On the bride's side is little 3-year-old Lo Fu-chen, hand held by his aunt.

he sat in for the bar exams, he failed; but in 1923, he tried for a third time, and succeeded. Out of the 42 newly appointed lawyers in all of Japan that year, three [3] were of Taiwanese origin; other than Lai Yu-ruo, Tsai Shi-gu [4] was also one. They were among Taiwan's pioneering class.

Becoming a lawyer took Lai Yu-ruo 16 years of blood and sweat; he was 45 years old when his dream was finally fulfilled. Although the journey had caused much hardship, the outcome proved that where there is a will there is a way, and he earned the respect of Chiayi's people. In 1931, by the time Shou-luan returned from Japan to get married, Lai Yu-ruo had acquired even greater stature as a member of the Tainan City Council. This position was similar to a postwar Provincial Councilman, except that one was appointed to the Council by government officials, not by the electorate.

Lai Yu-ruo's daughter's wedding was therefore a big event for all of Chiayi. After the wedding ceremony, everyone gathered for the customary photo-taking to remember the day by. Taking up the last few rows of the photo were Chiayi's most important and powerful businessmen and government officials, standing tall on their feet. Seated in the first row were the family members of the bride and the

---

[3] The three Taiwanese that passed the 1923 Japanese bar exam and became lawyers were Chen Tseng-fu (陳增福), Lai Yu-ruo and Tsai Shi-gu.

[4] Tsai Shi-gu (蔡式穀, 1884-1951) was very active in Taiwanese Autonomy Movement against the Japanese. He also took part in Taiwan Culture Association's numerous political and social reform activities.

groom. Lai Yu-ruo, seated to the left of the groom, represented the groom's family. At 60, he emanated both power and authority. On the other hand, to the right of the bride, representing the family on the bride's side, was a tiny, insignificant little three-year-old me.

It would be unfathomable to Westerners that I could be the person giving away the bride at the age of three, but according to the Taiwanese tradition, this arrangement was not unusual.

The Taiwanese society of the 1930's privileged the male. According to this tradition, the bride's mother was deemed incapable to give away her daughter. Instead a male must be found to take on this role. By right, it should have fallen upon her uncle, my father. However, my father was stricken by a contagious disease when I was ten months old, and died in a matter of days. As the only son of my father, I was his natural replacement so I ended up taking the seat next to the bride that day.

Age is no consideration in Taiwan's traditional scheme. One's position in the family tree hinges upon his or her relationship to the rest. A one-year old infant might be a forty-year old's "granduncle" and a twenty-year old woman might call a two-year old girl "grand-aunt." In Taiwan, there is nothing unusual about this; it is as natural as can be.

In my childhood, I was often given grown-up roles. Apart from giving a bride away at the age of three, I became the head of the household when I was merely thirteen months old. My mother and my older sister lived in said household, under my responsibility.

02

An Aunt Becomes a Mother,
a Mother Becomes an Aunt

RECORDED IN MY HOUSEHOLD CERTIFICATE
BOOKLET is an anomaly that deserves mentioning. In the column
for Mother is the name "Chu Lian" (朱蓮) and just beside it is the
name "Chen Chou" (陳醜), also with the word "Mother" scribbled
above it. This may strike you as strange, but it was merely another
reflection of our strange customs back then.

In the year 1736, two hundred years before I was born, my
ancestors sailed from Zhang Zhou in Fujian Province and set foot on
Taiwanese soil for the first time. Around this time, Chinese people
were leaving China, not only to go to Taiwan, but also to Malaysia
and Thailand (80 percent of Bangkokians have roots tracing back to
Fujian province).

There is a one-hundred-year-old hotel called E&O Hotel, in
Penang, Malaysia. Tombstones in the cemetery near it bear dates
from the early 18th century, around the same time as the year my
ancestors first arrived in Taiwan.

They settled their roots in Chiayi because it was a city (which
was called Chuluo at that time). The Los settled in O-A-Lai, an area
south of the city. Newly established in foreign soil, the migrants did
not know one another; there was much fighting. Unrest came to
characterize the Taiwanese society of that era. In the Lo family, there
is a story which has survived through many generations. According
to this tale, our entire village back then comprised of Los. Among
them was a feisty person called Lo An (羅安), who stood up for the
clan but ended up getting killed instead. The clan built a temple in

his honor, and the words "Lo An Saved Ten Thousand Men, but Ten Thousand Men Could Not Have Saved Lo An" were engraved in the temple.

In this new land, my ancestors endured great hardship and by the 19th century, managed to amass great wealth. It was said however that our ancestors were ill-tempered. Landowners in the past deemed themselves superior to everyone else. Once, on the first day of the Lunar New Year, a tenant farmer bearing customary gifts of chicken and vegetables paid a visit to my ancestor's home, hoping to get the lease on his land extended. A Qing Dynasty scholar (xiucai), my grandfather, or Ah Gong as he was called, happened to be sitting in the main hall of the ancestral home. He was deeply absorbed in a book, reading the lines out loud to himself, when the creaking sound of the approaching tenant's shoulder pole snapped him out of his reverie. Incensed, he leapt up and kicked the tenant as if he were a dog. Infuriated by such humiliation, the tenant went back to Minsyong, bought lots of betel nuts and bribed other farmers to join him in giving up my grandfather's land. That was how all forty hectares of paddy field went fallow the following year. A saying in the family goes: Ah Gong with his bad temper "felled forty hectares of paddy with one foot." At that time in rural Chiayi and Tainan, if you owned ten hectares of land, you were already considered wealthy. Forty hectares was really quite a lot. Each year this story is retold when it came time to commemorate Ah Gong. The food offerings would be plentiful. But as if to prevent Ah Gong's bad temper from passing down to me, my mother forbade me to eat any of it.

My father, on the other hand was born at the end of the Qing Dynasty, and grew up during the peaceful Japanese colonial period. He moved into Chiayi city and established himself in the busy downtown area.

Called Lo Cheng (羅程) (Lo Zhang Cheng (羅章程) according to family genealogy), he was the youngest of three brothers, and he was without an heir. His second elder brother Lo Ya (羅雅), on the other hand, had a household filled with many children. After his first wife died, he took a second. All in all, he had four sons and two daughters; I was the last of these six. At the time of my birth, my biological father Lo Ya was 48 years old and my little uncle Lo Cheng was 44 — he had not yet bore any children, which was a big problem.

According to Chinese tradition, every scion of a family must have his own male heir. Even if your brother had already produced one, the onus was still on you to have an heir to extend the family name. Like relay runners who must not drop the baton, for dropping the baton would mean that the race is over. Each master of the house must procure its own male heir, to prevent the house from "collapsing". This was to be ensured by any means. In cases where it was not biologically possible to produce an heir, the Chinese sometimes cheated by adopting the children of other relatives.

My little uncle Lo Cheng had married my aunt in 1919, and having tried for more than ten years, they were by then resigned to their infertility. After my biological mother became pregnant for

Lo was adopted by his uncle before he reached his first birthday.

the fourth time, my aunt begged of her, "If it's a son, you must give him to me!" Given the situation, my biological mother could hardly say no. Therefore, when I was seven months old, on the first day of January, I was taken to my aunt's home.

Thus it came to be that while I was still in baby clothes, the entire course of my life changed.

I would henceforth call my father my second uncle, my little uncle my father, my mother my second aunt, and my little aunt my mother.

This dramatic switch of fate might not sit so easily with people

Although Lo was adopted by his uncle, his biological mother lived just across the street. Therefore, he still enjoyed her tender care through his childhood.

nowadays — one might be bitter about being separated from one's natural birth parents, I suppose. But the truth was my life did not change for the worse as a result. On the contrary, I was the recipient of even more affection.

My biological mother had given birth to two pairs of sons and daughters. My adoptive father Lo Cheng said to her, "Since you are giving me a son, why not a daughter as well?" Thus my sister, Chao-rong (昭容), who was only two years older than me, also followed me into a different household. Remaining at the side of my biological mother were Fu-hui (福慧), my biological brother and Chao-yi (昭儀), my biological sister.

Who would have thought that fate would continue to deal blows to my biological mother?

Extremely gifted, Fu-hui was seven years older than me. In fifth grade, he already knew how to construct a darkroom, and develop his own pictures. He gained admission into the very prestigious Taihoku High School — not only Taiwan's sole high school at that time (its campus on Heping Road is now used by National Taiwan Normal University) but also a playing ground for future elites. Lee Teng-hui (李登輝, President of Taiwan from 1988 to 2000) was among its many famous alumni. Admission into this school was seen as a ticket into the nine Imperial Universities open only to those living in Japan and its colonial territories. The university entrance exam was particularly competitive. 40 people passed the year Fu-hui enrolled in school; of these, 34 were Japanese and only six Taiwanese.

Fu-hui happily packed his bags for Taipei. Before the first day of school, however, he suddenly came down with some illness related to his gallbladder. He was quickly admitted into Taipei Hospital. Second Uncle's second son Fu-yue (my biological half-brother) happened to be working in this hospital as Dr. Du Chong-ming's [1] assistant, and he took care of him. On the second day, Second Uncle, back in Chiayi, was reading a book when he came across the distressing words "father crying over his son," which he took as omen. Sure enough, the next day, news of Fu-hui's sudden death reached Chiayi. Fu-hui's body was cremated in National Taiwan University Hospital. I don't know why they never gave him a normal earth burial. I still remember being brought to the hospital and using a pair of chopsticks to pick up his ashes. I was only five years old then.

Fu-hui's departure left Second Aunt beyond grief. No one at home dared mention his name. The words "Fu-hui" seem to have been cremated along with his body. I never heard his name again.

When Second Aunt lost her only son, I became the substitute child and the one on whom she would dote. That was how I became a child with two mothers.

---

1 Du Chong-ming (杜聰明, August 25, 1893 ~ February 25, 1986) was the first doctor of Medical Sciences (equivalent to Ph.D.) of Taiwan. He received his degree from Kyoto Imperial University in 1933. His pharmacology research lab was the cradle of medical research in Taiwan. In 1954, he founded Kaohsiung Medical College (now a university) and became the first president of the college.

03

A Hundred Years Ago, Mother Was Once a Telephone Operator

THINKING BACK ON MY YOUTH NOW, it seemed as if I had always been precocious, assuming roles that were incommensurate with my age. At the age of six, for example, I moved to Japan and became an overseas student.

At the end of 1941, Japan bombed Pearl Harbor, declaring war on the United States. Before that, Japan had been fighting China for years. One might say that Taiwan was also at war. However, Mother had brought me to Tokyo not to evade war (after all Japan was at war too, like Taiwan) but so that I could get a good education. Nothing was more important than a good education, and she wanted only the very best for me.

Compared to the other women of the same generation, Mother was considered liberal. She had also experienced more than they had. She had not been sheltered growing up. Her father ran a mountain products business and also worked as a security escort for goods in transit. Around the end of the Qing Dynasty, there were still many mountain bandits. Traders worried that their goods would end up in those bandits' hands. As a result, people like my grandfather were in demand. They needed him to safeguard their goods. When I was in fifth grade, I gave a massage to my seventy-something grandfather. He showed me the tools he used to make his living — two knives. He even pointed to a deep scar on his shoulder, explaining that it'd come from a bullet shot by a mountain bandit. Coming from such a background, Mother must have naturally inherited a wild spirit.

She was also intelligent. She graduated top of her class in primary

Lo Fu-chen's mother is an independent modern woman. She was a career woman before WWII, and managed her own hotel after the war. The picture showed her walking on Tokyo street, in the 1940s.

school. She could even speak Japanese. It was a pity that she was born at a time when higher education was still withheld from the female gender. Chiayi's High School for Girls had not yet been set up. There was no way for her to continue her education. Around the time she finished primary school, Taiwan was embarking on a series of reforms to modernize its Qing-era villages. Society was on the brink of change as she left school. She was among Taiwan's pioneering career women.

Mother was born in 1900. That year, Taiwan was introduced to the telephone. 15 years later, because of her outstanding grades, and at the encouragement of her teacher, she confidently applied to be one of the telephone operators that Chiayi's Post Office advertised.

At that time, women mostly helped out with farmwork if they

100 years ago, telephones were not equipped with switchboards, and needed "exchange operators" to help connect the speaking parties. In the picture, the 3 on the left are female Japanese exchange operators, and the 3 on the right are Taiwanese exchange operators.

were poor or they stayed at home without lifting a finger if they were rich. Either way, it was not acceptable for women to take on work outside. The so-called "career women" back then were tea-pickers in the North, or working within the very small contingent of teachers. In the 1910s, no female typist existed yet, or female bus conductors, or saleswomen, or factory seamstresses. As a phone operator, my mother blazed the trail for future career women.

The telephone was an object that was both modern and Western. One might be tempted to imagine my mother wearing a starched white blouse to work, which was not the case. In the mid-1910s, Mother dressed the way all Taiwanese women dressed, in the Chinese-style attire of the Qing and the Ming Dynasties. She wore a blouse so long that it draped over her rear and a skirt so long that it covered her ankles. Cloth shoes, embroidered in silk, peeked out beneath the hem of her skirt.

My adoptive mother was a capable, savvy woman, different from my biological mother. They were classmates in primary school; one was the top student in the class, the other second. They had gotten along very well, and now they were sisters-in-law. Normally, though they might be in the same room, my biological mother would be doing needlework while my adoptive mother, on the other hand, busied herself with accounts or talked business with outsiders. Still, at the end of the day, she was a mother through and through. Raising a child was at the center of everything she did. She did not aspire to start a business of her own nor did she care for status or wealth.

When Mother (left) married into the Lo family during the 1910s,
Taiwanese women still dressed in cheongsam and long skirts.

When I was small I often complained of stomachaches; the doctor told Mother that she should give me foods that grew in cold area. She always remembered this piece of advice well.

At that time, cousin Shou-luan was studying medicine in Tokyo. Mother wanted my sister and me to go to Japan so that we would receive a better education and have a brighter future ahead of us.

In May, 1941, we boarded the ship and left for Japan. My mother was 41 years old; I was 6 then, my sister 8. Single-handedly, she took

Lo moved from Chiayi to Denenchōfu, Tokyo, with mother and sister to start life anew. The rented house was huge with a small Shinto shrine and a shrine gate in the yard. Their next door neighbor was the chairman of Morinaga Milk Candy Co.

Fu-chen and sisters in front of their home at Sakaemachi, Chiayi.

us across the sea by ship to settle down in a foreign land.

During Japanese colonial times, Taiwan continued to send its students to Japan for further studies. In 1925, there were some 800 Taiwanese overseas students in Japanese universities. By the time I was born in 1935, this figure had grown to more than 2000. The former editor-in-chief of the Mandarin Daily Newspaper Hong Yen-qiu (洪炎秋) also received his education in Japan, but in a difficult way. His father opposed the Japanese and forbade him to go to Japan. In an act of desperation, Hong Yen-qiu stole money from his father's bank account and escaped to Japan where a better education awaited. The opera singer Lyu Quan-sheng (呂泉生) had been inspired by Natsume Sōseki's[1] Sanshiro when he followed the male protagonist's footsteps to start life afresh in Tokyo. In the 1940s, Lee Teng-hui, graduated from Taihoku High School, and chose to study abroad at Kyoto Imperial University. I was just a six year old amid this growing wave of studying abroad in Japan. Mother took me by my hand and made that jump with her. To this day, I still think of that decision as my mother's greatest achievement, unthinkable for a widowed woman back then.

---

[1] Natsume Sōseki (夏目漱石, February 9, 1867 ~ December 9, 1916) was a Japanese novelist of the Meiji period (1868-1912). He is best known for his novels *Kokoro, Botchan, I Am a Cat* and his unfinished work *Light and Darkness*. He is often considered the greatest writer in modern Japanese history, and his portrait appeared on the front of the Japanese 1000-yen note.

04

Father Founded a Transportation Company and Even Built Bridges

To BE AN OVERSEAS STUDENT, you had to be from a rich family. I was no exception.

Lo Cheng, my father, was by all measures a successful businessman. I don't know the details of his education, but I do know that he was once a teacher at a public school in Meishan (formerly Xiaomei). During the Japanese colonial period, only those who had come graduated from Sotokufu National Language School or the High School for Girls could enter the occupation. My guess is that because my grandfather Lo Yu-dian (羅豫典) and my fifth granduncle had both been certified scholars (xiucais) under Qing Dynasty, and the Los of my father's generation and for the past generations before that had sat for the Imperial Civil Service exams, it was likely that my father was qualified to teach Chinese in a public school on account of a Chinese studies background[1].

At the end of the 1910s, Chiayi was on the cusp of exciting major developments. It had been a sleepy small city of just over 20,000 people. In the spring of 1919, the Chiayi School for Agriculture and Forestry (now a part of National Chiayi University) was declared open. A year after, work began on the Chianan Reservoir, a mammoth construction project that would span ten years. Its offices and work dormitories were based in Chiayi. These projects contributed to the dazzling development of Chiayi as a major city and attracted a great

---

1 The Japanese writing system is a combination of three character types: Hiragana, used for native Japanese words; Katakana, used for borrowed foreign words; and Kanji, Chinese characters. That's why my father, a Chinese language expert, could teach in a Japanese school.

influx of people. Before the end of the 1920s, Chiayi had doubled its population, making it Taiwan's fourth largest city after Taipei, Kaohsiung and Tainan, a position it managed to hold on to till the end of the Japanese colonial period. Back then, it was even more prosperous than Keelung, Taichung, and Hsinchu.

Word of Chiayi's population growth spread. Chiayi soon became known as the city of opportunity. Many moved to Chiayi, hoping to make it big. In 1922, from a nearby city called Puzi came a man, Lin Bao (林抱). According to Mother, he hadn't had much of a formal education, but he was street-smart and full of ideas. He saw a notice for a Court Sale, and reported it to my father. The two of them began a business trading foreclosed property, even, at one point, bidding for a cinema.

After this, Father ventured into a series of new and trendy undertakings. For example, in 1924, he was the first to import over ten machines specializing in manufacturing socks. More and more women were taking on work outside their homes with each passing day. Female fashion was undergoing a revolution. Chinese-style dresses were getting shorter and shorter, and the newly-revealed ankles beneath the hems of the dresses needed to be covered as a result. Female students also began to abandon the long skirts of the Meiji period for more modern knee-long skirts, which meant that they too needed socks to cover their ankles. Naturally Father's business proved lucrative. According to news reports, Chiayi saw six factories specializing in sock production grow within the next two years. These factories produced more than a hundred dozen pairs of socks every day, making it a combined output of nearly 1500 pairs of socks a day, which would be sold to all of southern Taiwan.

In 1925, cities like Chiayi and Xiluo were suddenly infected with a "rice futures" craze — not unlike the futures trading we know today. Rice was the subject of speculation. People who traded in "rice futures" were committed to investments pegged to a future price of the grain. The "Chiayi Chamber of Commerce" Father founded also ventured into this business, not only as an agent earning commission from each trade but also as a deader. The price of rice was very volatile, which meant only the smartest traders could survive. By 1927, the number of stockbroking houses in Puzi, for example, shrank from the original seven or eight to just two, one of which was Father's. This was testament to Father's business acumen. In 1934, the city of Dajia in Taichung saw a spate of bankruptcies related to rice futures trading that resulted in a few suicides. This caused a newspaper to remark that rice futures created wealth for a few; for the rest, it had brought only downfall. Father luckily belonged to the former camp. One day, after Mother dreamt of fireworks raining down from the sky, the winnings of 70,000 Japanese yens [2] fell in Father's lap. To place this in context, a policeman or a bank employee earned a monthly salary of only 20 yens at that time; ten years of work translated into 2,400

---

[2] Between 1910 to late 1930s the Japanese yen remained a rather stable currency. It traded against the dollar in single digits. But by 1945, the rate had inflated to 1 USD against 60 yens.

yens. To win 70,000 yens overnight was thus an unimaginably large sum.

A decisive man, Father knew to quit when ahead. In 1927, he closed his stockbroking business, and launched into a completely different direction with the opening of a bus transportation company.

Nowadays, next to airplanes, subways and express rail, bus transportation must sound pedestrian. But it must be remembered that it was only in 1912 that Taiwan saw its first automobile, brought in by a Japanese hotel owner based in Taipei. Soon after that, a cinema owner, also based in Taipei, bought a few buses and began

Lo's aunt Chen Hau (holding the steering wheel), both modern and spirited, is the 1st woman to get a driver's license in Chiayi.

a transportation business. In 1914, he expanded his business into Chiayi and used two buses to ply the short 15 kilometers between Xingang and Chiayi. That's when the people of Chiayi laid eyes upon their first automobile. But at that time, how many could afford to try such a newfangled and monstrous object? For a journey of a mere 15 kilometers, walking sufficed back then. Hence, the bus transportation company quickly went out of business in Chiayi.

For a while after that, car ownership increased at a snail's pace. Twenty years later, there were only forty automobiles in all of Tainan State, which included Chiayi, Tainan and Yunlin. At the end of 1927, when Father bought a bus in Tainan and drove it back to Chiayi, the vehicle was still as rare as a UFO sighting. According to Mother, because there were no bridges at that time, Father had to drive on the sandy river banks of Bahjang River. Fortunately it was in the thick of winter when the water had dried up. Back in the countryside of Chiayi, a boy who had never seen an automobile before was so scared by bus that he jumped into a ditch. Seeing the boy, the driver braked. In the next moment, the mother of the kid had pulled him out of the ditch and was "recovering his soul" via chanting and going through various gestures next to the bus. One wonders if she thought of the bus as some kind of God or Demon.

After they bought the bus, father and Lin Boa went on to apply for a business license and got it in no time. However, the onus of road-building fell onto those with cars, i.e., those who would actually use the roads. At that time, only Father and his business partner

Chiayi Automobile Company, founded by Lo Fu-chen's father, was the largest bus company in Chiayi before WWII. Lo was held by his mother (front row). Those standing in the back dressed in uniforms were bus drivers.

Lin Bao wanted to operate a transportation company from Chiayi, therefore, the responsibility of building roads fell on them. The first route they planned connected Chiayi and Beigang where there was a Matsu Temple [3]. This bus service would be in great demand among the temple's many worshippers. Along the way, however, the

---

3 Matsu is the Chinese goddess of the sea who is said to protect fishermen and sailors. Matsu is widely worshiped in southern coastal China and Taiwan. There are over 500 Matsu temples in Taiwan.

bus would have to make two river crossings: that of the Niuchou River just leaving Chiayi city, and then that of Beigang River before entering Beigang. Father paid out of his own pocket to construct a seventy-meter long wooden bridge over Niuchou River, and another over Beigang River. Including these bridges, over 20 kilometers of road were developed within a year. On the first day of 1928, Father's bus transportation company officially opened for business.

According to the elders, bus company owners eighty years ago were mostly concerned about the threat of flooding: at stake were the bridges that they had built. In order to prevent them from being washed away, Father would get his workers to dismantle the bridges at the first sign of continuous heavy rain, and stored the wooden logs somewhere safe. Only after the rain had passed, would they reconstruct the bridges. Taking apart and putting back together these connectors — it was as if they were playing Legos, albeit with larger pieces. The very idea seemed to have a touch of magic, as if coming straight out of *1001 Nights* itself.

05

A
Celebrity's Dog Caused Me to Hit My Head against the Wall

FATHER'S BUS TRANSPORTATION COMPANY
FLOURISHED, with buses traveling the northwest route towards
Beigang and the northeast route towards Zhuqi. Second Uncle, who
ran a bicycle retail business under the auspices of "Taijia Chamber
of Commerce," set up "Datong Automobile Company" in 1930,
which sent buses Southwest towards Xinying and West towards
Suantou (known today as Chiayi's Liujiao). The business of the bus
transportation company was run out of their homes, situated in front
of Chiayi Main Station, in the fifth section of what the Japanese
called Sakae-Machi. Today it would be beside Zhongshan road.
Just a stone's throw away from the Main station, it was a convenient
location. Second Uncle lived at No. 31, Zhongshan Road, Father at
No.21, opposite each other, their homes flanking one road. I was
born in Second Uncle's home, and when it was decided that I would
live with my adoptive father, it was just a matter of being carried
across the street.

Father was a man with great ambition, but he did not want to
have to socialize with Japanese officials. On paper, Lin Bao was the
director of "Chiayi Automobile Bus Company." However, it was
Father who truly controlled the operations, and who was responsible
for buying and selling cars.

One year, Taiwan's Automobile Association sponsored my father
to go on a tour to learn about the Japanese automobile industry.
It was the first time he had been to Tokyo, and there, he had his
first experience dining at a fancy Western restaurant in the Imperial

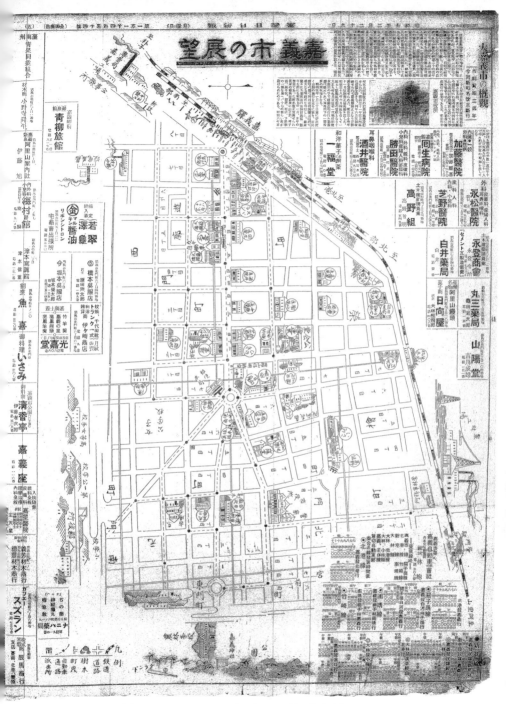

A full page 1932 newspaper advertisement. The dotted lines are
Chiayi Automobile's bus routes. The square on the bottom right
corner is the daily bus schedule.

Hotel. Like Taipei's Grand Hotel, Tokyo's Imperial Hotel was meant to host important visitors to the country. It was built in 1890, during the height of the Meiji Restoration Period, when the Japanese were unabashedly imitating everything about the West. In fact, the Minister of Foreign Affairs, Inoue Kaoru (井上馨), had said: "Let's make Japan a European country! Let's all be European!" With the blessings of the Japanese monarchy and some wealthy businessmen, he commissioned the very impressive and very Western Imperial Hotel opposite Hibiya Park. Imperial Hotel was, until after the war, the default choice of residence for all international celebrities paying a visit to Japan. In the 1930s, Babe Ruth [1], the king of home runs, and the deaf and blind author/educator Helen Keller [2] both stayed at the Imperial Hotel. In the 1950s, Marilyn Monroe [3] who visited Japan on her honeymoon also chose to check into the Imperial Hotel. Swarms of reporters crowded around her asking what she wore to sleep at night. Her ingenious reply? "Chanel No. 5," referring to the famous perfume. It was in that very hotel that she delivered the

---

[1] In November 1934, as the United States and Japan drifted toward war, a team of American League all-stars that included Babe Ruth, went to Japan. The all-stars stayed for a month, playing 18 games, spawning professional baseball in Japan, and spreading goodwill.

[2] Helen Keller (June 27, 1880 ~ June 1, 1968) visited Japan in 1937. During this trip, she was given an Akita pup as a present. When the pup died of canine distemper 6 months later, its brother was presented to Keller as an official gift from the Japanese government. Keller is credited with having introduced the Akita to the United States through these two dogs.

[3] Marilyn Monroe and Joe DiMaggio went to Japan for their honeymoon in February 1952. During the trip she took a four day detour to visit the U.S. Troops stationed in Korea.

famous repartee still known to many.

Western people would certainly feel at home walking into a Western hotel, but not my father. It was his first ever fine-dining experience at a Western restaurant. Seeing the table set with all manner of cutlery ranging in shape in size, he froze. But, as an experienced businessman, he adapted quickly. Upon his return to Taiwan, he said proudly to us that though he was caught off guard, he hadn't let any of his inexperience get the better of him. Out of the corner of his eyes, he slyly watched the person sitting next to and opposite him, and picked up whichever knife or fork that person picked up.

In his active years, new trends were being brought into Taiwan from all directions. To someone born and bred in Taiwan, it was like a country bumpkin experiencing the wonders of the city afresh. Many funny anecdotes inevitably resulted. Father's business partner Lin Bao was also at the center of many funny anecdotes that spread so far and wide that even my university classmates in Taipei had heard of them.

During the Japanese colonial period, everyone copied the Japanese. Answering the phone, we would even say *"moshi moshi"* instead of *"Wei-wei"* in Taiwanese. Lin Bao had his own modest way of answering the phone. He would go, *"Molosi, molosi, Sesha Lin Bao si,"* a beginning marked by a change of accent, followed by an ending that rhymed comically. *"Sesha Lin Bao si"* more or less meant "Your humble servant Lin Bao"; it was a memorable way of greeting a caller.

The most famous joke associated with Lin Bao centered on his proclivity for mispronunciation, for he had difficulty with languages. Invited to Japan to "*sisatsu*" (inspect) the automobile industry, he made it sound instead as if he was going to Japan to "*jisatsu*" (commit suicide). On his return, he meant to say that he would be "*soshiki*" (reorganizing) the company operations, but it came out as "*sōshiki*" (funeral rites) — and sounded like he would be mourning for someone upon his return.

It was hard to tell which of these anecdotes were true and which were false. Lin Bao had come to Chiayi by himself and became successful with only a primary school degree, even getting elected to the City Council. His ascendance was legendary. His fame inevitably invited jealous mockery. Some of the funny stories may have happened, but they may have also been fabricated. But I did in fact personally witness one famous Lin Bao anecdote.

After the war, as an eleven to twelve year old son of my father's, I received preferential treatment from Lin Bao. He gave me a special pass that I could flash upon boarding any of his buses to enjoy a free ride. This special treatment even extended to any companion as well. One day, my friend and I were on board a bus when it suddenly broke down due to engine failure. The bus driver sat, frowning. The army soldiers from China on board the bus got anxious, and made a lot of noise, but the bus driver only knew Taiwanese. Despite talking his mouth off, he couldn't get himself understood. At that time, one did not provoke military personnel. Someone rushed off to get Lin Bao, who immediately hurried to the scene, muttering to himself, "Why wouldn't anyone know how to say 'engine failure'?" From inside the bus, I saw a confident Lin Bao striding towards the Chinese soldiers, telling them: "bong bong bong — referring to the engine — sleeping," which immediately got his point across. There was no doubt that Lin Bao was a quick-witted person.

In another story related to Lin Bao, just before I left to study in Japan at the age of six, mother and I moved to Ximending's seventh section, to the right of the Main Station, next to Lin Bao. He kept a German shepherd, or a 'military dog', as it was called back then. I was small and short. The dog did not fear me and ran after me. Scared witless, I fled for my life, and ended up crashing into a wall, scarring my forehead. Though short-lived, this episode remains to date one of my most vivid memories of childhood. I will always remember it.

06

Eating the Rice Sent by Wang Yung-ching (王永慶)

AT CHIAYI'S XIMENDING, we lived next to another famous person — the businessman who would later become the Chairman of Formosa's Plastic Group. To many, Wang Yung-ching was the "God of Business." His enterprise, which had dealings all over the globe, had its humble beginnings in Chiayi.

Wang Yung-ching did not grow up in Chiayi; he was born in Taipei, Xindian. Like all youths at that time, he could either stay home and help with farmwork or he could find work outside — as a shop assistant or in some company as an odd job boy — what the Japanese called *kozukai* or *kozou*, or what the Taiwanese called *ginna gang*. So, around 1931, Wang Yung-ching left primary school, and like Lin Bao, moved down south to the prosperous new city of Chiayi, and, through the introduction of an uncle, became a *ginna gang* in a Japanese rice shop.

A year later, Wang Yung-ching ambitiously set up his own rice shop. He was only 16. One night at 2 am, a chef from a nearby inn came calling with an order for a bushel of rice to be delivered at once. Since he couldn't turn down the business, he got up to make the delivery, even though it was raining and he had no raincoat. He was thoroughly drenched by the time he got back. That night, he couldn't sleep because he was bothered by this thoughts: he only earned one sen (1 Japanese yen = 100 sens) for that one bushel; this business couldn't possibly be sustainable in the long run. The profit margin was laughably small. After all, at that time, a bar of Shiseido soap cost 10 sens and a tube of toothpaste 15 sens.

In his third year, Wang Yung-ching bought a machine and started his business of unshelling rice.

After a day in the factory, his entire body would be covered with white rice shavings. Although he could easily pop over to the Japanese public bath just next door for a hot, piping shower for 3 sens per bath, he'd rather stay at home and wash himself with tap water. This way, he felt as if he had earned an extra 3 bushels of rice every day! Over time, through thrift and hard work, he managed to amass a fortune. By the 1940s, he had saved up enough to buy 12 hectares of land in Yunlin, Dabei, with a business partner. Through sheer effort, he had finally become, "a landowner."

According to the research undertaken by Chiayi's Bureau of Culture, Wang Yung-ching's Wen Yi rice shop was located at No. 31, Ximending, Section 7, near the intersection of Guangning Road and Guangcai Road. Our family lived at No. 61 not far away. One of the drivers working for my father's bus transportation company was called Wang Zhen-po (王振波). He was a relative of Wang Yung-ching. Perhaps because of this connection, we would store the rice that we had harvested, set aside for our own consumption (i.e., the rice that hadn't been sold), in Wang Yung-ching's silos. Whenever we needed to make a withdrawal, we'd ask for it to be sent over. Wang Yung-ching was very good at keeping accounts, Mother once told me.

Through my early childhood, I would eat the rice that Wang Yung-ching had sent over, only knowing that I was eating the rice

Wang Zhen-po (middle), a relative of Wang Yung-ching, worked as a bus driver for Lo Fu-chen's (2nd from right) father's bus company during the Japanese colonial era.

of Wen Yi Rice Shop. I knew nothing about its boss. It wasn't until 1954, that I first met Wang Yung-ching. Mother was accompanying me to Taipei to enroll at National Taiwan University. By coincidence, Wang Yung-ching, riding a bicycle, spotted my mother and called out: "Mrs. Lo, where are you going?" That was when I first found out about Wang Yung-ching, the man who had been sending us rice all throughout my early childhood.

07

We Owned a Lake

At THE PEAK OF HIS BUSINESS, my father even owned a lake. Before our ancestors arrived in Taiwan, there was a scholar by the name of Chen Meng-lin (陳夢林) in Zhangzhou. He came to Taiwan under orders to write a report on Chiayi. He traveled all over Chiayi, and came to know the terrain intimately. North of the city, he discovered a lake of about 2,000 to 2,500 square meters. Since in all his research, he hadn't heard about any plan to develop a lake, he deduced that this natural landscape must have been there from time immemorial of heaven and earth. Seeing its water lilies "of unknown origin," he decided to give it the name "Lake of Northern Fragrance". From that point on, aspiring poets would come to the "Lake of Northern Fragrance" and celebrate its beauty with words. A shortlist of the best six landscapes in all of Chiayi would certainly include the "Lake of Northern Fragrance." If eight landscapes would be permitted, then it was surely possible to make a case for the lake in autumn, featuring its water lilies.

According to family legend, our family had once owned the lake during the Qing Dynasty, but then lost it. After my father and my uncle made their fortune, they intentionally reacquired the lake. They planted trees and flowers all around it, constructed a wooden bridge over it, and set up a pavilion by the edge. They also provided row boats, which could be rented by anyone. Boating was a popular form of leisure in the 1930s. In fact, when my father-in-law returned home for summer from his studies at Kyoto University, he often took my mother-in-law out to the lake on dates.

The Lake of Northern Fragrance used to be Chiayi's popular resort in the 30s. Boating in the lake was really romantic. After the war, the lake dried up and fell into a state of neglect. But recently, Chiayi government has restored it to its original state.

According to Mother, Father loved the Lake of Northern Fragrance very much; and he often spent whole afternoons by the lake, soaking in its carefree atmosphere, swaddling me in his arms. Only in the evening would a driver be sent to take us home.

The Lake of Northern Fragrance was only one of many properties that Father and Lin Bao owned. Father left the running of the boating business up to Lin Bao. In 1939, Chiayi's municipal government wanted the lake back. They'd give my family a compensation of 70,000 Japanese yens for it. We had no choice — and so the lake was lost again. However, this large sum of money, coupled with the combined rental incomes from our fields and the forty houses that we owned, meant that we could make the move to Tokyo comfortably.

08

A Six-Year-Old Overseas Student

MY LIFE IN TOKYO as an overseas student began quietly and peacefully in Denenchōfu.

We rented a house at Hisakahara, an area now known as Unokichō at Denenchōfu's center. My cousin Shou-luan lived only two to three kilometers apart from us, just a few subway stops away. Today, Denenchōfu is considered an elite suburb and this was still the case before the war. It had very pleasant surroundings and there was a stream (in which prawns lived) flowing through the area. One might compare the district to Tienmu of old Taipei.

We had a Japanese-style house and a Western style house. Both of them overlooked the same traditional courtyard. And once again, we lived next door to a famous person. Only a wall separated us from the Chairman of Morinaga Company, famous for its caramel candies.

In our courtyard was a large plum tree with persimmon trees on each side of it. In the summer, flowers would blossom on the plum tree. When they were done blooming, they became fruits to pluck. Autumn would follow, and it would be the persimmon trees that would be hanging with shiny yellow persimmons. We would take out the bamboo pole to pluck fruits from the trees. Although war was closing in surely, all of that was outside our peaceful courtyard. As a child, I did personally witness war and its effects, but my childhood was not the least bit scarred by any painful memory.

I had arrived in Japan in May, and Mother had enrolled me into Unokichō Kindergarten under the Japanese name: "Fukumoto Morio" (福本盛夫). We Los have for a while now used generational

Denenchōfu was already an elite suburb before the war.

Before the war, Tokyo was already very prosperous and well developed. It was a fad for Taiwanese youth to go there to study.

names. Father had the generational name of "Zhang" (章); I have the generational name of "Fu" (福); my children's the generational name "Tse" (澤). "Fukumoto" in Chinese means "originally Fu."

Years later, after I was appointed as Taiwan's ambassador to Japan, I received instructions from Tang Fei (唐飛), the head of the Executive Yuan, to host a welcome banquet in his name for the visiting Legislative Yuan delegation, headed by Wang Jin-pyng [1]. The delegation was on their way to Hokkaido for institution visits. At the dinner, I sat to the right of Wang Jin-pyng; Lo Fu-zhu (羅福助), a delegation member, sat two seats to his left. All of a sudden, Wang Jin-pyng turned to take a good look at Lo Fu-zhu, and then quickly turned his head to look at me. And as if a momentous realization dawned on him, he exclaimed: "The two of you are so alike!"

This didn't bode well. Although we were both in fact very tall with similar faces and our names were exactly the same except for one character, Lo Fu-zhu was notorious in the Legislative Yuan for his violent temper. In fact, under Chiang Ching-kuo's [2] military rule, when the National Police Agency did a "clean-up" of all the troublemakers, Lo Fu-zhu was among those locked up in prison.

So I asked Lo Fu-zhu, "Where are you from?" He said

---

1 Wang Jin-pyng (王金平, March 17, 1941 ~) is an influential Taiwanese politician. He was KMT party's Vice-Chairman from 2000 to 2005. Wang has been the Speaker of the Legislative Yuan since 1999.

2 Chiang Ching-kuo (蔣經國, April 27,1910 ~ January 13, 1988), was the son of Chiang Kai-shek. He succeeded his father to serve as Premier of the Republic of China between 1972 and 1978, and was the President of the ROC from 1978 till his death in 1988.

"Changhua." Like an accused pronounced innocent, I breathed a sigh of relief, saying: "Then we can't be from the same family. I was born in Chiayi. My family emigrated from Fujian Province more than 200 years ago." But Lo Fu-zhu countered, "Our family came from Chiayi." Ah! I still felt cursed. I managed to say, "Oh. Then we should get our DNAs checked."

Later, examining a sold family property record that covered with seals of over 60 names, I did in fact discover one "Lo Fu-zhu." Luckily, this relative did exist, and he did live in Chiayi. In short, he was not the Lo Fu-zhu I met that day from the Legislative Yuan.

09

Singing At The Top of Our Voices: "Chiang Kai-shek and Soong Mei-ling[1] Have Fled Into the Mountains"

---

1 Soong Mei-ling (宋美齡, March 5, 1898 ~ October 23, 2003) was a First Lady of the Republic of China, the wife of Generalissimo and President Chiang Kai-shek (蔣介石).

SEVEN MONTHS AFTER MY ARRIVAL IN TOKYO, Japan bombed Pearl Harbor, escalating World War II. A year later, when America first attacked Japan, I was at home. Most people's curiosity was at that time stronger than their fear. Everyone rushed outside to see what was going on. I kept shouting "Enemy planes are attacking! Enemy planes are attacking!"

Our music lessons in school began to take on an anti-American and anti-Chinese turn. One of the songs we were taught goes like this:

> Chiang Kai-Shek and Soong Mei-ling have fled into the mountains
> Oh Roosevelt, Roosevelt,
> We've gone after your disciple Churchill
> He's been knocked out and flattened!

My memory during lower primary school was very good; I also loved to sing. During wartime, the number of military songs must have been over a hundred. I knew all of them, more or less. I still remember the first song I was taught in primary school; it only had these lines:

> Everyone happily goes to school (みんなで勉強うれしいな)
> First graders (国民学校一年生)
> Everyone's happily doing exercises (みんなで体操うれしいな)
> First graders (国民学校一年生)

Japan could be the country with the most songs for children. During the Meiji Restoration period, music lessons were considered a very important component of modern Japanese education. Many schools started to teach their children English folk songs that they had adapted, replacing the English lyrics with Japanese ones. In effect, these English folk songs became songs for children. For example, the melody for"庭の千草"is adapted from an Irish folk song "The Last Rose of Summer."

Our house in Denenchōfu was much larger than that of the average Japanese. A female domestic helper had come with us from Chiayi. With her to keep the house in order, our day-to-day living was more comfortable than most others. At that time, Chen Tian-tsan (陳天燦), a cousin from my mother's side, whose mother had passed away, also lived with us. Mother enrolled him into an elite Japanese school so that he could go to university. One day, Tian-tsan brought me to Ginza. Wearing my student cap, I took large strides, happy as can be. It was very fashionable then to take pictures. There were people with cameras on the street, aiming them at us, then coming forward to sell us the pictures that they had taken. Whether we bought these photos or not was finally up to us. Since we were well-off, we did. Mother had also been similarly approached when shopping.

But as far what we wore and what we ate, we were not too different from the rest. During wartime, the government distributed the same rations to everybody, and all students had to wear uniforms.

Cousin (Chen Tian-tsan) took Lo for a stroll in Tokyo's Ginza area.
They were snapshot by a street photographer and left this rare
in-motion picture (taken in 1943). The line Tian-tsan was about
to step on was the streetcar track. On the background one can
see the classic street lamp and a hotel ad hanging alongside the
electric pole.

About a year after declaring war on the United States, Japan began to experience a shortage of commodities. Our family in Taiwan started sending us sugar in the mail. Since sugar was abundantly produced in Taiwan, sugar was just another commodity. However in Japan, sugar was quite uncommon. Mother could exchange the sugar for eggs, fruits and vegetables in the countryside. But the more precious the good, the greater greed it induced. Before long, our sugar started getting "lost in the mail." A needle was used to make a small hole in the envelope, and to extract all the contents from it. By the time the package reached us, it was as good as empty. My Taiwanese relatives outsmarted the dishonest mailman by making round sugar lumps each the size of a grape. To extract such sugar, you'd have to make a remarkably large, obvious hole. In this way, the theft was foiled.

With each day's passing, the standard of living deteriorated, and so did the taste of our white rice, which got mixed with soy pulp and wheat. At this time, pig liver was a source of unexpected solace. The Japanese did not eat pig innards. We Taiwanese on the other hand, prized pig liver for its nutritional value. To us, it was even better than pork.

I was only seven or eight years old at that time. I was carefully protected like a plant sheltered in a greenhouse — the temperature and humidity of its environment all controlled. Occasionally there would be a little variation in my environment, but this variation was limited to the taste of food. Little did I know that the small detail of

Well protected by Mother, Lo went through the war unscarred.

a change in the food was connected to a tremendous upheaval to the world outside.

10

Leaving Our Homes En Masse for Schooling in a Hot Springs Resort

ACCORDING TO THE JAPANESE SCHOOL SYSTEM, one started school in April. In April 1942, I entered primary school. Around this time, the Japanese invaded Hong Kong, Singapore, Burma, Malaysia and the Philippines — all these countries fell easily. But in July 1944, when I was in third grade, the tide turned. The United States started attacking Japan. American soldiers had advanced toward the Japanese gates. In just nine days, Saipan in the Pacific Ocean fell to the Americans, and the bombing of Japanese cities commenced thereafter. On July 22nd, the military general Tōjō Hideki stepped down after a series of defeats. Finally the ripples of war even reached us in primary school, who had been previously unaffected by the war.

In order to protect what the country deemed the future pillars of its society, Japan orchestrated a "dispersal" of its children to the countryside to keep them safe from War. Just as the Kuomintang called its forced escape to Taiwan in 1949 a "migration" to conceal its embarrassment, the Japanese hid the fact of its desperation by giving the move the more neutral term of "dispersal." In August 4th, 1944, Tokyo's first group of children were dispersed; 4800 students were sent to rural Toyama, 200 to 300 kilometers from Tokyo. Over August and September, a much larger group followed: a total of 350,000 students from third to six grade were "dispersed" to villages of varying distances from Tokyo. I was among this group.

My sister, a victim of the times like the rest of us, was also implicated in this unusual exodus. As a fifth grader, she was sent to

Toward the end of the war, Lo was dispersed with school to Funabara Hotel, a hot springs resort at Shizuoka-ken's Izu Peninsula.

the big temple by Hamana Lake at Shizuoka-ken. I was also sent to Shizuoka-ken but I was luckier. I got assigned to a hot spring resort at Izu Peninsula.

Our "dispersal" meant that we had to abandon not only our school, but also our families and parents. At the beginning, this harsh reality barely registered with us absent-minded third graders. All of us went in high spirits, our backpacks were crammed with delicious snacks that our mothers had prepared. When we arrived at what would be our new school, the luxury Hot Springs Resort Funabara at Shuzenji Onsen, some women from the local Patriotic Women Association came out to welcome us and to make us feel at home, like hotel *nakaii* (maids). As far as we were concerned, "dispersal" was just another name for "school excursion".

Funabara was a Japanese-style hotel. Our first day, we ate dinner around a long table in the tatami-style main dining room. The boys sat on one side and the girls on the other. We were all happy to be there. Then the teacher started a speech. Upon hearing "you can't go home anymore," all the girls burst into tears. The usually fidgety and restless boys suddenly sat still with arms crossed. We stared numbly at the girls opposite us. I didn't cry. None of us dared to cry for fear of being teased.

Children are touched only lightly by sorrow and happiness. With the passing of time, the sorrow of leaving home lightened as we discovered the wonder of life in the mountains. Each day, we followed a routine. After we got up each morning, we would wipe our backs in the morning with a dry cloth. Then, before breakfast, we would sing the songs that the Meiji Emperor himself had penned. We studied in the mornings, and planted sweet potatoes up in the mountains in the afternoon. After a few months, just when these sweet potatoes were ready to be harvested, we saw with our own eyes unwelcome visitors taking them from us, enjoying the fruits of our labors. These unwelcome visitors were not human beings but mountain boars.

At Shuzenji oranges were produced in abundance. We might get only one egg a week, but every day, we would be given a few oranges.

A male teacher by the name of Shimizu had his own room. A few of us boys often crowded outside his room to spy on him through the keyhole in the nights. It was probably better that we hadn't done so. Sometimes he would be roasting sweet potatoes, and sometimes even mushrooms. The sight caused our mouths to water. In the mountains, time dragged and we had so much free time. We stole Matsutake mushrooms and learned to roast them, copying our teacher. To make these mushrooms tastier we dipped them in soy sauce.

At the end of that year, knowing that we would be welcoming the New Year without our family, the Ministry of Education decided to alleviate our homesickness by distributing packets of Western biscuits to every child. These Western biscuits were already commonly available in Japan in the 1920s. But in the wartime of 1944, the biscuit factories were producing dry rations for soldiers. Biscuits had become scarce to a fault.

Packets of biscuits were sent to each makeshift school in the name of the Empress. History records indicate that each child received an entire package of biscuits all for himself. If memory serves me right, however, I only received three white coconut biscuits, not an entire package.

Since these had been bestowed on us by the Empress herself, it would not be respectful of the teacher to casually hand them over to us and watch us devour them immediately. To partake in these generous gifts, we had to follow a strict ritual. With our hands by our side, we had to stand and sing the national anthem while the biscuits lay on the table in front of each of us. I remember singing the national anthem while eyeing the round confections greedily — I couldn't help it. When the song was over, we began cramming the biscuits into our mouths. It was my first time eating real Western biscuit. They were the most delicious thing I had ever tasted.

After this episode, the situation took a turn for the worse. On March 10th, at dawn, American planes dropped petrol bombs on a sleeping Tokyo. Because the houses were made of wood, the fire spread quickly. More than a hundred thousand people died in a sea of flames. The tragedy was devastating. It proved that Japan no longer had the upper hand. Fearing that American troops would embark on Japanese soil — one of the possible embarkment spots was supposedly Izu Peninsula — the government ordered for us to move to Aomori situated in the North.

The siege of March 10th had been concentrated on Eastern Tokyo. Fortunately our home in Denenchōfu was situated in the West. None of my family was injured. Mother, in fact, worried about me. Not willing to let me go with my schoolmates to faraway Aomori, she rushed to intercept the relocation and to take me home. On the train ride back, we passed Yokohama. As we were about to enter Tokyo, I caught sight of the destroyed houses still smoking silently, sending out black wisps into the sky.

Against the general helplessness amid wartime, Mother's ability

The fourth graders went on a school outing in May. On August 15, Emperor Shōwa delivered the surrender speech.

and tenacity stood out even more. We moved to a different residence nearby just north of Tokyo, an area called Saitama-ken (Kitamoto city today). The house was not only the size of a mere 16 and 1/2 tatami mats [1], but we also had to share it with the landlord's family. This left us each with a private living space of about 6 tatami-mats, and 4 and 1/2 tatami-mats of communal space. In order to secure our survival, Mother often walked long distances into the countryside to get sweet potatoes from farmers, giving up clothes in return. She even learned to prepare the sweet potatoes like the Japanese by boiling cut strips and then leaving them out on the rooftop to dry. When we wanted to eat them, we would lightly bake them in our Japanese-style stove before putting them in our mouths.

Because I didn't go to Aomori with the rest of my school, I had to transfer to Saitama-ken, and pick up my studies there as a fourth grader. However, shortly thereafter, about four or five months later, Japan would announce its surrender. We would move again.

---

[1] The size of tatami differs between different regions in Japan. In the Tokyo area, tatami generally measures 0.955 m by 1.91 m.

11

Japanese Subjects No Longer!

On AUGUST 15, 1945, every household received news that the Emperor would be giving a speech. My family and my landlord's kneeled in the 4 1/2 tatami mat-sized communal space by the radio and awaited the "jade voice" of our Heavenly Emperor. When he announced Japan's surrender, my sister immediately cried while my cousin Tian-tsan whispered by my side: "We're no longer Japanese subjects! No need to kneel any longer!" At that time, my cousin was already in his first year at Waseda University's Engineering School. Evidently he knew much about the historical entanglements — both positive and negative — between Taiwan and China, as well as between Taiwan and Japan.

After that day, it seemed as if a new page had been turned in my life; a new chapter was about to begin.

Now that war was over, all military personnel slowly resumed their civilian posts amid a city of ruins. Many set up makeshift shelters, and cooked food in them. Actually, food was scarce but because we were Taiwanese, we got assigned a greater share. Mother said to me, "Our Japanese neighbors treated us so well in the past. Now that they are experiencing hardship, we should give them some food."

Children are always quite estranged from reality. Even amid hardship, they can be counted on to find a spot of joy. My playmates and I found that many of the pipes in the destroyed houses were half-exposed. These were inevitably made of lead. We dug them up and melted them to make pellets that we could play with. Sometimes we even used the pellets to strike birds down. We then roasted the birds to feed ourselves.

In the sky, apart from small birds, there were also big American birds flying low one after another, looking for signs of revolt perhaps. After all, it had only been a month or two ago when the Japanese, young and old alike, armed with sharpened bamboo sticks, had sworn to fight the Americans until the bitter end.

One day, soon after, I had my very first sighting of Americans at Kitamotojuku. Around me everyone was suddenly shouting at the top of their lungs "アメリカ兵" ("Americahei", which means American soldiers). But it was only a jeep carrying a few soldiers in khaki uniforms, some white and some black. Unlike Asians, there was something very eye-catching and colorful about them. This was my first time laying my eyes on whites and blacks.

I was thrilled by their strangeness. Some of the Japanese manga (comic books) that I had read alluded to Japanese conquests in Southeast Asia. The Pacific Islanders would invariably have dark skin, shiny black eyes, and white teeth. I had therefore seen black people in manga before. However in the manga, they didn't have hair, unlike these people in front of me.

Shortly after this wonderful sighting, we moved back to the big house we rented in Denenchōfu. Lucky for us, nothing had been destroyed. Having lost touch with our Taiwanese relatives for two years, we could not rely on backup. If something had happened to our home, we would have had to sleep in the streets.

Luckily for us too, Cousin Tian-tsan became an interpreter for the US army. I was able to get my hands on rare American chewing gum, chocolates and even a three inch-long harmonica. I treasured that musical instrument which I treated as a toy and put it to good use every day.

One day, my cousin invited two or three American soldiers back home. They brought more wonders with them. A tall and strong American soldier even brought a chicken with him. He shocked me by eating half of it all by himself — what a different breed the Americans were from us!

At the end of the visit, these soldiers jumped into their jeep. As the jeep drove off, the Americans in the back started scattering candy. A bunch of Japanese kids squealed with glee and ran after the moving vehicle, finding joy amid the post-war destruction.

It was during this time also that I glimpsed a hidden side of the Japanese. After the war, I returned to No.3 National Primary School in Unoki to continue fourth grade. That year, I got second prize in a calligraphy contest in Tokyo city's primary school category. For this contest, participants could decide for themselves what to write. My teacher suggested that I write "道路を汚すな国の恥", meaning "a dirty road is a country's shame." I guess my teacher wanted to express that, even if Japan had lost in the war, one's dignity must still be preserved. As a Japanese, one must uphold Japanese values at all times and not lose sight of our immaculate and law-abiding national character.

Japan's first post-war Prime Minister Shigeru Yoshida had said something similar, "Though Japan may have lost this war, we must still uphold our Japanese spirit. That we may not invite pity." No doubt, this same Japanese spirit brought about Japan's swift recovery and high economic growth during the Showa Period.

12

Learning Mandarin Chinese in Japan

As THE JAPANESE REBUILT THEIR NATION, I prepared to go back to Taiwan to resume my Taiwanese identity. During my Japanese childhood, I had gone by a Japanese name and had operated completely as a Japanese. I had topped my class and served as class monitor. I had not been the victim of any prejudice. Even at home, I spoke Japanese to my mother. We did not speak Taiwanese, just like many overseas students nowadays do not speak Mandarin with their family members but speak English instead. It was indeed a curious situation, brought about by curious circumstances. I had been born in Chiayi and moved abroad to Japan at a young age. And now, before moving back to Taiwan, I had to pick up not Taiwanese but Mandarin Chinese first, so that I could connect with the new circumstances in Taiwan.

When the war ended, the Taiwanese in Tokyo came together to form an association in support of our fellow men. Mother and I went to the association to collect the supplies that the UN distributed to every household. But there was another reason for us to go there. The Taiwanese Association in Ryogoku offered many classes. One such class that I enrolled in was Mandarin Chinese. So, in the spring of 1946, when I returned to Taiwan, I already knew basic Mandarin pronunciation, unlike my classmates.

As a Taiwanese going to Ryogoku for lessons, I was treated as a victor of the recent war. I could ride the bus for free on a special bus pass. Even when we rode to Nikko, the famous tourist spot outside of Tokyo, we didn't have to pay a single cent. It was a surreal but a wonderful time for the Taiwanese living in Japan. One day you were a Japanese subject; the next, you crossed over to the victor's side.

On February 2, 1946, we finally set off for home, boarding a ship bound for Taiwan called Higawa-maru (冰川丸). This day happened to be the first day of Taiwan's Lunar New Year. Because the Japanese did not go by this calendar, it seemed even more significant that we were setting off on this day. It was as if our lives immediately switched from "Japanese" to "Taiwanese."

The journey by sea lasted four days and three nights. On the fourth day, at dawn, Taiwan finally came into sight. Eager for our homecoming, we all crowded the deck to look at Keelung Harbor approaching in the distance. In Japan, bananas were not readily available unlike in Taiwan where it was grown. My twelve-year old sister shouted excitedly, "Someone's selling bananas!" Shortly after, she shouted, "Chinese soldiers!" — also a new thing for us. The Japanese manga that I had read liked to emphasize the looseness of their gaiters when alluding to Chinese soldiers. The Chinese soldiers that I saw now in front of me did indeed wear their gaiters differently from their more disciplined Japanese counterparts.

We had to wait until nightfall before taking a South-bound train. The platforms we passed were unlit. It was pitch black and crowded. People fought to board the train. Someone even climbed in through the window. It felt strange to be back again. A voice said repeatedly in my mind "So this is Taiwan."

Back in Chiayi, Second Uncle (my biological father) was concerned

After the war, Lo (back row, 4th from right) came back to Taiwan and entered Chuei Yang Elementary School in Chiayi. No one can miss KMT's party emblem on the school building the soon he enters the school.

about me. Seeing that I couldn't speak a single word of Taiwanese, he invited Mother's former Chinese teacher to give me lessons. For my first lesson, he taught me the Three Character Classics: "Men at their birth are naturally good. Their natures are much the same. Their habits become widely different." He would speak one phrase in Taiwanese and I would repeat what he had just said. According to past custom, the Three Character Classics was taught to five and six-year-olds but I was learning them as an eleven-year-old. My educational journey (becoming an overseas student in Japan at six, learning Mandarin pronunciation at ten) was surely unique.

Matching my badly spoken Taiwanese was an outward appearance that made me stand out from the rest of the Taiwanese children. For example, everyone was barefoot, but I wore leather shoes. This in itself was not a big deal but I was also the only one carrying a doctor's briefcase to school, an accessory that was more suited for a village elder. All of my classmates used a big piece of cloth to wrap up their books and slung the resulting cloth bag across their backs after tying a knot with the ends at the chest. This was how Taiwanese children had carried books since the Japanese colonial period. To be honest, I don't know how I acquired the briefcase. Second Brother had been a doctor, but it wasn't his briefcase. Anyway, in the eyes of the other kids, I must have come across as a self-important piece of shit from head to toe, one that needed to be "fixed." I was in fact "fixed" one day, by a kid that they pushed out to challenge me to a fight.

13

The Scar of the 228 Incident: A Chiayi Perspective

ONE YEAR AFTER OUR RETURN FROM JAPAN, the infamous 228 Incident (also called 228 Massacre) erupted on February 28, 1947. Under the Kuomintang's rule, frustrations had accumulated. It took only one incident of abuse by an inspector (who beat up a woman found selling contraband cigarettes) to trigger this explosive counter-reaction. It reverberated around Taiwan and provided an opportunity for all to vent. Protests against the government arose everywhere.

At the beginning of March, some students from Changhua and Taichung gathered on Main Street between Chiayi Station and the central fountain to give a speech calling for further rebellion against the ruling party. Their emotions fanned. A group of militia took over City Hall, forcing the mayor (sent from the mainland to govern us) and his troops to withdraw to Shuishang's airport in the south and to Shanziding and Hongmaopi in the east. Clashes ensued, resulting in a death toll of over three hundred people from both sides. Others died in the surrounding chaos. The standoff lasted seven or eight days. During that period, many respected Taiwanese elders shuttled between the two camps trying to negotiate a truce — but to no avail. Finally, after receiving additional backup (from Mainland China), the military forced their way into Chiayi city and acted with hardened vengeance. People were arrested left, right, and center. Those who resisted were killed.

From the first day that gunshots were heard ringing continuously in Chiayi, Mother acted quickly to remove twelve-year-old me and my sister from the bloodshed. We headed south for Shuishang where First Aunt (on my father's side) would give us refuge in her home. But who would have guessed that we were not alone in retreating there? Gun-toting civilians surrounded the airport. I saw with my own eyes defeated militia walking in threes and fives through the town. Muddied and using their rifles as crutches, they seemed to have walked right out of an American Civil-War movie.

Mother fretted that Shuishang would prove unsafe, so she decided to bring us to the east, up into the secluded Meishan hills where we would hide with another aunt's family. But, as the Chinese saying goes, 'man proposes, God disposes.' Gunshots soon started in the night. The next day, Mother immediately took us out of the hills and back to Chiayi via Zhuqi.

Dark clouds seemed to follow us wherever we went. With no place deemed safe enough to hide, we were in despair.

My Second Aunt's brother, Chu Rong-gui (朱榮貴), had once been a speaker on Chiayi's City Council. Although he had already retired from the post at the time of the 228 Incident, he was nonetheless an important figure in the city's politics. Since Second Aunt was my biological mother, I called him First Uncle. After the 228 Incident, First Uncle was arrested. But why? Nobody knew. Everyone in the Zhu family was worried. In order to save First Uncle, Second Aunt, knowing that an important commander was in town, threw caution to the wind and left the house in a formal cheongsam to seek a redress. In front of the municipal hall, she knelt holding a placard demanding that the wrong be righted and stayed in that position for hours. A small and weak woman pleading with the mighty military to release her brother.

Second Aunt did in fact save her brother. A week later, he was released. First Uncle's good friend, Dr. Pan Mu-zhi (潘木枝), however, was not so lucky.

In the period just after the war, the opinion leaders in Taiwan were doctors, lawyers, and respected scholars. A city council would be comprised of irreproachable men without a blemish on their records, unlike how it is today. To stem the rebellion, the Kuomintang government decided to punish these opinion leaders to set an example for the rest. These punishments were lawless to the point of being barbaric. In the morning, soldiers would make their arrests, tie their victims' hands. Wooden boards with their names written were attached to their backs. They would be paraded on a truck driven through the city's main streets until it finally stopped in front of Chiayi Station. With their legs wobbly from the ordeal and their bodies bent out of shape, these poor souls were made to jump down from the truck. Without ceremony they would be shot at close range and their bodies left exposed on the street long after their execution. (It was forbidden to claim these bodies until the sun had set.)

In the eight days from March 18 to 25, three public executions took place in Chiayi. Each time, the same ritual was observed — from tying the victims' hands to their backs, to parading them through the streets, to leaving their dead bodies on the ground for all to see. The first time it happened, I was not around to see the parading and the executing, but I did go to see the dead body lying in front of Chiayi Station afterwards. At that time, I did not know who he was, but I later learned that the body belonged to the Chair of the 228 Cleanup Committee, Chen Fu-zhi (陳復志). He had been spearheading the efforts to negotiate a peaceful resolution, but instead he was charged with "masterminding" the revolts. It was most tragic, to say the least. The second time it happened, I didn't know about it. The third time, the senior artist Chen Chen-po (陳澄波) and Dr. Pan Mu-zhi were among the four city councilors who were executed.

I still remember that day clearly. I was standing on the second floor balcony of our Renai Road home with Second Uncle. Because of its proximity (only two hundred meters) to the station, we witnessed the shootings with our own eyes. When the truck had passed in front of our home earlier, I still remember Second Uncle, seeing Dr. Pan Muzhi tied up on the car, turning to me sorrowfully and said, "That's Mu-zhi *sen-na*."

In Chiayi, First Uncle was certainly not the only one to call Dr. Pan Mu-zhi, Muzhi "*sen-na*" — a term reserved for respected elders. He was much admired for his medical skill. Before the 228 Incident, he was even elected to the position of deputy speaker on the City Council. In the year 2012, an exhibition was held to commemorate Dr. Pan. His fourth son, Pan Ying-ren (潘英仁) and my high school classmate, asked me to give a speech at the opening. The former Vice President Xiao Wan-chang (蕭萬長), who was also in attendance, said it was Dr. Pan who cured him of his poor health when he was young. The day Dr. Pan died, his mother had sent him — an eight-year-old then — to light an incense stick before Dr. Pan's body.

The eight-year-old Xiao Wanchang hadn't been the only one to pay respects to Dr. Pan this way. In fact, immediately after the execution, someone laid a thurible and packets of incense by his side, so that others could come forward and pay their respects to their Mu-zhi *sen-na*. When Dr. Pan was finally brought back home by his family on a stretcher, thurible after thurible could be seen on the ground, along the way with many lit sticks planted in them. This was everyone's way of sending off our beloved doctor.

I was twelve and still did not understand politics. But from the way the elders talked about his death that day, I got the impression that all of Chiayi had been dealt a severe blow. To think that such a good man that was respected and loved by one and all, could have been butchered so senselessly. It was a day of great heaviness.

14

Passing the Night on a Ping Pong Table in a Military Police Station

WHEN THE TRAGIC AND SENSELESS 228 INCIDENT OCCURRED, I was still very much a child. Trauma was in the air. I knew that something had happened, but I didn't understand what exactly. However, an incident about two years later awakened me to it fully. I was fourteen years old, in my second year of junior high, when a military officer pointed a gun at me and escorted me to a military police station, where I was detained overnight.

Mother often reminisced about my studious younger self. She said I would wake up early in the morning without any fuss. She would walk me to school, hand in hand, and I would go obediently. I did well in primary school. In fact, I had the best grades in class. In the 1940s, after I graduated, I entered "chuzhong" (初中, junior high), not "guozhong" (國中, middle school) as they call it now. If you are a Taiwanese between 55 and 60 years old now, you would have taken entrance exams for junior high. It wasn't until 1968 that these entrance exams were abolished to make way for the new system (in which everyone had to go through 9 years of compulsory education). But, in my time in 1948, a common entrance exam hadn't yet been devised. I had to sit for an exam for each school I wanted to get into.

I looked up to my cousin (also my biological second brother) Fu-yueh (福嶽). You could say I even worshipped him, for I wanted badly to follow in his footsteps. He was older than me by twenty years and was among Chiayi High School's second group of students during the Japanese colonial period. He did so well in school that he earned a free pass to enter Taipei's School of Medicine (now NTU's College of Medicine) without having to take the entrance examination. In 1924, he received his doctorate from Taipei's Imperial College of Medicine and became the pride of the family. I vowed that I would also get into Chiayi High School. It was the only high school that I applied for, and I did get into it. On the first day of school, entering the school gate flanked by two grand rows of coconut trees standing upright like two rows of soldiers welcoming a foreign dignitary, I muttered to myself: "Yes, I made it!"

During the Japanese colonial period, high school students would wrap their books with a big piece of cloth and carry this bundle by their hip. I entered Chiayi High School in 1948, the third year after the war. Lots of military clothes and supplies now flooded the market. There were even shops specializing in selling these products. The first modern book bag I laid my eyes on was made out of the same green canvas material that had been used to make military clothes and parachutes. And shortly after, I started carrying a canvas book bag to school. There wasn't any rule against them.

In my first year, building off of the hard work during my primary school days, I still got fairly decent grades. However, from my second year on, my grades slipped. I started to "sweep the streets." I liked to play tennis then. I would meet my tennis buddies to play tennis and then get snacks together. After eating our fill, we would loiter in the streets — this was then known as "sweeping the streets."

In the second and third years of junior high school, one never seems to run out of energy. My schoolmates would get into fights at the slightest provocation and it'd often be against a group from another school. It was no secret for example that Chiayi High School students looked down on Chiayi Agricultural & Forestry School students. Back then, traditional fertilizers (i.e. shit) were still being used in farms so my schoolmates would joke about Agricultural students "carrying shit for a living". Fights would break out as a result, and sometimes these fights were taken to Chiayi Girl's High School so that the fighters could show off in front of the girls.

At that time, Chiayi High School saw itself as a stepping stone to a tertiary education in a university, and therefore superior to the Agricultural, Forestry, Commercial or Industrial schools, whose students entered the workforce immediately upon graduation. Ironically, it is Chiayi Agricultural & Forestry School now that has overtaken Chiayi High School to become a university whereas Chiayi High School still remains a high school. Fate is indeed fickle.

But when my classmates were rounding up a group for a fight, they wouldn't ask me along. Although I was of a relatively big build, I wasn't what you called a fighter. Compared to the rest, I belonged to the scholarly type. Out of loyalty or friendship perhaps, they left me alone. When I went with this same group of friends to college in Taipei, they continued to treat me with kindness and understanding. It was out of this same loyalty and friendship that they would exclude me from their drinking sessions. They knew that I did not like to drink.

During my second year in junior high school, our teacher

organized an excursion to Taichung. On the day of the outing, something or other happened to our teacher. He didn't show up. We had no way of reaching our teacher — cell phones did not exist yet, nor were public telephones common. Young people in a group often get up to do things that they otherwise wouldn't think of doing alone. We decided to take the trip to Taichung by ourselves.

At Taichung, we got off the train and checked into a hotel, even though my good friend Tsai Shun-li (蔡順利) and I had not brought our IDs with us. It was 1949, and the Kuomintang was wary of public places like hotels that might act as hotbeds for Communists or resistance groups. As such, it was not unheard of for military police to show up at a hotel and do spot-checks on guests. You had to produce an ID if you didn't want to get into trouble.

By a stroke of bad luck, we got spot-checked by a military police officer with a mainlander accent. When Tsai Shun-li and I couldn't produce our documents, he immediately pointed his gun at us and then escorted us out. I was so frightened that I just did as I was told, barely registering the roads or buildings that passed us by. At the military police station, an officer at first gave us a look of pity, saying, "Because the two of you are just students, I'll let you sleep on the ping pong table." Yet, in the next moment, he growled, "If no one comes to bail you out within 24 hours, I'll send you to Fire Island **1**." I was then only fourteen years old, what did I know of Fire Island?

---

1 Fire Island is located in the Pacific Ocean, 33 km from Taiwan's east coast. The Kuomintang Government built a prison there especially for felons and political prisoners. The Fire Island Prison was infamous for its cruel and inhumane treatments to the inmates.

That night, dazed and scared, I drifted off to sleep on a ping pong table. The next day, Mother and Second Aunt rushed over to take me home. Needless to say, they were shocked and worried.

In comparison, junior high school students today are much better protected since the teachers know to toe the line. It's frowned upon for a teacher to air his political opinions or even reveal his political leanings. But 60 years ago, at least at Chiayi High School, when politics extended its monstrous tentacles toward the school, its gate automatically opened, its walls fell, the invaders practically met with no resistance, and the students were left unprotected. Once, the military police drove their red jeep into our school. The entire third-year cohort was made to assemble in front of them. A student was yanked out and taken away in the jeep. Apparently it was because he had distributed some pamphlets in Puzi.

This arrest would never have been permitted in a true democracy. Although we were all indignant about it, none of us organized a revolt. But, even so, something stirred in each of us — the beginning of a political consciousness, perhaps. For example, when Hsieh Tung-ming[2] came to Chiayi High School to give a talk on the magnificence of Chinese culture and how we Taiwanese should be proud to be part of it, I had an inkling that I was listening to propaganda. The night

---

2 Hsieh Tung-ming (謝東閔, January 25, 1908 ~ April 8, 2001) was a Kuomintang member. When he went to Chiayi High School to deliver a speech in 1948, he was the vice director of Taiwan Education Department. He later became the Vice President of the Republic of China (1978 to 1984).

I spent in a police facility, coupled with my experience of the 228 Incident, had left a deep impression in my heart. I had seen for myself the superciliousness of the Kuomintang ruling party and I knew that those in power surely did not treat us as equals. In their eyes, we were beneath them. Chiayi High School was in the east, on a hill slope. Its classrooms were set higher than its sports field. From Chiayi High School, you can, as you might from Hsinchu High School today, look down on the city. Since my home by the Main Station was located in the west, I had more time to "sweep the streets."

When my grades slipped, Mother didn't nag. She only said, "You do have a brain. You just haven't applied yourself." At that time, Mother was too busy running her hotel to supervise me.

During wartime in Tokyo, we had been cut off from our Chiayi relatives and friends. Our first day back in Chiayi, after the war had ended, we hadn't stepped out of the Main station when mother said she missed our old home and the forty or so houses we owned and rented out. She wanted to see them. But what greeted us instead of them was an entirely new building with red scrolls plastered over the walls congratulating the owner on his new business and the sign read "Fuda Hotel" (福大旅社) over the entrance. We were still registering the sight when a woman stepped out and greeted us "Ah, you're back!" It was my uncle's daughter-in-law. That was when we found out that the Americans had bombed every Taiwanese city, including Chiayi. Our old home had been destroyed. Fu-zhi (福祉) had built up this hotel after the war.

But Fu-zhi didn't know anything about running a hotel, so it was decided that Mother would take over. Many Japanese traditional hotels were in fact managed by women, known as "joshō" (女將, female boss). Mother, who had received Japanese education and had lived in Japan for couple of years, was both the obvious and natural choice to run the business.

In front of Chiayi Main Station were other, smaller, hotels, more like inns. Our family hotel was bigger. The post-war years were a period of recovery, but also, potentially a period of great opportunity for every sector. Our hotel bustled not with tourists, but with businessmen from all walks of life looking for their breaks. Some came by themselves. Some sold medicine. Some others were in the import/export business.

At that time, only extremely rich people could afford to go abroad for business. Taking a civilian plane was not common. Expressways had not opened yet, and very few people owned private cars. For traveling within Taiwan, most people relied on transportation by rail or by buses traveling ordinary roads. Our family hotel was situated in a prime location by the Main Station and on any day, we'd get a lot of walk-ins. When this was coupled with mass reservations by a tour company that delivered busloads of 40 to 50 people at a time, our entire hotel would be veritably abuzz with guests.

Though Fuda Hotel was a business, it was also our residence. My mother, sister and I lived in one room while my aunt and her two kids lived in another. In the crowded hotel, I don't remember

Lo's biological mother (fron row, 3rd from left) and adoptive mother (front row, 3rd from right) sit together for this group photo in front of Fuda Hotel on Jan.1st, 1961.

ever having my own desk, or ever leaning over a table to bury myself in homework. I only remember not caring much about exams after my second year, not bothering to memorize any English vocabularies before my English tests. My grades as a whole were losing their luster.

But just before graduating from junior high, I did experience a jolt of self-awakening. I had been too lazy and I wanted to change my surroundings.

Around this time, Tsai Shun-li, the classmate who had been detained in a military police station with me, appeared again. He had played too much, and now he couldn't graduate from junior high school. He wanted to see if he could get into senior high school. One day, he told me, "I have to go to Tainan to sit for Chang Jung Senior High School's entrance exam. Why don't you come with me? We can explore Tainan after I'm done." As an afterthought, he added: "National Tainan First Senior High School is also holding its entrance exam that day. Why don't you take it and see how you do?" What happened thereafter was completely like a sitcom. The star of the show did not get into Chang Jung Senior High School, but the supporting actor earned a place at National Tainan First Senior High School.

What would have been even more unimaginable, back then, was that this fluke outcome was based on a 15-year-old's whim and a proposition from his classmate. It heralded not only his departure from Chiayi but the beginning of his journey to the other side of the globe. In fact, a journey to the farthest corners of the world so that for 30 years he could not go back. In a way, that 15-year-old would leave Chiayi forever.

15

Many Famous Classmates at National Tainan First Senior High School

IN 1952, I got into National Tainan First Senior High School. The 200 people admitted in my year were divided up into four classes (A, B, C, D) according to the number of strokes in their family name. "Lo" had a high stroke count, so I was assigned to the D class. Our third year, we were divided up once again. Those studying Science made up three classes. Those studying Humanities — who were in the minority — made up the D class. Chen Lung-chi (陳隆志), who later became a law professor at Yale, thus switched from B to D class.

Chen Lung-chi, an authority in international law, would later be a long-time guest speaker at Formosa TV. However in his youth, he was already celebrated nationwide for coming in first place every year in his studies. As our valedictorian at National Tainan First Senior High School, he won a position to study law at National Taiwan University, where he would also be at the top his class. In his second year at National Taiwan University, he took the exams to qualify for civil service. He came out as the top scorer. In his third year, when he took the exams to qualify for court judges, he was again awarded the highest marks. He probably got addicted to taking exams for he even sat for the diplomat qualification exam in his fourth year.

Chen Lung-chi was National Tainan First Senior High School's pride. National Tainan First Senior High School was indeed known for producing many top students, apart from him. This might be partly attributed to the high standards expected of every student. Nowadays, high school students take graduation for granted, but back then, out of the 200 students who entered high school with me, only

170 or so graduated. More than ten percent had to repeat the final year. In fact, there was nothing terrible at all about these students' results. It was just that the teachers at National Tainan Senior High School were overly severe with their grading. Take my group for example. According to school regulation, seven of our best students should have been guaranteed places in National Taiwan University. But because only one met the requirement of an average score higher than 85% across all the subjects, only that one person in our entire group got the coveted spot. Although some people had to stay back a year, this was no setback in the larger picture. Some of these repeat students nevertheless got into National Taiwan University and went on to get American doctorates. Some others became high-ranking officials in the Kuomintang government.

Among my famous classmates were ex-Minister of Transportation Kuo Nan-hung (郭南宏), who had excellent grades and went to America for his Ph.D., before returning to Taiwan where he was given a high-ranking position in the Kuomintang government.

Ex-Mayor of Taipei City Huang Ta-chou (黃大洲), ex-Chancellor Su Jun-shiong (蘇俊雄), ex-Mayor of Tainan Chang Tsan-hung (張燦鍙) etc. were all classmates from my year.

In 2012, our class organized a reunion at a coffee shop in Taipei. I was slightly late. As I entered the room, I saw many familiar-looking faces around the tables which were arranged to form a square. No name cards had been put on the tables. There were about 30 people who already took their seats freely in the crowded room. I simply

There are many famous figures among Lo Fu-chen's National Tainan First Senior High classmates: Chen Lung-chi, law professor of Yale; ex-Mayor of Tainan and WUFI chair Chang Tsan-hung; ex-Minister of Transportation Kuo Nan-hung; ex-Chancellor Su Jun-shiong; president of Kaohsiung Medical University Tsai Ray-hsiung; president of North America Taiwanese Professors' Association Huang Tong-sheng; and former top representative to Switzerland Liu Kuan-ping.

羅福全(Lo Fu-chen) 蘇俊雄(Su Jun-shiong) 郭南宏(Kuo Nan-hung) 黃東昇(Huang Tong-sheng)
陳隆志(Chen Lung-chi) 張燦鍙(Chang Tsan-hung) 蔡瑞熊(Tsai Ray-hsiung) 劉寬平(Liu Kuan-ping)

took any empty seat that I could find.

Chang Tsan-hung suddenly discovered a strange phenomenon. He rose, addressing everybody, "Have you noticed? Those sitting to this side are all "green"; those sitting on the other side are all 'blue!'" [1] If he hadn't mentioned it, I would probably not have realized it. But sure enough, Chen Lung-chi and Chang Tsan-hung from the World United Formosans for Independence sat together. They had respectively been the best and the second best students from our graduating class who went on to become anti-Kuomintang activists, campaigning for Taiwanese Independence within the US. Former top representative to Switzerland Liu Kuan-ping (劉寬平) also sat at Chang Tsan-hung's side. In the 1960s, Liu had been the Vice Chairman of the World United Formosans for Independence. I was also a member of this group. Had it not been for the fact that I had arrived late, I would probably have sat next to them. Opposite from them sat Huang Ta-chou, Kuo Nan-hung and ex-Chair of the Kuomintang Discipline Committee Li Tsung-jen (李宗仁), who had all been high-ranking officials in the Kuomintang at one point or another. In between them, on the third side, were mostly doctors who took a back seat to politics.

We were all seventy-seven years old. Many of us were grandfathers with white hair. In our youth, because of our different fates, we

---

[1] In Taiwan, "blue" refers to the Kuomintang camp and its supporters while "green" refers to the DPP camp and its supporters.

had taken separate paths, and stood by our divergent politics. All the differences between us that had developed over the decades since we left school seem to encapsulate Taiwan's post-war political development itself.

Looking back, what proudly united us all as seventeen and eighteen-year-old high school students were our cap badges identifying our school. The Kuomintang party hadn't been in Taiwan for very long but high school had already acquired a strong military character. All high-schoolers wore the same khaki-colored uniform, and the same military type of caps that you see on today's police officers. Every high school student wore the same attire. The only thing that differentiated one student from another school's was the copper badge on his cap. Proud to belong to our school, we did our utmost to polish this badge, so that it would shine from even afar and let one and all know which school we came from. The more fashionable among us would scrunch the cap in the middle until it was sharply raised. When we were outside riding our bicycles, these crooked hats would draw the bashful gazes of female students despite themselves. These constituted some of the games that we would play as youths in the 1950s.

16

Shiy De-jinn (席德進) Was My Art Teacher

My HIGH SCHOOL YEARS TOOK PLACE IN THE EARLY POST-WAR period when one colonial power was phasing into the next. During this time, the Mainlanders that "retreated" en masse from China to Taiwan were still considered a special new group. Older Taiwanese, a generation or two before me, were suspicious of these newcomers. Some were angered by their presence. Others simply alienated them because of the language barrier. Some others refused to let their daughters get married to these Mainlanders. As for those of us in high school, because we had Mainlander teachers, we got to experience the new culture that they brought along with them.

In Chiayi Junior High School, I had a Physics teacher from a Hakka background. Athough he had studied Physics in an imperial university in Japan, he did not speak good Mandarin. As such he was at a loss sometimes when he had to teach in that language. Saying the Mandarin for parabola, he fumbled: "throwing a straight straight line." The dawn of a new era exposed the former elites to many linguistic torments. As for me, I was among the first group of students after the war who had had the benefit of a Chinese education. I was taught Chinese in primary school when the Kuomintang took over. Though my Mandarin was not perfect, it was good enough.

At that time, the teachers in National Tainan First Senior High School were curiously split by origin. Taiwanese teachers largely taught Physics and Mathematics, while humanities like Chinese Literature, Geography and History were largely taught by Mainlanders. My

Mainlander teachers exerted great influence on me. As an editor of a bulletin board, I once put up a Chinese essay that I myself had written about a mid-autumn festival I had spent abroad away from home. In the essay, someone had given me a piece of mooncake, which I ate while listening to music and admiring the moon. Perhaps the essay expressed a certain loneliness that resonated with my history teacher Xue Yun-yu (薛蘊玉) who was after all living in Taiwan away from her own homeland. She admired it greatly. She and my English teacher Dong Shi-chi (董世祁) had both graduated from Beijing University, so she asked him who the author of the essay was. My English teacher then praised my essay in front of the entire class. So encouraged, I became more and more enthusiastic about Chinese literature. I committed to memory the ancient Chinese poems in my Chinese textbooks. Even to this day, I still know many of these verses by heart. However, since I used Mandarin to memorize these verses, it's only in Mandarin that I can recite them.

In my first year at university, Professor Ye, who taught us Chinese literature, discussed the death of Yang Guifei [1], with the ancient seven-word poems by Bai Ju-yi [2] entitled "Song of Everlasting Regret" as his

---

1 Yang Guifei (楊貴妃, June 26, 719 ~ July 15, 756) was known as one of the Four Beauties of ancient China. She was the beloved consort of Emperor Xuanzong during his later years. The emperor's guards demanded that he put Yang to death because they blamed the rebellion on her cousin Yangzhong and the rest of her family's corruption.

2 Bai Ju-yi (白居易, 772-846), was a Chinese poet of the Tang Dynasty. He was one of the most prolific of all Chinese poets. He developed a style that was simple and easy to understand, making him the most well-loved and widely read of all Chinese poets.

starting point. An-Lushan had rebelled. Emperor Tang Xuanzong hurriedly fled Chang'an (capital of the Empire) to Sichuan with Yang Guifei. They didn't make ten kilometers out of the capital when the escorting guards refused to go further. They demanded that Lady Yang be put to death, as a condition of escorting the Emperor to Sichuan. Emperor Xuanzong only hid his face as the soldiers dragged his beloved consort from him and hung her. Her golden and jade trinkets fell to the ground in her struggle. As Professor Ye spoke of this moment, I repeated the following lines, word for word, in my mind:

> Troops refused to advance
> which seemed more hopeless indeed
> The crown had to strangle his sobbing
> beauty before his steed.
> Her jewelry scattered all over the ground yet
> no one would care,
> Among which was a green jade
> hairpin with a gold sparrow so rare.
> The emperor had no choice but to sacrifice her;
> he sadly covered his face,
> Blood dripped and tears dropped
> when he looked back at the very place.

There were many sides to my Mainlander teachers who weren't

always pro-Kuomintang. The teacher who taught me Chinese literature at National Tainan First Senior High School was pretty daring. He once scribbled a poem by Mao Zedong on the blackboard entitled "Shen Yuan Chun." (〈沁園春〉) In those days, it was banned to refer to the Communist leader, certainly in the context of a classroom. I remember he didn't say much about the poem. He only made two short statements: "This was written by Mao Zedong." "He wrote very well."

Lo has enjoyed drawing ever since he was young. Occasionally, he would sketch down what caught his eyes when traveling. These are Muslims in the Philippines' Mindanao Island.

In 1975, Lo went to India as an economic consultant and took part in India's national development conference. The Indian people are eloquent and love to debate. Both in and outside the conference hall were filled with heated debates. Lo drew these humorous sketches, indicating that the conference building was overwhelmed by noises, and the crow was crying, "What is development? Don't disturb me."

In Chiayi Junior High School, I had another Mainlander teacher, who would later be famous. He was the painter Shiy De-jinn. That year, our class had two art teachers — one Taiwanese, the other Mainlander. Each taught two classes. The Taiwanese, Lin Yu-shan (林玉山), had been famous since the Japanese colonial period for his glue paintings. I wasn't his student. The art teacher who taught my class was Shiy De-jinn — who wasn't 30 years old yet.

I was probably the best painter in my class. But when Shiy De-jinn organized a class-wide painting competition I did not win. The winner had submitted a passable landscape of the fields that we saw each day on the way to school, while I had submitted an "imitation" painting of a postcard of Kaohsiung Main Station that I had at home. I was drawn to paint this scene because of its attractive composition. I liked the green trees by the station. But in the end, I only was awarded second place. Sensing my disappointment, Shiy De-jinn pointed at my painting and asked: "Have you been to Kaohsiung?" I shook my head. He said, "Since you haven't been to Kaohsiung, how can you paint Kaohsiung Main Station? This isn't Art." At that time, I interpreted his statement being that Art is that feeling engendered in the artist reacting to his subject.

Shiy De-jinn was still young then. He had thick eye brows and a set of piercing eyes. His skin was shiny as glass and his face was white as porcelain. At that time his hair was still the same as everybody's, cropped short. It was only after he went to New York and returned to Taiwan that he started to keep it long the way the TV host Zhu

Geliang (豬哥亮) kept it (Similar to the Beatle haircut). I remember a habit of his. He often unconsciously brought the tips of the fingers on his right hand over his forehead to gently brush his hair.

The Shiy De-jinn who taught me wasn't yet famous. It was only after he left Chiayi for Taipei, then New York, then Paris before coming full circle back to Taiwan, that his reputation grew. He never blindly submitted to Western Art. Instead, he pursued Chinese Art that "took inspiration from its immediate environment." He even took pains to research ancient Taiwanese temples and ancient architecture and wrote a book entitled, "Taiwanese Folk Art." We have him to thank for the Lin An-tai Historical House in Taipei. Without his valiant efforts, the building would never have been preserved.

17

Nowadays Universities Admit Tens of Thousands of Students, But in the Past They Only Took Two Thousand

In 1954, when I graduated from High School, the university path that stood before me was not the "narrow doorway" that people spoke of in the 1970s and the 1980s; it was a mere crack. Today in Taiwan, there are over a hundred universities. But fifty years ago, the only university in existence was National Taiwan University. Other forms of higher education did exist. Among the public schools were Taipei's Municipal Teacher College (now Taiwan Normal University), Tainan's Municipal Engineering College (now National Cheng Kung University) and Taichung's Municipal Agricultural College (now National Chung Hsing University). That year, for the first time, the four public schools held a joint entrance examination. National Taiwan University admitted 1,052 students; the other three colleges each accepted over three hundred students, making a total of only 2,100 university students that year. Compared to the grossly inflated figure of over 100,000 new students accepted into university each year today, it may give you an idea of how much more difficult it was to get into university back then. At that time the only private college was Tamkang College of English (now Tamkang University), which held a separate entrance examination, and thus offered those who had been turned away a final chance of promotion to the elite corps of university-educated intellectuals.

Among the humanities students just getting out of high school, the most popular and the most obvious aspiration was to get into Law and to become a lawyer. In 1954, only National Taiwan University had a law school. That was my original ambition as well, except I

never forgot how a cousin of mine had once sued his own father —
how ridiculous that this was permitted under the law! That was why
I ruled out the idea of studying Law.

I considered History. I did love history. Moreover, I didn't want
to let down my History teacher who so admired my essay on the
bulletin board. For that same reason, I always strove to get the highest
marks for that subject. But I also knew that if I studied History, it
would be hard to get a job afterwards, so I ruled it out too.

So I decided on Economics. At that moment, I didn't overthink
it. In Chinese, the characters for Economics (經濟), was embedded
in the Classical Chinese "經"國"濟"民 ("Managing the Country and
Saving the People"), which felt like a heroic thing to get into. You
could help your country amass riches. What loftier ambition was
there? So I took the plunge. Some of my classmates, on the other
hand, decided to study Mining and Metallurgy with the thinking
that impoverished China would likely develop its Mining industry.
There would surely be potential there. Our choice of concentration
went hand in hand with our patriotism. In high School, we were
constantly exposed to China's buzzwords, symbols and signals. I
loved to read books, so I devoured books about the formation of the
Republic of China. In my childhood I even thought that I would set
up a bookstore one day and call it "Chenji" (全記) because the name
had such a charming Chinese quality to it.

At that time, a lot of people simply didn't understand what
Economics was. Even when I had graduated, my relatives still asked

me: "Ah Chuan (my Taiwanese nickname), now that you've finished university, will you be going to Medical School?" They seemed to think that the end point of all studies was to become a doctor or a lawyer.

Lo chose to enter NTU's economic department, the largest department in NTU at that time.

Little did they know that the world outside Taiwan was ushering in a new era.

The year I entered University, it had been a full nine years since World War II ended, the world had taken off its helmets and parked its cannons. Whether your country won or lost, it was now time to roll up your sleeves, get back to work on recovering your economy, and concentrate on bringing prosperity to your people. As such Economics was a tremendously popular subject. In National Taiwan University, for example, the 160 graduates studying Economics constituted its largest department. At that time though, Economics still encompassed Sociology since it did not exist as a department.

Using direct, layman language, my National Taiwan University's graduation yearbook defines the raison d'être of Economics. Though the average person thinks that one studies Economics in order to "strike it rich" — which in and of itself, is not a bad thing — one studies Economics in fact so that one's whole country as a whole can "strike it rich," or in order for the entire world to "strike it rich."

Though the yearbook explains the subject quite well, it also made the claim of having 20 "learned scholars" in its department. My personal experience, however, told a different story. In fact, only Professor Shi Jian-sheng (施建生) alone had studied abroad in the US — at Harvard, no less — but he had only received a Master's degree. At that time, there was no one in Taiwan qualified to write an Economics textbook. The textbooks that we studied were all imported foreign textbooks. The teachers taught Economics in the classroom by reading out the textbooks line by line. We'd copy each line as it was read. As students we would joke about our teachers behind their backs, saying that they graded our scripts by turning the electric fan on the heap of our papers. Whichever got blown the furthest would get the highest score.

Only two or three teachers stood out. The Dean of the Economics school Chang Han-yu (張漢裕), who taught History of Capitalism, had received his Ph.D. from Tokyo University where he had co-translated with his professor Otsuka Hisao (大塚久雄) a book on the history of Economics. It won the approval of British academia, proving that his methodology was up to scratch. Another professor Hsing Mo-huan (邢慕寰) taught us Economics Theory. Years later, when I went to the US, I could understand my lessons thanks to him. The third professor who taught us Accounting was Chang Guo-wei (張果爲). He had studied abroad in Germany, and had once been the Finance Minister of Fujian Province. When he left his post, it was filled by Yen Chia-gan (嚴家淦) who would later become our Vice President (from 1966 to 1975). Whatever course Chang Guo-wei taught, I would pick. When I graduated from University, Professor Chang invited me to be his teaching assistant, but my heart was not in academia at that time so I politely turned him down. In the end, he picked someone one year my junior, who would later go on to be the Chief Financial Officer for the Kuomintang in the 1980s and 1990s. He was China Development Financial's former Chairman Liu Tai-ying (劉泰英).

Liu Tai-ying was the student of former President Lee Teng-hui; so was I. At National Taiwan University, the only truly useful class I took was taught by Professor Lee Teng-hui. He had just come back from Iowa to lecture on Agricultural Economics, but in doing so, he introduced to us the latest Economic Theory, "Linear Programming."

Among the sociological sciences, I still believe Economics to be the best subject of them all. There's a reason why the Nobel Prize is awarded for Economics. However, I only recognized and understood this deeply after I had gone abroad to the US for further studies.

18

For Organizing a Graduation Dance, Our Class Rep Got Demerit Points

AFTER THE WAR, as benefactors of US military and economic aid, we looked up to the superpower, worshipping anything American. Its great shadow loomed over all of us, extending even into the popular culture of campus life. We were most crazy about American movies and American pop music. Among the biggest hits in Taiwan was "Seven Lonely Days" by Georgia Gibbs — it was even translated into Chinese as "給我一個吻" ("Give Me a Kiss").

The year I entered University, LPs of American popular music started selling in Taipei's Ximending. Listening to American music, you were considered hip. Profess a love of Taiwanese songs, you were considered a country bumpkin.

At that time, American burgers were considered a luxury food. I ordered it once at Ximending's Kissling, but it came sandwiched with a piece of fried egg — surely un-American. Two other restaurants offered hamburgers in Taipei: Sullivan opposite Kissling and Moulin at Zhongshan North Road. It was commonly known that Moulin was more high-end than Kissling.

While at university, my wife Chin-fun's (清芬) family hosted a female Canadian reporter by the name of Ruth Lor in their home. Once, returning from the US Military Club or the Restaurant at the Privy Council — I'm not sure which — Ruth brought back a hamburger. They treated it as the rarest of foods. Using a knife, they solemnly divided it up. Everyone got a taste of a real American hamburger.

As for the American hotdog, it existed in Taiwan then as well. It was also extremely rare, unlike today, where you can find it readily available at any supermarket.

American dances also were popular, figuring prominently in campus activities. The Chinese for "派對" ("party,") became a buzzword. Without doubt, the most popular song was "Tennessee Waltz." The lyrics to this song told a tragic story:

I was dancin' with my darlin'
To the Tennessee Waltz
When an old friend I happened to see
I introduced her to my loved one
And while they were dancin'
My friend stole my sweetheart from me
I remember the night and the Tennessee Waltz
Now I know just how much I have lost
Yes, I lost my little darlin'
The night they were playing
The beautiful Tennessee Waltz

But I guessed that nobody really understood the lyrics. Everyone was just intoxicated by the foreign melody and the foreign voice, soaking in the fashionable atmosphere of the music.

Through organizing these dances, the male students not only bonded over a collective activity, but they were also able to check out the girls and look for girlfriends. The dances provided an opportunity for them to interact with their female counterparts up close. The female students at that time were just also getting into American fashion. Western clothes seemed to brim with vigor. Pom pom dresses, one-pieces that reached the knee, sleeveless dresses were all the rage. Especially around this time, the US started sending overseas Chinese students to Taiwan on sponsored visits. Most of these overseas Chinese came from Malaysia, Singapore and the Philippines. But we also welcomed second-generation Chinese immigrants from Australia. Compared to Taiwanese girls, they were more liberal and wore brighter clothes, which inevitably got the boys even more excited about going to the dances. However, it was still forbidden on campus to organize one. If you wanted to dance, you had to do it elsewhere.

In Taipei, there were a few places where American officers could dance, like I HOUSE which was back then located in Da'an Park at the corner of Xinyi Road and Xinsheng South Road. In Chinese, I HOUSE got translated as "國際學舍" or "International Hostel." To people born in the 1950s or 1960s, the impression they have with I HOUSE would be a place for book fairs. But for us 70-year-old generation, the "International Hostel" was where international visitors on cultural or academic exchanges went to socialize with locals. Occasionally, there would be "dance parties" organized by international or overseas students. These parties were guaranteed to be very Western affairs.

Chin-fun was five years younger than me, but because she started school two years earlier than average children, she was only three years my junior. She studied History at National Taiwan University. According to her, Chiayi's Air Force Club also held dances for fun-seeking military officers. Students could attend, but they had to register with an ID.

Through my four years at university, the dance I remember most vividly was the one on the eve of my graduation. As per custom, Economics majors held a gathering to thank their teachers. We chose to hold the event on the second floor of the law school. That night, excitement was in the air. Thanking our teachers was in fact the last thing on our minds. When the gathering finally came to an end, we hurriedly sent off our teachers, locked up the doors, and then converted the premises to one giant dance hall. However, after a night of fun, we found out that the class rep had racked up two major demerit points[1].

When the gathering transformed into a dance, I didn't stay for a single dance. During my four years at university, dances were like far-off rainbows with their multi-colored hues — they didn't have anything much to do with my life.

From a young age, I was often lonely, living with only my mother

---

[1] The merit system is used by schools to regulate student behavior. Depending on the seriousness of the offense, the student gets a warning, a minor demerit, or a major demerit. Three warnings add up to one minor demerit, three minor demerits add up to one major demerit, and three major demerits will get one expelled from school. For male students who have to fulfill a compulsory 2-year military service upon graduation, the major demerit record automatically disqualify them from sitting in the military officer examination.

and my sister. When I grew up, I found socializing difficult. Mixing in a group and making small talk were not my favorite activities. I did like to make friends, and what I liked about making friends was developing deep relationships and becoming confidantes with these friends. I guess I was an introverted university student; I never went to a single party.

Another reason for my introversion was that I never lived in a dormitory. For my first three years at university, I rented a house outside campus by myself. Dormitory students however, regardless of their chosen discipline or year, spent day and night together. They ate, showered and studied together. Their constant interaction naturally extended to other activities outside of school. Living in a dormitory, in other words, provided more opportunities to cultivate extroversion.

19

Fighting for a Photo of a Swedish
Actress with a Girl

IN MY FOURTH YEAR AT UNIVERSITY, Mother was visiting me in Taipei when she bumped into her old friend Mrs. Mao. At her passionate and sincere invitation, I moved into her single-story Japanese-style house for a year. It was located at Zhongshan North Road, Alley No. 2. Back then, we didn't use xiangzi (巷子) or alley, we used the term tiaotong (條通).

"Tiaotong" or "dōri" was a usage left over from the Japanese colonial period. Mrs. Mao's house was in a large residential area located to the east of Zhongshan North Road, Section One and to the south of Nanjing East Road. Called "Taishocho," it was considered an elite neighborhood and spanned nine alleys. Taiwan's first medical PhD Dr. Du Chong-ming (杜聰明) and the founder of Hua Nan Bank Lin Hsiung-chen (林熊徵) both lived here. However, they were assuredly in the minority group. Most of the residents were Japanese. After Japan lost the war and the Japanese officials based in Taiwan retreated back to their country, these houses became the property of the Kuomintang government. High-ranking officials moved in. Among these officials were ex-president Chiang Ching-kuo (son of Chiang Kai-shek), who was then the Chair of the Veteran Affairs Council — he lived at Alley No.4. His residence would be where the Chang-an Branch of Hua Nan Bank is today, along Chang-an East Road, Section One. It was almost back to back to Mrs. Mao's house at Alley No.2 — I recall seeing military guards at his doorstep.

Chiang Ching-kuo's mother's surnam was Mao, but she was of no relation to Mrs. Mao. Her husband, Mr. Mao Chao-jiang (毛昭

江), was inherently Taiwanese. He came from a very famous and respectable family in Tainan's Liujia. His two brothers-in-law were both famous doctors in Tainan. The first of them, Wu Sin-rong (吳新榮), was both a writer and a doctor. The second, Wang King-ho (王金河), had eradicated Taiwan's Blackfoot disease [1]. Mr. Mao's father Mao Jing-tang (毛敬堂) once operated a brick factory called "Chishan Tile Production Private Limited", and had even served as a Member of Parliament in Tainan State. In the 1920s when the colonial government built Wu Shan Tou Reservoir, they had taken back a big piece of his family land.

The Japanese colonial period lasted fifty years (1895-1945). Taiwan had many good geographical factors going for it. It was also Japan's first colonial outpost. Under Japanese rule, water reservoirs were built, the quality of its rice improved, superior Hawaiian sugarcane was introduced, agricultural methods upgraded, and rice and sugar production were stimulated. In every aspect, life became better for the Taiwanese. However, Korea had a different experience under Japanese rule. Under thirty-five years of Japanese rule (1910-1945), Korea was not only left to fend for itself (the Korean economy was in shambles), but the Japanese also built their Governor-General Office

---

[1] Blackfoot disease (BFD) is an endemic peripheral vascular disease confined to the southwestern coast of Taiwan. It was so named because of its gangrenous appearance involving the feet of the patients. In severe cases, the patients' feet or legs had to be amputated. BFD was associated with the consumption of inorganic arsenic from the artesian wells.

Building inside the ground of the Gyeongbokgung Palace[2] and used high pressure tactics to force Koreans to work in Japanese mines. To the Japanese, Taiwan was a good colony, bringing the Japanese many benefits. Korea, on the other hand, brought only losses.

Among the older Taiwanese, those who were rich were mostly landowners. They got even richer as production increased. With wealth, they could afford to send their children to Japan for studies. Mr. Mao Chao-jiang thus studied Law at Kyoto University. After the war, he served first as the principal of Tseng Wen Junior High School. He then came to Taipei to be the Manager of the Provincial Taiwan Cooperative Bank. That was how he came to live at Alley No.2.

Mr. Mao was a very strict father. He expected much of his children. At six and seven in the morning, his children were already up listening to Professor Lilian Chao's (趙麗蓮) English lessons broadcast over the radio. But Mr. Mao also had a romantic side. It was said that he had gone to great lengths to court Mrs. Mao. He often traveled to Jiadong, south of Houbi, where Mrs. Mao lived. Houbi was situated more than ten kilometers away from Liujia. At night, after his visits, he worried that the long walk home might be dangerous. He often slept in a straw house midway between Houbi and Liujia belonging

2 Gyeongbokgung was the former Korean Imperial Palace. The Japanese deliberately built their Governor-General office building there (1916-1926). In doing so, all but 10 of the 400 palace buildings were demolished. It was long felt by the Korean as a symbol of Japanese Imperialism. The Governor General office was demolished in 1995.

In his 4th year at the university, Lo lodged with the Mao family. The Mao's second daughter, Chin-fun (back row, 3rd from left) later became Mrs. Lo.

to duck farmers. After they got married, whenever they quarreled, Mrs. Mao would jokingly complain that had it not been for Mr. Mao's persistent courtship, passing his nights in that duck coop, she wouldn't have agreed to marry him.

Mr. Mao's daughters were all very pretty. Like me, the eldest daughter, Mao Tsan-ying (毛燦英), was doing her final year at National Taiwan University, except that she was majoring in Foreign Languages. Her English was top-notch. Not only had she been elected to be class rep, she had even won a debating competition and represented Taiwan at the Asian Youth Meeting in Korea. On campus, everyone said that there were two beauties: Lin Wen-yue (林文月), from the Chinese Literature Department, one year my senior, and Mao Tsan-ying from the Foreign Languages Department. Many boys snuck into the Humanities School to steal glimpses of these two.

Romance eluded the nerdy twenty-two-year-old me. Many classmates were jealous of my proximity to Mao Tsan-ying since I lived with her family. But nobody knew that during my one year with the Maos, I was responsible only for house-sitting. When my male classmates rang the doorbell at the Mao residence for Mao Tsan-ying, I would go to open the door, and greet the person at the door, "Oh, it's you!" — that was it.

Mr. Mao's second daughter Chin-fun was just beginning her studies in the History Department of National Taiwan University in my senior year. One day, I was walking out of the house as she was entering. We collided into each other. I had always seen her as another plain-looking straight-haired high school student. But that day, because she was about to enter university, she had permed her hair, which she didn't want anybody to see yet because she was still shy about it. Seeing her like this for the first time, I experienced "a spark." But, nerdy as I was, I didn't pursue it any further. A few years later Chin-fun would become my wife, but that is another story.

Chin-fun remembers an episode from the past which proves how innocent I still was when I lived at her home. At that time, I was not Mr. Mao's only house guest. The Mao family also played host to the son of Dr. Chang from Chiayi Hospital. This master Chang majored in Law at National Taiwan University, but his passion was in the movies, and he often analyzed the movies that he saw. When his father went to the US for medical training, he brought back many movie memorabilia and movie star photos as gifts for his son. At that time, no foreign movie star visited Taiwan nor were DVDs invented yet. So movie enthusiasts in Taiwan could only content themselves with collecting photos of movie stars. Master Chang gave us some photos to split up between ourselves. Who knew that Chin-fun and I had our eyes on the same photo of Ingrid Bergman? To decide who would get it, we played a finger-guessing game which I won. Unthinkably, I took the photo and just left. Even after so many years, Chin-fun still holds this ungentlemanly act against me. How could I have refused to give up a photo to a girl!

20

Learning Proper Dinner Etiquette before Going to Study Abroad

IN 1958, after I graduated from university, I should have entered the army, but that summer, I went to take an exam to see if I qualified to study abroad.

In the 1950s, studying abroad was not just a matter of having the money, and getting admitted into the university. In the post-war era, Taiwan's economic situation was still rather dire. Without foreign exchange reserves, the government fretted that US dollars would follow the overseas student abroad. As a result, you had to prepare enough foreign currency as a deposit before you could leave. Later, as the number of applicants got higher and higher. The government decided it needed to control the number of people leaving the country. In 1953, the first exams determining if you could study abroad were introduced. In the first years, the total number of students that made the cut each year was somewhere between 200 and 500.

From today's perspective, an exam to determine whether you qualified to study abroad must come across as suspect. Taiwan at that time had no Ph.D. programs, and the number of homegrown Master's degree holders was regrettably small — and these were restricted to Literature or Law graduates. The government probably knew that they should have encouraged the trend of overseas education because that would surely nurture a core of elites that would help build up the nation. Ironically, the government structure itself had set down many barriers. It must be remembered how perversely the government was structured in those years. After all, the one at the top of the government had not been democratically elected, so he treated

Taiwan as he would a birdcage in his palm. He did not wish for people to freely leave Taiwan to see the sights of other countries, nor did he allow non-state-owned magazines and newspapers to operate. He wanted control of everything, including the number of young people seeking knowledge outside of Taiwan's borders. He wanted to build barriers, to restrict the numbers of students going overseas.

At that time, there were a lot of overseas students whose intentions were indeed to escape the island forever, and never come back. These students nursed hopes of settling down in the US. Although the popular catchphrase "Come, come, come to National Taiwan University; Go, go, go to America" had not emerged, the common perception was that if you had graduated from National Taiwan University but did not go on to further your studies in the US, you were as good as a country bumpkin. Not passing this exam that qualified you for study abroad got you mocked as "a person who can't get a wife." A person whom nobody wanted — what a fearful condition! Even though I didn't really want to go overseas and I had no intention of becoming a scholar, I took the exam anyway.

One of the subjects [1] they tested was your ability in the language of the country you wanted to study abroad in. Because I had lived in Japan as a child, I thought it wouldn't be so bad to go back to Japan

[1] The qualification examination for students wanting to study abroad included 4 subjects: Chinese; language of the country you want to study in; a combined test on your knowledge of Chinese history, geography and political thoughts; and one subject from your majoring field. The exam was abolished in 1976.

and visit again. So I signed up for this test. I didn't prepare for it at all, but the moment I saw the test, I knew that the questions had been set by my teacher Hsing Mo-huan, so I quite enjoyed completing them. My foundation in Japanese was still good after all those years. I passed the test easily and ranked as the eleventh best scorer among all the test-takers.

The Ministry of Education required everyone who passed the exam to attend a week of classes. Overseas students were a rare breed and were highly respected. The Vice President himself, Chen Cheng (陳誠), showed up to give a lecture at the main hall of the old National Taiwan University Law School at Syujhou Road, where our weeklong classes were conducted. The Law School never had any need for concern over security, but that day, because a Vice President was on its premises, guards were deployed everywhere and nobody was allowed to enter or leave without checks.

This week of classes was remarkable for another reason. Worried that our overseas students would embarrass themselves abroad, the government held etiquette classes as well. They taught everyone how to hold a knife and a fork to eat a steak, and how to wear a proper suit to attend a formal dinner. In the end, however, we didn't get a chance to apply these lessons once we were overseas. Who would invite a poor student to a formal dinner? Those who arrived in the US immediately understood that the American society was more relaxed. It was simpler than we had imagined. There weren't many constraints. The society simply wasn't formal. In fact, from my own observation, Americans did not subscribe to European manners. They often picked up a knife with one hand to cut the meat, only to pick up the fork afterwards with the same hand to eat.

When my wife Chin-fun left Taiwan, it was also the same. My mother-in-law, who was very fussy about appearances, thought that Chin-fun would be invited to party after party in the US, so she prepared many sets of cheongsams and evening gowns, even going to the extent of matching them with handbags. But it was mostly for naught. In the US, Chin-fun was so busy that she even had to squeeze time to wash plates, let alone attend a dance. Mother-in-law's painstaking efforts did not entirely go down the drain though. Mrs. Jessie, the American woman who welcomed foreign students at Chin-fun's school once invited Chin-fun to attend an evening with the Philadelphia Symphony Orchestra. So she did get to dress up after all.

21

I Wanted to Open a School at the Age of Twenty-five

AFTER UNIVERSITY AND COMPULSORY MILITRY SERVICE, many crossroads lay ahead of me. From the start, I was free to choose. But over time, because of the changes to the world outside, I ended up going down a path that I never would have imagined taking.

I never wanted to be a "pure scholar." Rather than publishing essays and becoming a famous academic, I had seen myself going into the real world to tao lor (work). But I had become disillusioned with society. It bothered me that everyone had to be bribed with red packets. For example, when I wrote to ask for my certificate of military service, I didn't hear back for a week. Someone told me that I should send the office a bag of sausages; that did the trick immediately. When my mother came back from Japan, the Customs Officers confiscated some of the things she brought back. Apparently, if we wanted them returned, we had to bribe them.

Some of the Economics graduates ended up working for Customs. Naturally I was not predisposed to this idea. Some went to the bank, and sat counting money all day — this was not my style. Opening my own business, well, that couldn't be done in those days without also having to socialize over drinks — so I also ruled it out.

I was twenty-four or twenty-five. I had passion and energy to spare. I only wanted to find something in Taiwan that I could do.

My third aunt's husband was called Lin Mu-gen (林木根). He was well known in Chiayi. During the Japanese colonial period, he had a villa sprawling well over two hectares near Taiwan Forestry

Research Institute and Chiayi's head-water area. The villa comprised of traditional courtyard houses and a Japanese-style house. There were many fruit trees, artificial hills (rockworks) and waterfalls. It was also located at the edge of a cliff, with a grand view. Although the villa wasn't as impressive as the Lin Family's villa in Wu Feng, there was certainly a classical refined air about it. Lin Mu-gen even gave it an elegant name to go with it "暮庵" ("Mu An", i.e. Sunset Hut).

In my third year at University, I had gone to visit Lin Mu-gen who had been hospitalized at National Taiwan University Hospital. I found out that he wanted to put this villa on the market. Thus a plan formed in my mind. When I graduated, I would like to do something meaningful. Following this thought, I asked a friend one year my senior, Hung Teng-kun (洪登坤), to be my co-investor. We would invest over two hundred thousand NTD (New Taiwan Dollars) into this property, and convert it into a school. At that time NT$200,000 was an amount you stood to take home if you won the first prize in the Lottery. It cost less than NT$100,000 back then to buy a house in Taipei.

The Taiwan Forestry Research Institute nearby was cultivating mahogany trees. Mahogany was highly-prized by European furniture makers. I eagerly bought over 50 saplings to plant back at home. Mahogany takes a couple of decades to fully mature. I was already looking far, far into the future. I told Hung Teng-kun jokingly that in 30 or 40 years down the road, I could chop one down for my daughter's dowry when she came of suitable age.

At that time, I was also a big fan of the 4 to 5 A.D. Chinese poet Tao Yuan-ming [1]. I loved, for example, the feeling he evoked with the lines "At eastern hedge, I was plucking chrysanthemums/when I suddenly saw the beauty of Nanshan (the southern mountains)" so I had even picked a name for my school, after these lines: "Nanshan High School".

I rounded up seven or eight of my Chiayi High School classmates (we hadn't even hit 30 yet, at that point) and floated the idea of running a school together where teachers would live alongside their students. Everyone was thrilled by this idea. All our romantic and passionate visions for the school poured out; our discussions soared. And so it was decided that we would do it.

After getting approval from the Ministry of Education, I applied for the green light from the county level. But this was where I got stuck. They wanted money. One day, an official from Chiayi County's Education Division made an appointment with me to inspect the grounds of the prospective school. He waited in front of his office, dressed in a Western suit, as if expecting me to pull up in a Benz. I arrived instead on a bike. When we got to the villa, he took out a tape measure and made like he was using it to take measurements — of well over two hectares of land! Their decision came by mail soon after.

---

1 Tao Yuan-ming (陶淵明, 365-427 AD) was a Chinese poet who lived in the middle of the Six Dynasties period (220-589 AD). He is often regarded as the greatest poet during that period. In his poems the theme of countryside solitude particularly resonates. Therefore, he is regarded as a Fields and Gardens poetry poet or a "recluse poet."

There was no outright rejection but they needed to study the proposal further. I knew then and there that it was not going to happen.

There went my dream of starting a school. Shortly after, someone pointed another way.

An alumnus of NTU's Economics Department and a very intelligent person, Wu Chin-liang (巫欽亮) had gone to Fengyuan to set up a woodwork factory just after the war. There, he caught the attention of the former secretary to the President Liao Liau-yi's (廖了以) family. He was soon married to Liao Liau-yi's eldest sister. After their wedding, they emigrated to Brazil where his business grew into a formidable empire. Today, many years later, their son has been elected to Senator.

Wu Chin-liang was not only my senior (albeit by six or seven years) but also a close friend of the family. The Los and Wus have helped each other out for generations. His father Wu Chen-hsiang, in addition to being my father's friend, had also been my mother's public school teacher. What's more, he even matchmade the two of them. As children, Wu Chin-liang and his brother had gone to Japan to study. It was our family that had given them financial aid. On account of our generations-long friendship, Wu invited me to Brazil to carve out my career.

Today, Brazil's per capita income is about US$11,000 compared to Taiwan's US$20,000.[2] But more than 50 years ago, Taiwan was still

---

2 In 2012, Brazil's per capita income was $ 11,208 and Taiwan's per capita income was $ 20,574.

struggling economically. Our per capita income then was US$160 while Brazil's was already US$2,000. In the 1950s and 1960s, many Taiwanese longed to leave Taiwan. If one failed to get into an American or Japanese school, Brazil was considered a very good third option for opening up one's horizons. At that time, Brazil's arms were wide open to foreign workers. No wonder there was a wave of Brazil-bound Taiwanese emigrants.

The Japanese also went. In fact they were the earliest to go, and they went in the largest groups. They were also very systematic about their emigration (be it to Brazil or Hawaii). They would go into agriculture and develop new lands. On the other hand, the Chinese were savvier. They eschewed farmwork for restaurants or small businesses in the city.

At that time, the Fujianese emigrating to Southeast Asia or Taiwan had any one of "the three cutting instruments," as it was said, to earn their living by. One group would pick up scissors, open tailoring shops, and make new clothes. Another would pick up vegetable cleavers, open restaurants, and prepare delicious meals. The last would pick up shears, open up barber shops, and trim hair. When the instruments earned the immigrants enough money, they proceeded to the next step-lending money at high interest rates. These overseas Chinese would band together as a group, help each other along, and maintain an area of the city purely for the Chinese, i.e. establish a Chinatown. The Japanese did not set up Japanese Town.

To me, Brazil was still too far away, and I was still a little green

In 1960, Lo (middle) and friends Huang Tong-sheng (2nd from left), Chen Lung-chi (2nd from right) left Taiwan on the same plane. Lo went to Japan to study at Waseda University, while Huang and Chen went to the United States.

1961, while studying in Japan, Lo went to Atami hot spring resort with friends Lai Chia-shing, Hsieh Nan-chiang, and Chang Hong-shi (from right).

While working for his master's, Lo attended both Tokyo University and Waseda University and tried to build a firm foundation for his future career.

when it came to doing business. I was also not all that passionate about making money. I took a step back, and thought, since I already passed the study-abroad exam, I'll go to Japan.

I successfully applied for a place in Waseda's School of Politics and Economics. I would leave Taiwan in

August, 1960. On the day of my trip, central and southern Taiwan was experiencing a flood that saw fields turning into seas. Trains were not in service. Instead, military planes filled in as transport. I flew out of Chiayi on a military plane, then when I got into Taipei, switched to a civilian carrier. I was on my way to Japan to be an overseas student again.

22

Forty-three People Secretly Becoming Sworn Brothers in a Hotel

AYEAR LATER, I came back to Taiwan for my summer vacation. The second day, I went to find my best friend, Tsai Shun-li. Instead of welcoming me with open arms, he looked at me with a panic-stricken face, and blurted, "How dare you come back?" This was how I found out that in my year away, many of my Taiwanese friends had been tormented and left at the gates of Hell. Tsai Shun-li had been arrested by the Bureau of Investigation and locked up for half a year. He was beaten until he was almost half-dead. His family pitched together four hundred thousand NT dollars to bail him out. But Liu Chia-shun (劉家順) was not as lucky.

Liu Chia-shun had studied at National Taichung First Senior High School. He was thin as a pole, and his eyes were very sharp. With his outstanding grades, he had secured himself a spot at National Taiwan University. But having matured young, he had many ideals. Not content to study medicine, the most popular choice at that time, he threw himself into Political Science instead. The night before he was supposed to leave for the US to further his studies, he heard from the Garrison Command Headquarters that his passport had been suspended. Never mind that his air ticket had already been bought. Half disbelieving this news, he thought he'd try his luck anyway the next day. He was stopped at the airport and forbidden to board his plane. Over the next few days, bad luck pursued him like a series of bullets, Liu Chia-shun got called up by the Bureau of Investigation for a talk, and then got sentenced to eight years in prison by the Court of Law.

What crime they had been guilty of, nobody could say. In that era, the Kuomintang detained whomever they wanted. There was no need of justification. We could only deduce that these arrests had something to do with a meeting at Guanzihling a year ago, where forty-three of us secretly became sworn brothers. Kuomintang's intelligence must have found out about it somehow.

In the summer of 1960, my ex-classmates were finishing their military service, and many of us were preparing to go abroad to study. Among them was Tsai Trong-rong (蔡同榮), a Legislative Yuan member today. Tsai was my ex-classmate from junior high school. During his university days, he studied Law at National Taiwan University. He already demonstrated a flair for leadership. For example, he was elected to be Chairman of the Student Representatives Union. Seeing that we would soon be going down our various paths, Tsai Trong-rong didn't want us dispersed. He organized a get-together in hopes that we would be able to do something for our society in the future. In all honesty, at twenty-five years of age, we had no solid plan, no agenda at all. We were discontented with Kuomintang's tyranny, and only knew that the onus was on us young people to topple the regime.

Nowadays, through Facebook, it's easy to make plans with a bunch of friends to meet at a restaurant or to go cycling. This would have been unfathomable back then. At that time, under martial law[1], you had to apply for a permit for a gathering of more than three

---

[1] Taiwan's period of martial law has lasted from May 19, 1949 to July 15, 1987, 38 years and 57 days.

people. To get a big group together, a few core hosts would privately invite their classmates, who would then ask their classmates, thus extending the network like the spokes of an umbrella. As a cover, we would be organizing this group outing in honor of Tsai Trong-rong's departure and this send-off would take place at a Hot Springs Resort in Tainan's Guanzihling.

June 19, the appointed date for this secret gathering, finally arrived, bringing with it a strong typhoon. The rain came down in torrents, and the wind howled — all the better perhaps to conceal our secret gathering. We were not intimidated by the typhoon and stuck to our plan to meet up in the mountains. I got on a bus with Tsai Shun-li, but it would not go beyond Hsien Tsao Pu. So we put on our raincoats, got off the bus, and walked in the strong wind for three kilometers (bearing our torches as we did) and found ourselves at Guanzihling's Ching Ler Hotel.

We had planned for 70 to 80 people that day, but only 43 made it. Among them was Huang Kun-hu (黃崑虎), who is actively involved in the Taiwan Friends Association today. We had booked the entire hotel that day. There were no other hotel guests except for us. That night, at Ching Ler Hotel, with no peach blossom forest or incense from the time of "The Three Kingdoms [2]," we sat on tatami mats,

---

2 The Oath of the Peach Garden is a fictional event in the historical novel *Romance of the Three Kingdoms* by Lo Guanzhong. This event is set at the end of Eastern Han Dynasty (184-220 AD). Liu Bei, Guan Yu and Zhang Fei took an oath of fraternity in a ceremony in the Peach Garden, and became sworn brothers. Liu Bei would later became the first emperor of Han Dynasty.

Lo and Tsai Shun-li are like brothers. They braved winds and rain and went up to Guanziling in a typhoon day.

talking heatedly about our common cause, while the typhoon was unfolding outside. We promised to be at one another's weddings and made a pact to come together the second day of each New Year.

When we all agreed to be sworn brothers at Guanzihling, we did not mention a word of politics. But now that a few of us had been arrested, the rest of us were constantly spooked — would a special agent appear from nowhere, point a gun at us and escort us away? To escape from arrest, Huang Kun-hu left his Tainan home to hide in Hsinchu's woods up in the mountains. Tsai Shun-li also told me not to look for anyone from this group. He added grimly that if I got arrested, I should not, even if I was tortured, reveal the pact of brotherhood we made at Guanzihling.

23

Getting Engaged During White Terror

THAT SUMMER WAS LIKE A BAD PRANK PLAYED BY THE GODS. I was terrified of being arrested, so I locked myself up at home all day while depressing cicadas screeched outside, making the atmosphere even tenser. On the other hand, I was elated that my marriage was going to be finalized at last. Lucky for me, Chin-fun would be my life partner.

At the start of the summer, I took a ship designated for overseas students returning to Taiwan. Mother arrived in Taipei, where she would stay a night at Mrs. Mao's before continuing to Keelung to greet my arrival. That night, mother said to Chin-fun: "Chin-fun, Chin-fun, tomorrow our Ah Chuan is coming back, let's go to Keelung to welcome him home." Chin-fun was a very considerate girl and agreed at once. At midnight, she started to feel that something was not quite right. According to the Chinese calendar, she was twenty-two and about to graduate. She worried that by her going, as such a young girl, to welcome home a male, it might be taken as evidence of a boyfriend-girlfriend relationship. So, come five or six o'clock, at daybreak, she apologized to mother and said she wouldn't be accompanying her to Keelung after all.

Mother's first trick didn't work, so afterwards my relatives and friends got more aggressive in trying to get Chin-fun to marry me. Mother, Aunt, and mother's friend, one after another, paid visits to Mr. and Mrs. Mao in an attempt to persuade them to marry Chin-fun off to me. In the end, Mrs. Mao, partly as a way of paying back the favors, partly out of courtesy, made Chin-fun visit our family in

Chiayi, saying, "Come with me! Otherwise it'd be very paiseh — betraying their kindness! We are not strangers to them, are we?" Once in Chiayi, Chin-fun seemed surprised to see so many other people coming along to watch the show — and what's more, it seemed as if our parents had already warmed up to the idea and were now bent on becoming in-laws.

That day, I brought Chin-fun alone to "Sunset Hut" to let her see my once-upon-a-time dream and the mahogany trees that I'd planted. It was mid-summer. Chin-fun was wearing a short skirt, and both her legs got bitten by mosquitoes.

But the mosquito bites weren't the problem. The problem was Chin-fun, who wasn't quite ready yet. At university, she had always played the role of "relationship counselor" — she had never been in love herself before. Now that she was the one to confront the question of marriage, she was at a loss. She hadn't even worked a single day of her life yet, but she had now to seal her romantic destiny! No wonder she panicked. To make things worse, all my relatives and friends wanted to see me quickly engaged, while I was still in Taiwan over the summer, before I returned to Japan. That day, leaving Chiayi for Taipei, she cried all the way and even lost five or six kilograms shortly after.

Although free love was already practiced in the 1960s, obeying the wishes of your parents and letting them run your destiny was still a strong traditional imperative. If you weren't completely repulsed by the other party, you would probably accept your parents' choice of a life partner for you. So, at the encouragement of her parents, Chin-fun accepted the arrangement.

I felt terrible not giving Chin-fun enough time to come to a decision. But I had a friend whose family ran a lumberyard. They had hired a few thousand retired army soldiers to build a mountain road through Danda Mountain at Gigi in Nantou, and therefore had some military connections. He told me privately that the Garrison Command Headquarters had sent people to ask him about what I was doing in Japan. Of course he didn't betray me — he was after all a friend — but nevertheless this ominous message added great pressure. I wanted to end my summer holidays in dangerous Taiwan as soon I as could and rush back to Japan.

According to Taiwanese engagement ceremony tradition, I needed to go to Chin-fun's home in Taipei to "wear a ring". Fifty years ago, unless you had something urgent to communicate, you would use the telephone. Otherwise you communicated by mail. So I wrote my friend in Taipei and told him about my getting engaged in Taipei. When I got his reply, sent to my Chiayi home, I saw that the envelope had been opened and then resealed. Quite obviously, I was under surveillance.

A few days before my engagement, I boarded a North-bound train alone. Not long after, a man with a crew cut — the kind that army men sport— took a seat very close to mine. My heart sank. When I got off the train, would he take out a gun from his pocket, press it against my back, and then, in a low voice, tell me to follow him?

All trip long, my fellow passenger was silent. My heart was beating through my chest. Was he indeed someone who had followed me to this train, or was he just another traveler?

Patches of green and blue sped by outside the window. The train was transporting me towards my destination. In my heart, I sighed. I did not know if I would get a chance again to set my eyes on such scenery.

Time dragged. Every second felt like three minutes. After what seemed like a long while, we made it past Central Taiwan, and finally reached Yangmei, Taoyuan. My good friend Tsai Ray-hsiung (蔡瑞熊) was in Yangmei doing his military service. He was the valedictorian of Kaohsiung Medical University's first ever class. He would later become its principal. When I was in senior high, I often stayed over at his place. This time I said I would drop by. When the train came to a stop in Yangmei, I jumped out of the compartment, and, without turning my head back, walked resolutely towards the exit. There I showed my ticket to the conductor and quickly turned my head. I heaved a sigh of relief when I saw no one had followed me.

The engagement took place two to three days later. I rushed back to Japan soon afterwards.

24

The Unbelievable Economics Department at Tokyo University

My PROFESSOR AT WASEDA WAS A SPECIALIST IN STATISTICS. Because my grades in this subject at NTU were not bad at all, I was made a secondary teaching assistant in my sophomore year. As a rule, M.A. students are offered secondary teaching assistantships. Only Ph.D. students got to be primary teaching assistants. However, being appointed to a mere secondary teaching assistant was cause enough for celebration. It meant your ¥100,000 school fees would be waived and you also drew a salary of ¥4,500 a month, enough to rent a room the size of four and a half tatami mats.

As a secondary teaching assistant, I had to take attendance for every class. Among the students studying at Waseda was former Prime Minister Mori Yoshirō. Forty years later, when he took over the office, I was Taiwan's top representative to Japan. We talked about our shared past at Waseda and I even joked to him: "I probably called out your name during those years."

One day, the chair of the Economics department at National Taiwan University, Chang Han-yu, paid a visit to Tokyo. He had graduated from Tokyo University. The moment we met, he encouraged me to transfer to Tokyo University. He said I had to go there if I was serious about my studies. At that time, there was some flexibility in the university admission process. Tokyo University offered a special M.A. program. If you attended classes in this program for a year and passed the examination, you would be admitted into Tokyo University. A graduate of Tokyo University, Dr. Chan Han-yu wrote a letter to his alma mater strongly recommending me. That was how I entered Tokyo University and became a student of Professor Ōishi Yasuhiko. Before the war, whether at Tokyo University or Kyoto University, you could not study Modern Economics. Economics was still very much under History or Marxist Economics. Ōishi Yasuhiko was Tokyo University's only full Professor schooled in Modern Western Economics.

One may think of the Japanese as a punctual society, but this punctuality didn't seem to apply to campus life. I reported at 10:10 am to a class that was supposed to start at 10:20 am, only to find

While studying at Waseda, Lo rented a place close to Tokyo University, and also enrolled in Tokyo U's special MA program.

myself alone, waiting for the class to start. At 10:20 am, when students were supposed to be streaming into the classroom, no one had appeared yet. During my time at National Taiwan University, if the teacher still hadn't shown up after 15 minutes, it meant that class had been cancelled and students were free to go. In Professor Ōishi's classroom, I waited until 10:35 am. Seeing that 15 minutes had passed, I concluded that class had been cancelled. Still, something didn't feel right, so I decided to go to his office to take a look. What do you know, Professor Ōishi was still seated casually at his desk. I frowned, and said "Class was supposed to have started fifteen minutes ago, but there's no one in the classroom." Calmly, he gestured for me to sit and we started a chat. At 11am, we got up from our seats and walked back to the classroom, where all his students now sat waiting.

There was a famous young professor from the Economics Department at Tokyo University by the name of Negishi Takashi, who went to Stanford University after graduating from Tokyo University. In the US, he had published many articles. Among the Mathematical Economics scholars in Japan, Negishi Takashi was probably the very best. We all wanted to read his English articles, even if we struggled to understand them. The US had produced two giants in the field: one being Paul Samuelson from M.I.T. and the other, Kenneth J. Arrow from Stanford University. At that time, the Mathematical Economics Department at Stanford was considered the best in the country, and Negishi Takashi had been an associate professor there. But, back at Tokyo University, his academic brilliance and the aura

Taken at Waseda. Shirts and hand-held square bags were standard
attires of Japanese graduate students at that time.

of his Stanford career were no match for traditional Japanese set. He was given the lowly position of Assistant Professor. Sitting in Ōishi Yasuhiko's classroom, I saw how the full professor sat to one side, from his position of power, while Negishi Takashi was called to the front of the classroom, to "give his report."

In reality, although Ōishi Yasuhiko was a full professor, he did not possess a Ph.D. In the past, Ph.D.s were hard to come by. It wasn't just a matter of finishing a course and completing a Ph.D. dissertation within three years. You had to have achieved something and acquired a reputation before you could be assessed for the title. For example, before and after the war, many doctors were given their Ph.D.s only after they had worked for some time, and had submitted a dissertation. The Economics Department at Tokyo University in the 1960s was still a very conservative place. A higher position in the hierarchy meant you were always in the right. If professor Ōishi Yasuhiko was not actually a Ph.D., you could not stay at Tokyo University and hope to get a Ph.D. yourself.

Although this way of doing things would change shortly, six or seven years later, I felt very stifled at Tokyo University where these conservative values were so deeply ingrained. If I stayed long-term in Japan, when would I get my Ph.D., if ever? I decided that it was only a matter of time that I must go. In addition, since arriving at Tokyo University, all I saw were English books. Everyone was carrying nothing but English books. Rather than study from English books at Tokyo University, I might as well go to the US.

Having set my mind on further studies in the U.S., I asked Professor Ōishi Yasuhiko, "Ten years from now, which fields in Economics will hold the greatest prospects?" He told me, "Econometrics and Regional Science." Both these new fields had Statistics and Mathematical Economics as their foundation. My mentor in Waseda had been a specialist in Statistics. My grades in Statistics at National Taiwan University were the best compared to that of my other subjects. Encouraged, I went to the American Press Office to gather research on American Universities. I discovered that the leading school for Econometrics and Regional Science was University of Pennsylvania. That was when I set my mind not just to go to the US, but also to attend University of Pennsylvania.

25

American Policemen Gave Me a Lift to My Protest

IN THE EARLY 1960s, there was already a common saying: "The moon in the US is bigger than that of Taiwan." On August 6, 1963, I finally set foot on American soil and experienced the America of my dreams.

I had boarded a propeller plane from Japan, but back then it was not yet possible to fly directly. It was necessary to make three stopovers before reaching our destination. The first stopover was in Hawaii, my first time on American soil. The passenger sitting beside me was the wife of an American soldier based in Japan. She complained, "You can't find good steak in Japan." The moment we landed, she headed straight for a restaurant to satisfy her craving. When I found my way there eventually, she was already cutting into her steak.

Picking up the menu, I ordered a hamburger steak for a buck. I can't say I still remember the taste of that hamburger steak, but my gaffe with tipping is still vivid to me. In a way, you could say it was my first real experience with Western culture.

Before going to the US, my Japanese professor had gently reminded us that tipping was customary practice. You had to tip everywhere. But I only knew the half of it. After my meal that day, I got up with my check, walked over to the cashier, and attempted to present my tip to her in person. She seemed shocked to see my extended hand. What was the money for? It was only afterwards that I realized tipping is done by leaving money on the table, never directly to the staff. Similarly, it's good etiquette to leave a tip for hotel staff on the pillow before checking out of your room.

Nowadays, when young people go to the US, whether to further their studies or to travel, it's just a matter of crossing borders and experiencing a fresh curiosity about everything foreign. However, those in my generation who went to the US experienced strong cultural displacement that we might as well have been reborn. What was most revealing to us was witnessing what democracy meant.

When I was studying at Waseda University, my schoolmates had hung an anti-American Imperialist slogan from the statue of Waseda's founder, Okuma Shigenobu. If that itself had been an eye-opener, then experiencing American democracy was downright shocking.

Six months after my arrival in the US, a group of overseas Taiwanese students organized a protest against Taiwan's 228 Incident on February 22, 1964, in Washington D.C. Growing up in Taiwan, I could not conceive of street protests. That day, however, I would be part of one.

Those of us overseas students taking to the streets might be what you would call amateur protesters. We were certainly not as comfortable as American protesters, who marched with such conviction. They believed that speaking their minds was a God-given, inalienable right. Though we were physically in the US, our hearts were still "made in Taiwan." We carried signs, on which were written "Long Live Taiwanese Independence!" or "Taiwan has the right to decide for herself!" or even "Down with Chiang Kai-shek!" Passionate as these slogans seemed, the thirty of us walked silently with stoic faces. We made our way through the park and around the

Washington Monument, sticking to the prescribed route.

Of course Kuomintang special agents had their cameras ready, snapping pictures of our faces up close. Their cameras were so close that they couldn't have been thirty centimeters from our faces. It was as if they were making mug shots of their Top 10 Most Wanted. Chen Tung-pi (陳東璧), future top representative to Canada, was one of the protesters that day. Because he was afraid of creating trouble for his family back in Taiwan, he had come to the protest disguised. Chin-fun and I had given him a white pillow case to wear over his face (which he did after cutting out two holes for his eyes). He looked like a member of the Ku Klux Klan. Camera clicks were even more relentless around him that day.

In contrast to the fearlessness of the cameras around us, we were like innocent children, silently accepting of being photographed. Not only did we not tell these agents to stop, we didn't even dare to mutter a word, let alone start a fight. At this point, we must note the role of the American police, as our protectors that day. While we marched through the streets, policemen flanked us on both sides. Instead of waving their batons and barking orders at us to break up, the policemen waved their batons to make sure that our path would be smooth. They accompanied us to make sure that our safety was in no way threatened. This was the real eye-opener. The police I had known in Taiwan and in Japan were first and foremost extensions of our colonizers. They conducted themselves as if they were above us. They operated by inducing fear in the people they were supposed to protect.

A few years later, I would once again experience democracy in action through the American police. On the afternoon of March 26, 1968, Liu Wen-ching (柳文卿), a Japan-based supporter for Taiwanese independence, went to the Immigration Bureau to submit a routine report. Instead he was unexpectedly detained. Although forceful extradition had already been outlawed a year earlier, the plan was to put him on the first plane back to Taiwan the next day. That night, after hearing the news, Koo Kuan-min [1] came up with a plan to stall for time which involved rounding up ten men, driving in 3 cars, to stage a fake car crash against the Japanese police cars. He reasoned that if the extradition could be delayed, they would have time to take legal action against the stubborn bureaucrats to reverse the process. Faced with the forced extradition of one of their own, everyone threw caution to the wind. Among one of those who partook in the plan was the former top representative to Japan Hsu Shih-kai [2]. He signed up for the riskiest role — the driver of the car that would be involved in the fake crash. Apparently, he even told his wife, "If I were to die, you have my permission to remarry." However, due to a series of accidents, the car crash never happened. The ten desperate men

---

1 Koo Kuan-min (辜寬敏, Oct. 15, 1926 ~) is a Taiwan entrepreneur and an active member of Taiwan independence movement. He was once the director of the Youth Division of WUFI-Japan.

2 Dr. Hsu Shih-kai (許世楷, Ko Se-kai in Taiwanese) is a Taiwanese historian, politician, and diplomat. He is an important leader of the Taiwan independence movement, and was appointed as Taiwan's top representative to Japan from 2004 to 2008.

tried to pull off a kidnapping on the runway. After a scuffle involving much pulling and tugging on the tarmac, Liu Wen-ching was still extradited. The ten men, including Huang Chao-tang [3] and Hsu Shih-kai, were detained for three days and two nights.

To protest Liu Wen-ching's forced extradition, the WUFI-US headquarters decided to organize a protest targeting the Japanese embassy in Washington DC. Coincidentally, Dr. Martin Luther King, the human rights leader had just been assassinated the day before. Many blacks resorted to violence, throwing gas bombs and setting cars on fire. The whole Washington DC was filled with fire and smoke, which caused the sky to turn black. The pink cherry blossom trees alone blossomed, seemingly indifferent to the chaos happening all around the city.

Washington DC regulations decree that protests must be held at least five hundred meters away from the entrance of any embassy. That day, I marched with the chairman of WUFI-US headquarters, Dr. Chen I-te [4], carrying the Taiwanese flag, but nobody paid attention to us. The police had been dispatched to resolve the street

3 Dr. Huang Chao-tang (黃昭堂, Ng Chiao-tong in Taiwanese. September 21, 1932 ~ November 17, 2011) was an important leader in Taiwan independence movement. In 1960, he and some friends founded Taiwan Youth Association in Japan and published Taiwan Youth magazine advocating Taiwan independence. He was the Chairman of World United Formosans for Independence from 1995 until his death in 2011.

4 Chen I-te (陳以德, born 1930 in Taiwan) is one of the early US-bound Taiwanese overseas students. He and friends John Lin (林榮勳), Jay Loo (盧主義), Tom Yang (楊東傑), and Echo Lin (林錫湖) founded "The Formosan's Free Formosa" in 1956, which later expanded and became "World United Formosans for Independence" (WUFI) in 1970.

violence caused by angry blacks. Suddenly, we found ourselves close to the Soviet Union's embassy. A policeman emerged from nowhere and barred us from going further. "What do you want?" We replied that we wanted to go to the Japanese embassy to make a protest. He said, "This is the Soviet Union's embassy, don't you know where the Japanese embassy is?" When we both shook our heads, the policeman asked us to get into his patrol car. In the end, he gave us a lift directly to the entrance of the Japanese embassy, never mind the five hundred meter regulation. That was how Chen I-te and I arrived at the Japanese Embassy, where we submitted our protest letter.

26

The Son of the British Prime Minister Mops the Floor in the US

ONE DAY, in my first or second year at UPenn, I went with a friend to the school cafeteria to get a meal. Something caught the attention of my friend, whose gaze latched onto a young cleaner working not far from us. He gestured for me to turn around and take a look, too. He said in a low voice, "That fellow that you see there mopping the floor — he's Harold Wilson's son." Needless to say, I was shocked. Harold Wilson was the British prime minister at that time. Robin Wilson, his son, had come to UPenn to get a Master's degree in Mathematics. The fact that he was also doing menial chores part-time completely subverted whatever class-related expectations I had learned in Taiwan. Back home, if someone was a member of the ruling class or belonged to a wealthy family, his children enjoyed all sorts of special privileges. This unwritten rule was widely accepted as a fact. For example, in the 1950s, when Chen Lu-an, the son of Chen Cheng, the Chair of the Executive Yuan and second only to Chang Kai-shek in all of Taiwan, was about to graduate from high school, it was suddenly decreed that high school graduates were eligible to study abroad. Some of my classmates at Tainan First High School hitched onto the very same ride out.

Because Robin Wilson represented such a contradiction to my Taiwanese experience of class, my interest was piqued. On another day, I was once again in the student cafeteria when I saw a female cleaner. She had stacked quite a few plates on one hand that had gotten too heavy for her. Trying to balance the plates, she stumbled and as a result, the plates scattered everywhere. Robin Wilson was the first to rush to her side with his mop. At that moment, I felt that I had not come to the US for nothing. I learnt that day what is meant by democracy. The son of a British prime minister was a citizen of the country just like anyone else's son. He did not get special treatment. He held a cleaner's job. He mopped the floor, a very ordinary and menial task. He was serious about his job and respectful towards a fellow cleaner. Class did not enter into the picture. This was a true democracy.

I had come to the US by myself, after Chin-fun and I had gotten married in Japan. I worked hard every day. I was in the library from eight in the morning and I left the library only at midnight. On November 22, 1963, around 3 or 4pm, the custodian suddenly walked in to announce an early closure of the library. Only when I stepped out of the library, did I get wind of the news that was on everyone's lips. President John F. Kennedy had been assassinated. I looked up at the sky and thought of President Lincoln. He too had been shot by a white man while fighting for equality.

For the next three days, news of the assassination ran continuously around the clock on ABC and CBS, without a single ad interrupting the TV broadcasts. All of the US fell into a panic and mourning.

It was difficult to tear oneself away from the TV, such was the magnetism of the news. I too kept vigil in front of the TV, transfixed by every detail. Two days later, I was watching the live broadcast of Lee Harvey Oswald's arrest when suddenly the unimaginable happened again. The alleged assassin was assassinated. Along with everyone else watching at that time, I saw Lee Harvey Oswald keel over and die.

After Kennedy's assassination, Vice President Lyndon Johnson rushed and caught the next plane for the White House. While in midair, he was sworn in as President. When his plane landed, he had become the new president. The reporters swarmed to welcome him and had already forgotten about Kennedy's widow, Jacqueline. From the televised footage, I saw her opening the car door by herself. It didn't open the first time she tried.

During the three days of continuous coverage, numerous interviews were conducted. The Americans that I saw on television were sincere but frank, respectful but daring to speak their minds, capable of independent thought but also open-minded enough to assimilate other opinions. Collectively, they impressed upon me what a mature democratic society should look like.

The famous Japanese architect Andō Tadao (six years younger than me) once said that President Kennedy, his brother Robert Kennedy and Martin Luther King were the heroes of our time. In fact they were saints, sacrificing for their ideals of peace and equality, even if it got them killed in the end. Andō also said that those of us who lived in the same era as these heroes were truly lucky because we could experience the political change they brought. I share this conviction and I think I was even luckier than Andō for being in the US at that time.

27

Shouting at Robert Kennedy

AFTER PRESIDENT KENNEDY WAS ASSASINATED, Robert Kennedy, his brother and the Attorney General, decided to run for President and took part in the Democratic Party's primary. He even came to UPenn once to canvass for support. I squeezed my way to the front, and shouted, "Please support an independent Taiwan! Support Taiwan's separation from China!" Shouting this with me was Ou Jong-shiong (歐炯雄), who was studying Biology at UPenn (He would later become a professor at Chang Gung University). Ou's father was Ou Ching-shi (歐清石), the famous anti-Japanese colonial administration attorney.

Against the backdrop of recent advances in human rights for African Americans, I thought of the military rule that continued to oppress the Taiwanese people, depriving them of freedom. All through those years, I actively campaigned for an Independent Taiwan the best I could.

Politically, the world was split into two camps at that time. Those who flew the flag of "Communism" and those who flew the banner of "Democracy." Neither was willing to cede to the other. The US placed Taiwan on the side of "Democracy." To the US, Taiwan represented "Democratic China," and even set up a "committee of one million members" in opposition to Communist China. Support for a Democratic China was immense.

However, here was where Taiwan did not see eye to eye with the US. A "Democratic China" was laughable. We, Taiwanese, would neither be Democratic or Chinese. In order to get our dissenting

Taiwanese voices heard, we discussed and decided to focus our efforts on three Harvard professors with the greatest influence on US policy vis-à-vis China-Taiwan relations. These professors each had Chinese names: Fei Cheng-ching (費正清, John King Fairbank), Lai Hsiao-he (賴孝和, Edwin Reischauer) and Kung Chieh-jung (孔傑榮, Jerome Alan Cohen). The last, a scholar of Qing Dynasty law, had nurtured deep ties with Taiwan over the past few decades. In fact, among his former Taiwanese students were: current president Ma Ying-jeou (馬英九), former Vice President Lu Hsiu-lien (呂秀蓮), and his very first student from Taiwan, former Minister of Overseas Community Affairs Council Chang Fu-mei (張富美).

Professor Reischauer had also taught a student from Taiwan, Chen Hsien-ting (陳顯庭), who became his teaching assistant. Chen happened to be my senior at National Tainan First Senior High. It was through his arrangement that we both met Professor Reischauer at Chen's house. Professor Reischauer's first words well demonstrated his willingness to support the younger generation. "Today, I'm not going to be the one talking. I'm here to listen to what you have to say."

I was still young and would speak non-stop if egged on. I said, after the Treaty of Peace with Japan, Taiwan's status was never clear. Chang Kai-shek's rule had been decided by Douglas MacArthur as trusteeship. But what I most wanted to get across was that not all Taiwanese were on Chang Kai-shek's side of wanting to take back China. We wanted to have the right to decide our own future.

Professor Leischauer said that it was the first time he had ever heard a Taiwanese person speak about China-Taiwan relations with such passion and such depth. The meeting that day was supposed to take one hour, but in the end, it lasted three hours.

That afternoon, Chen's little brother Chen Heng-chao (陳恆昭), also a student at Harvard, was getting married in an auditorium at Harvard. We were all invited. Attending the ceremony were about one hundred Harvard professors and students. Not being from Harvard, my colleagues and I naturally congregated to one corner. When Professor Leischauer went onstage to give a speech as one of the wedding's witnesses, he unexpectedly gave acknowledgement of our group. "Those guys over there are fighting for Taiwan's independence," and even summoned us to the front. There, he raised a glass of champagne, and toasted loudly, "For the Republic of Taiwan." All my life, I had never felt as grateful as I did that moment. It was as if someone had finally understood and acknowledged publicly the never-ending journey that we alone had embarked upon.

28

A Letter from the Young Lee Chia-tung[1]

1 Lee Chia-tung (李家同, born 1939 in Shanghai, China), also known as Richard C. T. Lee, is an educator, writer, and opinion leader in Taiwan. He has been the president of 2 universities (National Chi Nan Univ. and Providence Univ.) and acting president of National Tsing Hua Univ.

I WAS BY NATURE A SHY PERSON. But the foreign soil of the US and the gentle wind of its democracy soon changed me. I ripened from a green fruit, and dared, for once, to express my bold colors.

In August 1963, when I first arrived in Pennsylvania, the new semester hadn't yet started. One day, I was in the school library looking for Japanese books when someone came over to say hi. I asked in English, "Are you from China?" "No." "Japan?" "No." Finally, I asked, "Then where are you from?" It turned out that he was from Gangshan, Kaohsiung. His name was Su Chin-chun. He graduated from National Taiwan University's Department of Electrical Engineering and was getting his Ph.D. at UPenn. Not long after, the Chair of the World United Formosans for Independence (WUFI) Chen I-te got word of me and drove down to invite me personally to join his organization.

After school opened, I attended a meeting held by the Taiwanese Association of the Greater Philadelphia region. I don't know what they saw in me, but I was picked immediately to lead their group. Perhaps because they perceived leadership in my tall build. Perhaps because they majored in Science and spent all their time holed up in a lab, I was comparatively freer with time as a Humanities major. In any case, I grew more extroverted as a result.

I had always loved to sing, so I rounded everybody up for sing-alongs. We would sing the heartwarming anthem "Our Taiwan" that the anti-Japanese lyricist Tsai Pei-huo (蔡培火) had written. It never failed to put us in a happy mood. I also took everyone to the Taiwanese Association in New York where we sang in larger numbers. The Taiwanese Association of Greater Philadelphia came to be recognized as one of the better led Taiwanese associations. Before long I was asked to be the Vice President of the Taiwanese Association of East Coast America.

When I was not studying for my Ph.D., my life on the East Coast in the 1960s constituted of joining political activities organized by the Taiwanese Association and the World United Formosans for Independence (WUFI). However, these organizations were different at heart. Members of one group did not always belong to the other. But, from the perspective of the Kuomingtang Party, joining a Taiwanese Association when a Chinese Students Association already existed for overseas students from Mainland China was as suspect as joining WUFI.

In reality, the Taiwanese Association was founded on very innocent intentions, to support compatriots on foreign soil. Upon getting my first job after graduation in 1968, I was sent to Pittsburgh where I got to know the local Taiwanese, and together we started the Pittsburgh Taiwanese Association. There was a backyard attached to the house I bought. I also held a good job and had a steady income, unlike many poor students. Some members of the Association wanted to get married in Pittsburgh, even though it was tens of thousands of miles away from their family. But they could not afford to rent a commercial venue. So Chin-fun and I would invite them to use our backyard, holding the wedding ceremony and the subsequent party with the lowest possible budget. The women would make egg rolls and spend $80 on potato chips, $20 for a cake, and $60 for a priest to administer the wedding. The bridal gown and sash — as well as the tears from the family — would be foregone. All in all, the cost wouldn't even total $200.

Many years later, we bumped into one of these brides that got married for cheap in our Pittsburgh backyard. Chin-fun and I didn't recognize her, but she could not resist coming forward and expressing her gratitude to us. Not only did she get married in our backyard, she and her husband had even spent their wedding night in our attic.

At the beginning of my third year in Pittsburgh, as a result of the Treaty of Mutual Cooperation and Security between the US and Japan, Okinawa was handed over to Japan, along with it was the disputable Senkaku or Diaoyu Islands. Much outrage ensued. Many youths took to the streets to protest the injustice. Some of these were overseas students from Mainland China. They were born in China and had lived in China for some years before moving with their families to Taiwan. Now they were nostalgic for what they thought of as their homeland. At the same time, they recognized that the Kuomintang's plan to reclaim their homeland would never bear fruit. Moreover, they felt helpless against the crazed mission to re-educate the masses (i.e. the Cultural Revolution) that began in 1966. Right up to the incident of the Diaoyu Islands, they had been angered by what they perceived as Chiang Kai-shek's lack of resolve. They placed their faith in the Communist Party instead. Even though our aspirations and political views were inevitably differed, we, as overseas students in the US, entertained high hopes about China's future as we all enjoyed the freedoms of living in the land of Democracy.

From the summer of 1971, overseas students of Taiwan and Hong Kong origin from all over the US took part in a series of debates about nationality. The last debate, also the biggest, was held at the Universtiy of Michigan at Ann Arbor (it would later be known as the "Ann Arbor meeting"). More than 400 people, including the children of influential Kuomintang party members, partook in this largely pro-China debate that lasted 3 days. It ended on the 5th of September with the conclusion that the Communist government should be the only entity representing Chinese people. If the Diaoyu Island activists began at first by unanimously opposing Japan, they now split into two groups, one gravitating towards Beijing, the other towards Taiwan, each with different hopes.

Although the Ann Arbor meeting was pro-China from the outset, I showed up, the only one pushing for an Independent Taiwan. Before the meeting, Hu Pu-kai (胡卜凱) the son of the longtime Legislative Yuan member of Hubei origin, Hu Chou-yuan (胡秋原), wrote a letter to me, inviting me to share my pro-Taiwan sentiments at Michigan. I happily accepted. This was what I had learned from being in the US. Express one's view and to listen with an open mind to a differing stance; and to respect that differing stance.

That said, the conference was ultimately not a pro-Taiwan platform, and the two opposing camps were sharply pitted against each other. My ex-Schoolmate from National Taiwan University Lai Chia-hsing (賴家興) decided to accompany me. Although Lai Chia-hsing was also a Ph.D. (from Kyoto University) and a scholar at heart, he was also a well-built level 3-certified Judo expert. He volunteered to be my bodyguard.

It turned out that I had nothing to fear. When we arrived, our hosts were courteous to a fault. Onstage, I gave a speech on behalf of the World United Formosans for Independence, emphasizing that in the future, the country known as Taiwan would not be divided by Mainlanders, Taiwanese or Chinese. As long as you hoped to live in Taiwan and strived for its future, that would be enough for you to be called Taiwanese. I also remembered encapsulating it all with the following statement. "The Kuomintang party does not represent the Chinese."

Those students who came to the meeting that day had probably never seen a pro-Taiwan person in the flesh. Many were curious about me. When I left the stage, 20 to 30 people lined up to speak to me.

Back from the Michigan conference, I immediately attended a Taiwanese Association meeting in Pittsburgh, where I gave another speech. By coincidence, the famous History professor Hsu Cho-yun (許倬雲) was in the audience. He was five years older than me. Professor Hsu was already a very respected academic at the University of Pittsburgh where he was teaching courses on ancient Chinese history and pre-Qin Dynasty history (2100 BC ~ 221 BC). My talk intrigued him. He later approached me to ask if he could join the

Taiwanese Association. I replied, "Of course, you're very welcome."

Hsu Cho-yun's ancestors were from Jiangsu, China. Ordinarily, a Mainlander like him wouldn't have joined a Taiwanese association. Among the overseas students at that time, those of Taiwanese origin were usually pro-Taiwan. Mainlanders, on the other hand, were usually pro-China. This seemed only natural.

For a while, Hsu Cho-yun and I got along very well. Although I worked at a civilian company, I taught part-time every now and then at University of Pittsburgh. The two of us might have even be considered colleagues. Cho-yun's wife was of Taiwanese origin. Sometimes Chin-fun and I invited them over for dinner. Other times, we were invited to their homes. Never once did I suspect his motive for joining the Taiwanese Association since he didn't seem to be the kind who would rat on others. Despite our fundamental difference in opinion, I thought that we could still be friends.

Once, when Cho-yun had to go back to Taiwan, I drove him to the airport. He said to me, "I will be going back to meet Chiang Ching-kuo (son of Chiang Kai-shek). Do you happen to have any suggestions for the Kuomintang Party?" I said, "If they really want to ease the domestic tension, they should unconditionally release the political dissidents that they imprisoned."

Since the Ann Arbor meeting, more and more Mainlanders had come to know of me. Even Lee Chia-tung, today's respected opinion leader and former president of National Chi Nan University, had solicited an article from me.

Among the publications published by overseas elites in the US was a biweekly founded by Chang Hsi-kuo called *Wild Grass* (《野草》). After Chang left the US, the task of commissioning articles fell to Lee Chia-tung. In 1972, Lee wrote me, emphasizing the magazine's political stance. "Never neutrality for neutrality's sake. Encouraging justice through freedom of speech." According to Lee, *Wild Grass* sought to represent every political angle. "This is its mandate." In the past, *Wild Grass* had debated Taiwan's secret trials and the infamous Lin Biao incident[2] in Mainland China. By soliciting an article in which I would elaborate further the ideals of my camp, Lee showed his willingness to present a divergent view. He hoped that it would further the understanding between our two camps. I graciously accepted his solicitation. I said, "People who disagree should exchange their differing viewpoints even more." That was how it was like for our generation of overseas students living in the US. Even if we fundamentally opposed each other, politically, we could still conduct ourselves in a civilized and open-minded way. We worked hard at achieving our opposing goals, as our words to one another remained civilized.

---

2 In 1971, Mao Ze-tong's vice chairman and designated successor Lin Biao perished in a suspicious plane crash over the Mongolian desert, following what appeared to be a failed coup to oust Mao. Following his death, he was condemned as a traitor by the communist party of China.

29

PhDs Take On Naval Divers t Williamsport

IN THE 1960S AND 1970S, Taiwan's Little League baseball team won game after game on American soil at Williamsport, Pennsylvania, bringing much glory to the Taiwanese of that generation. Since I lived in the vicinity, I went for two of the first three competitions.

In 1969, we were represented by a team called Golden Dragon. By the time this was reported in the newspapers, I had already gotten wind of it through a newsletter sent by WUFI encouraging overseas students to attend and cheer their compatriots. I designed a bronze trophy that with the phrase, "Viva Our Little Brothers!" engraved in English and Chinese and "Pittsburgh Taiwanese Association" at the bottom.

WUFI also decided to hang a banner which read "Team of Taiwan" and the Chinese words "台灣隊加油" ("Go, Taiwan, Go!") to let everyone know that one of the two teams playing on the field that day hailed from Taiwan. Despite our lofty-sounding title, "World United Formosans for Independence," we only had a couple hundred members in the US. That day, over 200 Taiwanese from different Taiwanese associations came to Williamsport to watch the game, but only 20 WUFI members were on site. Yale Professor Chen Lung-chi gave a speech. Lai Wen-hsiung (賴文雄) and Cheng Tzu-tsai (鄭自才) held the banner while I stood at the center. Cheng Tzu-tsai would later be one of the main players in an assassination attempt on Chiang Ching-kuo in New York.

The game started smoothly without any hitch. That year, the

Golden Dragon team was led by the Secretary-General of Taiwan's Baseball Association, Hsieh Kuo-cheng (謝國城). His son Hsieh Nan-chiang (謝南強), who had been my classmate in the Economics Department at National Taiwan University, also came to watch the game. Seeing me, he joked that his role there was to oversee the laundry of the team's smelly baseball uniforms. Naturally, I presented the trophy on behalf of WUFI.

The game ended with Golden Dragon as the winners. This was Taiwan's first win at Little League World Series in Williamsport. We all were smiling proudly from ear to ear. The next moment, however, five or six Chinese men built like martial-art experts emerged from nowhere to snatch away the pole that Cheng Tzu-tsai was using to hold up the banner. A fight then ensued. The troublemakers realized that they were outnumbered by people from the Taiwanese camp and they quickly retreated.

At 1971 Little League World Series, Chair of WUFI, Chang Tsan-hung, was informed beforehand that the Kuomintang was mobilizing their supporters to the baseball stadium. He thought of an ingenious idea to rent a plane that would display a banner with the Chinese words "台灣獨立萬歲" ("Long Live Taiwanese Independence") followed by "GO GO TAIWAN." Some joked, "Taiwan has an Air Force!" But in truth, it only cost $260 to hire the pilot. On the ground, the Kuomintang party made and distributed tens of thousands of Chinese flags to the spectators at the baseball stadium. Still, the sea of flags they waved were no match for our plane circling above.

At the next series in 1972, still sour at what had happened a year ago, the Kuomintang Party sent massive reinforcements to Williamsport.

A friend's son, who was still in elementary school, came up with a great idea. Using a potato, he carved out a seal of Taiwan. He stamped the shape of Taiwan on flyers that were distributed at the stadium. This boy, Chang Yi-jen (張怡仁), would later become a distinguished student at West Point. In fact, so distinguished that he was one of those honored with a face-to-face meeting with US President Ronald Reagan (It was customary for the US President to meet the top six students from West Point every year.)

In Taiwan, military school would only be an option if you didn't get into university. That is not the case in the US. To American students, military school represented both a challenge and an honor. Entry into West Point was highly coveted. To get into West Point, you needed to have Harvard-level intelligence and an even better physical shape. A West Point student did not have to pay for his education, but in return he had to serve 5 years after graduation. Upon completion of military service, he was free again to choose his own path. Chang Yi-jen ended up going to graduate school at Columbia University.

Young Chang Yi-jen's peaceful act of distributing flyers was no match for the violent atmosphere in the stadium that day. Before the game, we heard that the Kuomintang Party would be sending sixty Boston-trained naval divers to the stadium. Now, sixty may not sound like a big number, but we were grossly outnumbered.

Upon hearing the news, a few of the Taiwanese association members chickened out. In the end, only sixteen of us showed up fearlessly at the stadium, with bandanas on our heads to express our resolve.

Being outnumbered wasn't our biggest problem. We were PhDs, not fighters. "Cracking eggs against a rock" was more like it. Chang Tsan-hung came up with an idea. We would all keep a hidden stash of salt in our pockets. If push came to shove, we could throw the salt in our aggressors' eyes. Of course, none of the salt ended up being used.

Next to the Williamsport stadium was a little slope, where the sixteen of us stood. When the game ended, the sixty naval divers armed with iron bars wrapped in cloth surrounded us. A reporter from China Times shouted "They're one of us too! Don't beat them up!" Ironically, that was when the iron bars started swinging. Not knowing how to fight, I was beaten all over and I still have a scar to show from this incident. My glasses were smashed as well, so I couldn't make out what happened afterwards.

But Chin-fun saw it all. She had brought our two sons along and was standing on the other side of the slope. With one hand, she held the hand of six-year-old Ted and she carried two-year-old David in the other arm. Seeing that we were getting beaten up from afar, she panicked and yelled at an overweight police officer, who was also watching the violence unfold and not thinking at all to intervene. "What's the matter with you? Why aren't you doing anything?" No soon after the words came out of her mouth when three Chinese men shot out of nowhere and pushed her roughly and spit out the question, "Does your husband belong to the World United Formosans for Independence?" Before Chin-fun had a chance to reply, a police helicopter arrived at scene, scattering the sixty men and saving the day.

With my hand injured, I could not drive the car. A friend drove us two hundred kilometers back to our home in Pittsburgh. That night, Chen Gu-ing (陳鼓應), a former Professor of Philosophy at National Taiwan University visited me, marveling at our courage for taking on the sixty naval divers. I said, "To each his own. Beating up

Taiwan's little league baseball team Golden Dragon came to Williamsport, Pennsylvania to compete for the world cup. Taiwanese overseas students went as a group to cheer them up. WUFI hang a banner which emphasized this team is from "Taiwan."

someone simply for disagreeing with you, that's just plain barbaric."

Those few years at Williamsport, I deeply believed that we were simply a group of intellectuals inspired by the democratic air we breathed in the US. We decided to do something about the unjust system oppressing our homelands. We couldn't not do anything. We all wanted the best for our homeland, and to do so, we had to help bring about change. We had no knives or guns. We were only scholars who wanted to make a revolution happen. The Kuomintang party lumped us with the Communists, but this was in fact a perversion on their part. We were nowhere as large as the Communist Party for one, and certainly not the terrorists or evil people that they made us out to be.

Our headquarters in Pennsylvania rented a Post Office box (P.O. Box 7914). Because phone calls were expensive at that time, all communication was conducted via mail. The first time I went to collect letters at the post office, I was approached by an FBI agent. The first question he asked was, "Are you a communist?" During that time period, there was nothing more loathsome in American eyes than a Communist. Without a doubt, someone from the Kuomintang had (mis)informed the FBI about us.

If you take away the label of "World United Formosans for Independence," what remains? — The conscience of a thinker and the passion of patriot. Every week we would hold our meetings. And every week we brought to the table the aspirations we held for Taiwan's future and the question of our inalienable democratic rights. My son

David had a hard time understanding this. He asked, "Every week you keep talking about Taiwan's future. Aren't you tired?" I quoted Martin Luther King's famous line back at him. "I have a dream!" Now why would I ever be tired?

30

Bringing Bananas to America

IT WAS GENERALLY UNDERSTOOD THAT TAIWANESE OVERSEAS students in the US during the 1960s scraped by on the most meager of means. Taiwan's per capita income at that time was $160. We were allowed to take out only $200. The Korean students said that this was still more than what they were allowed to take out — $160. No doubt, the war had inflicted poverty on all of Asia. I was fortunate to come from a more affluent background. Mother gave me $2,000 that she had illegally obtained from the black market for me to smuggle out. This was the same amount managed by another ex-classmate from my NTU days, Hsieh Nan-chiang. His father, Hsieh Kuo-cheng, was at the time Assistant Manager at the Taiwan Cooperative Bank (He also was the secretary-general of Taiwan's Baseball Association. He would later come to be known as the Father of Taiwan's Little League Baseball).

Taking $2,000 out of Taiwan was considered a big deal. At its peak exchange rate of 1 USD = 46NTD, $2,000 was equivalent to 90,000 NTD. You could buy half a piece of property in Taiwan with that money. However, at Customs, you didn't need go to great lengths to conceal this money. It sufficed to put it in the pocket of your pants. Out of respect, customs officers did not subject students going overseas to a body search.

However, once you landed in the US, the money diminished in value, like a giant becoming a dwarf. The first time I ate a steak in an American restaurant, I spent nine to ten dollars in one shot. It was more money than what an entire semester at National Taiwan

University had cost me (the tuition was 240 NTD for one semester). One semester's fees at UPenn, on the other hand, cost $500. One spent on average $1 every day on food alone. The $2,000 would last at most a year. That's why, even though Hsieh Nan-chiang and I were from affluent backgrounds, we still had to work part-time like the rest.

When I first arrived in the US, before I even started school, a student senior to me with good intentions handed a restaurant menu to me. Seeing the confused look on my face, he explained, "You have to memorize this if you want to work as a waiter." It was commonly understood that overseas students all waited tables, so that they could pay their tuition. Being a waiter qualified you for tips. It was better than being a busboy which paid little.

In the end, I didn't become a waiter. One day, I saw an ad in the school paper seeking house painters. With two other international students (one Japanese, the other Korean), I applied for the job. I was the only one who dared to reach for the highest spot. Growing up, I had never done anything so menial. I couldn't help boasting about it when I got home that day.

Afterwards, I found another job at a hospital. This one required me to work from six to eight in the morning. All I had to do was deliver newspapers to the bedsides of two thousand patients. One month's work brought in $160, almost the same as an average full-time worker. On a monthly basis, Chin-fun and I spent $60 on food and $40 on rent. The remainder was allocated for books. A book at that time cost about eight to twelve dollars.

The average overseas student had it much harder. If he was from a poor background, he really had to be careful how he spent his money. My friend, Su Chin-chun (蘇金春), who came to the US after graduating from the electrical engineering department at NTU, got into this mindset from the moment he left Taiwanese soil. Most take a plane to get here but he made the slow journey by sea to the US's West Coast. It wasn't even a normal passenger ship that he took to cross the Pacific Ocean but a cargo ship, as if he was a piece of cargo.

Some overseas students used the time on the cargo ship to work part-time and earn a bit of pocket money. I don't know if Chin-chun

Owing to the great per capita income disparity between Taiwan and the United States, although Lo is from an affluent family, he and wife still led simple life in the US, and Lo even delivered newspaper part time.

The early Taiwanese overseas students tended to be poor, hence their weddings were often very simple and without their parents' participation. Usually the bride and the groom would go to the church accompanied by friends, and let the priest marry them.

Lo let friends use his home to hold the wedding reception. He helped setting up wineglasses.

worked or not, but I do know that he took a stash of mullet roe, a Taiwanese and Japanese delicacy, and a basket of bananas on board with him. At sea, if the weather was good, he would take the mullet roe out to sun on the deck. If the ship rocked, causing the mullet roe to slip back and forth, he was busy making sure that the roe didn't slip off the deck. Stopping over in Japan, he sold the bananas and mullet roes at inflated prices. With the money, he bought a windbreaker jacket and a camera before continuing on his journey.

When the ship docked on the US's West Coast, Chin-chun got off the boat and boarded a Greyhound bus headed east. At that time, a $90 ticket covered travel for 90 days. With this ticket, Chin-chun crossed the country before finally arriving at the University of Pennsylvania.

In the 1960s, Taiwanese overseas students in the States all lived a frugal existence. Wang Po-wen (王博文), who was two years older than me, saved money on a book bag by taking the doctor bag that his father used on outpatient visits. By the time I arrived in the US, he had already earned his Master's degree and started working. There were pear trees in the backyard of the farmhouse that he rented in the countryside. Usually farmers would allow the pears to fall naturally to the ground, where they could be eaten by horses. To think that a fruit we considered precious was fed to horses! Po-wen saved these pears. At gatherings, he often brought baskets of pears along, which we would eat with hearty enjoyment.

Before going to study abroad, you'd hear about the struggles of overseas students. But only the actual experience gave you a true understanding of the pressures of surviving abroad. Whether you were good at your studies or not, studying abroad represented a challenge in itself.

For our era of overseas students, the 1,000 out of 10,000 university graduates who qualified to go abroad, were considered society's crème de la crème. Even though we didn't have much in our pockets, our aspirations were grand. Almost everyone enrolled in prestigious schools. Our fathers and brothers back home borrowed money from relatives so that we could study abroad in the US. Even the most ungrateful one would apply himself with great determination to his studies as if his life depended on it.

31

Taking Classes from a Nobel Prize Winner

N O OVEREAS STUDENT COULD AFFORD TO LET HIS GUARD DOWN. At UPenn, I, too, worried constantly about my studies. Among my professors who were all world class economists, Lawrence Klein was especially acclaimed for his genius. When he was only 23, he got a Ph.D. at M.I.T. for a thesis entitled, "The Keynesian Revolution." When I took his course, it had been in print for more than thirty years.

When Klein taught at the University of Michigan, he may have joined the Communist Party. In the early 1950s, during the anti-

While studying at UPenn, Lo worked as Professor Lawrence Klein's research assistant. Klein was awarded the Nobel Economic Science Prize in 1980 for his contribution to the field of econometrics.

Lo became the student of Nobel Economics Laureate, Lawrence Klein, and received his doctorate from UPenn, an Ivy League school.

Communist McCarthy years, no action was spared to weed out Communists from governments and other public institutions. It was the same in academia. Accusations were not without ramifications. White Terror enveloped the entire public sphere. Klein was forced to leave the States for Kansai University in Japan and Oxford in England. In the late 1950s, Klein returned to the US, resuming his position at Michigan University and then moving on to UPenn. For his contributions to the field of econometrics, Klein was awarded the Nobel Prize in Economics in 1980.

In the 1960s, Econometrics was still considered a new field of science, founded by Paul A. Samuelson (May 15, 1915 - Dec. 13, 2009), the second Nobel Prize winner in Economics. He was truly one of the greats who broadened our understanding of Economics. In 1941, at his thesis defense at Harvard, his examiners, who were all respected names in the field, were stumped by his presentation and all looked at one another. The question wasn't whether Samuelson had passed, but whether they themselves had understood what Samuelson had just said. They questioned whether they would pass themselves. His dissertation would be the cornerstone of the new body of knowledge known as Mathematical Economics.

Klein had studied under Samuelson, the pioneer of this new American-dominated field. As a lecturer, Klein was very gentle, speaking to us as if we were equals in conversation, and often dwelling on the philosophical underpinnings of the subject. He didn't talk in equations or formulas or take us step by step through calculations. Deeply loved, he was well sought-after by students. In my first semester, my English was still not very good, and neither was my Mathematics for that matter. For my so-so performance, I only got a B⁺. So, I did not get to be one of his prized students. Of the 30 plus students in his class, only 4 or 5 got A's, 10 got B's, and the rest received C's or D's. He could be very harsh in his grading.

Honestly speaking, PhDs were not easily given out at these prestigious universities. Morris Chang (張忠謀), C.E.O. of Taiwan Semiconductor Manufacturing, had once been an overseas student in the US. He had gone before me. After getting his Master's, he spent two consecutive years from 1954 to 1955 sitting for his Ph.D. qualification exam at M.I.T. — but all in vain. The US was a meritocracy. If you got stuck at a bottleneck, as Morris Chang had been, you were discouraged from squandering your time and encouraged to leave academia.

The university system in Japan, on the other hand, was not at all like that. For example, at Tokyo University, students would knock on the doors of reputable professors in the hope of taking their classes. Not-so-good professors, on the other hand, would be shunned. To be taken on by a reputable professor was not an easy thing. But once he agreed and you became his protégé, you were pretty much guaranteed good grades (even if he had high expectations for you as a student) and everyone more or less got A's. At Waseda, I had gotten straight A's. When my professors at UPenn saw my transcript, they were surprised. With a smile, I said, "Getting a B in Japan is quite difficult."

Bright-eyed students at American universities were also on the lookout for the best professors to latch on to. However, the professor-student relationship in the US was less formal compared to that relationship in Japan. At times, after a certain point in the relationship, some students would even call their professors by their first names. I still remember my first exam at UPenn. After three hours of hard work, everyone still had their heads buried in their exam papers. Nobody had handed in his booklets yet, but the professor wasn't hurrying anyone. In fact, he cheered us on, asking us what we wanted to eat. Then he left and returned with coffee and donuts. This professor had a very interesting background. His brother was the great Paul Samuelson and his uncle was Kenneth J. Arrow. Both were Nobel Prize winners. Obviously, having such a distinguished set of relatives may not be a good thing, which is why he later changed his name to Robert Summers. 'Summers' sounded close enough to 'Samuelson', but was different enough to get him out of Samuelson's shadow. However, it was his son, Lawrence, that did him proud and made the 'Summers' name what it is today. Lawrence Summers became the Secretary of Treasury in 1999 until 2001, then the President of Harvard until 2006, and the Director of the National Economic Council under Barak Obama from 2009 to 2010.

During my first year at UPenn, a colleague of Chin-fun's brother-in-law at Tohoku University flew over for a campus visit. I was asked to show him around. The Japanese professor was keen on accompanying me to my classes to experience an American-style education. But at the end of the class, unable to conceal his shock, he kept asking me what happened. What had happened was, while the teacher was lecturing onstage, one student who was smoking a pipe had asked a series of questions to the lecturer. He was waving his pipe higher and higher with each question. The Japanese professor thought the student in question was quite out of line. I said that despite the casual atmosphere of our classes, our American professors could be very strict in grading. At the end of every semester, they would invite their students to their homes for dinner parties, but this friendly gesture had nothing to do with our grades. From my own experience, the US was still the best place for education.

In my second semester, I elected a class on statistics taught by a Greek professor called Phoebus Dhrymes. He awarded me 90 points, which placed me at the top of the class. Shortly after, I hit jackpot when he asked me to become his teaching assistant. Things got better from then on. Dhrymes' Ph.D. dissertation at M.I.T. was very well-regarded in the field. He was extremely knowledgeable. Klein had founded an academic journal called the International Economic Review and he invited Phoebus Dhrymes to be its editor-in-chief. The two had great respect for each other and often got together for discussions. It was through Dhrymes that I finally got Klein's attention. At that point, he was looking for research assistants to help him with his work on a large-scale Econometric model. I was invited to join the team, and henceforth became one of his protégés.

32

The Magnificent Computer Capable of Processing 43K

I WORKED AT PROFESSOR KLEIN'S RESEARCH LAB AS A STATISTICS research assistant. Klein was experimenting with a groundbreaking economic model that applied over 1,000 equations to map a model for the US economy. If this model was successful, it could be used to make many predictions. For example: should today's stock price go up by 5%, you could input this variable into the model, and it could tell you what effect that 5% increase in stock price would have on the US economy.

My job was to make calculations, but it was the kind of calculations required of an economic model. It was one that couldn't be done with pen and paper. It wasn't a matter of simple arithmetic. It was a mind-boggling dance involving over a thousand equations applied to a massive number of variables. In short, it was the kind of calculation that only a super-sized computer could handle.

ENIAC, commonly acknowledged as the world's first computer, was introduced in 1946 at UPenn's Moore School of Electrical Engineering. It was not until 1964 that I first set my eyes on a computer. Someone born then would be 50 years old today.

The computers then were different from the ones so commonly used today. You had to input your source data on a piece of paper. The size of which resembles today's "preference card" for universities that senior high school students in Taiwan fill out. They were called "punch cards." On each punch card were rows and rows of numbers. To input "A," you would have to punch X number of holes. To input "B," you would have to punch Y number of holes. There was a logic behind all this. There was a female typist handling all this inputting. In the 1960s, computers were already widely being used in American companies, especially in their human resource and accounting departments.

The volume of data handled by Klein's economic model was massive. We would often use up 30 boxes of punch cards a day. Each box contained up to 2000 punch cards. In other words, I would handle tens of thousands of punch cards each day. What I did at that time closely resembled what grannies in Taiwan do, when they go to wet markets. I would load a little pull cart with boxes of these punch cards, and wheeled them to the computer center at the Wharton School of Business.

Desktops or personal laptops did not yet exist. The computers that I encountered filled up entire rooms. In a room of more than 330 square meters, there would be units of refrigerator-sized computers. Each stood next to one another as many as twenty units side by side. Punch cards were fed into them, stored into diskettes and processed. A printout on paper would produce the results of the calculations. Because the amount of data I brought in each time was massive and took the computers a long time to run, the processing would often be done overnight. So, it became a routine that I would lug the boxes in at night and picked up the result of the calculations the next day.

If I remember correctly, the first model that we used was an IBM 7094. Subsequently, we switched to the largest computer center at Westinghouse Electric. The model there could handle a whopping

There was no PC in the 60s. Computers were huge, and often occupy a whole room. (Courtesy of University Archives, Columbia University in the City of New York.)

43 K. At that point, impressed by this magnificent capacity, I felt I was doing a very important job. Who'd expect that the file size of almost any digital photo today would easily surpass that?

33

A Ph.D. Certificate that Even a Ph.D. Can't Read

In MY SIXTH YEAR IN THE US IN MAY 1968, I spent more than three months working on my Ph.D. dissertation, entitled "The Growth Models of Two Regions." Although it was only 100 pages, it was rather original. Typically, a dissertation is followed by a defense, but after I submitted my thesis, my supervising professor Ronald Miller called me to tell me, "Everyone agrees that it's good." So I passed without even having to do a defense.

My Ph.D. degree was in Regional Science. If you just glanced at this title, it didn't seem at all related to Economics. But in fact, in the 1950s and 1960s, "Regional Development" was a very trendy term.

Lo (front row, 3rd from left) joined experts from other countries in Austria, and tried to find solutions for world problems.

The whole world was in the process of expansion. City planners, economists, geographers were often brought together in one room to rack their brains for the optimal strategy for a city or a region's development. The Chair of our department, Walter Isard, was a very ambitious man. He attempted to bring all these fields of knowledge together under the umbrella of "Regional Development." He decided to call it "Regional Science," so that it could be construed as a branch of scientific study. In 1960, Regional Science officially became a new discipline at UPenn, founded by Walter Isard.

Regional Science was a groundbreaking new branch of economic theory. It focused on economic growth, and attempted to provide solutions to the problems introduced by urban and agricultural expansion. Often its starting point was the gathering of statistical data related to the land being considered: its ecology, its environment, the resources available to the region, its human population, and its means of transportation. The data would then be inputted into economic models, and the conclusion of these calculations were subjected to further analysis.

At that time, everyone in the world was going to the US for their education, including the British and the Brazilians. Studying in the US was like studying at a kind of United Nations. Among my classmates were people of English, Thai and Indian nationalities. William Alonso, the very first Ph.D. in Regional Science, was from Argentina. He would later become a professor at Harvard. I was the 13th Ph.D. in my field.

Lo in front of the statue of Benjamin Franklin. Franklin is both the founder of UPenn and a member of the "Committee of Five" that drafted the <u>Declaration of Independence</u>. Lo took this picture on the day he received his doctorate degree.

I could only recognize my name in English, "Fu-chen Lo" out of the 70 over words printed on my Ph.D. certificate bestowed by the UPenn. A typical certificate would record the date of certification, but I couldn't even discern which of the words corresponded to the relevant month and year. I only knew that these words were in Latin. Using Latin for their official certificates was a long-held tradition at UPenn.

The school was founded in 1740 by Benjamin Franklin. It is one of eight Ivy League schools. While its contemporary North America colonial schools busied themselves on churning our clerics, Benjamin Franklin had conceived that the institution would produce world leaders, not only in business and government but in other public sectors as well. Today, it has groomed many of the most outstanding contributors in the fields of humanities and business. It's for a good reason that the Koo's behind Taiwan Cement and CTBC Financial Holdings insist on sending their sons to UPenn's Wharton School of Business.

A few years ago, Tamkang University invited me to teach there. According to protocol, I was asked to produce my Ph.D. certificate. When they saw the simple black and white certificate without a golden seal, or colorful school logo, or golden frame, they were shocked. Looking at this thin and seemingly photocopied document, the administrator couldn't help herself and said, "What is this?" Then, she half-joked, "Do you have another?"

34

My Friendship with Ikuda Kōji (生田浩二)

M<small>Y FIVE YEARS AT UPENN WOULD BE SPENT</small>
BUILDING THE MOST precious foundation of my life. It
was a continual grind, but it also brought me many rewards, and
determined the heights I would rise to for my career afterwards.
Everything went smoothly and I was immensely happy. There was
only one thing about that time that brings me some sadness — the
passing of my good friend Ikuda Kōji (1933-1966).

Kōji was a very young man and had already become a minor
figure in modern Japanese history — he was also a genius. Majoring
in Economics and Law at Tokyo University, he was at the top of
his class all the way through. In 1960, the US wanted Japan to sign
the Treaty of Mutual Cooperation and Security, allowing the US
to station its troops in Japan. This would elicit the greatest wave
of protests that Japan had ever seen since the Second World War.
From senators to labor unions and students, everyone protested this
imperialistic imposition by the US. As many as 600,000 people
surrounded the parliamentary building. Some students even forced
their way into the parliamentary sessions. President Eisenhower's visit
to Japan was cancelled. Amid these passionate protests, a student
movement emerged led by Kōji, a fervent anti-imperialist if there
ever was one. He had even been appointed to Secretary General of
the Japan Revolutionary Communist League. For his involvement
in the Communist movement, he was arrested and sentenced at first
to one and a half years in jail. Later, the sentence was reduced to a
probation, so he ended up staying out of jail. Two years later, he gave

up on Communism, and came to the US to become an expert in American capitalism.

Kōji was two years older than me, but he came to the US a year after I did. We were both in the same Regional Science department, and both been recommended by the University of Tokyo's professor Ōishi Yasuhiko to come to the US. That's how we came to know each other. Kōji was brilliant. Breaking a historical record, he took and passed the Ph.D. qualifying exam after only one year where I did it in two.

We shared a common language between us — Japanese. My wife Chin-fun and his wife Kyoko (恭子) also got along very well. Kyoko was a high school mathematics teacher before coming to the US. She had lived a life of great hardship growing up. She had lost her father, a naval diver, at a young age, when his submarine sunk, leaving her and her younger sister orphaned.

We often hung out together. When the World Expo was held in New York from 1964-1965, the four of us went to the Flushing venue and marveled at the enormous globe constructed out of stainless steel. We posed for one of the few photographs we have together in front of it.

In the spring of 1966, tragedy occurred. Kōji and Kyoko lived together in an apartment near school. One day, perhaps because of a stray cigarette carelessly disposed at the foot of the building, the entire apartment caught fire, engulfing them in flames. The Japanese overseas student body differed from the Taiwanese overseas students

Ikuda Kōji and wife Kyoko were all smiles in front of Philadelphia's Museum of Arts.

body in two respects. First, Japanese overseas students were fewer in number and secondly, Japanese students all wanted to return to Japan after completing their study in the US. Because the US represented a temporary and seasonal stopover, Japanese students did not think of forming an association to support one another. Upon their deaths, there was no Japanese association to take care of such matters. The responsibility fell onto me to organize both their funeral and their memorial.

Kyoko and Kōji had neither close Japanese friends nor family in the US. Their remains had to be returned. I suppressed my grief from losing two of my best friends. I wrote their names "生田浩二" and "生田恭子" in calligraphy on separate pieces of paper that I then pasted onto their urns. I got these urns delivered to the Japanese consul, Miyazawa Yasushi (brother of former Prime Minister Miyazawa Kiichi), at the consulate general of Japan in New York. The consul was moved by the fact that a Taiwanese would go to such lengths for his Japanese friends. I remember him saying as much. I would later come to learn that Kōji's brother had used the calligraphy I wrote on the urn for Kōji's gravestone. This was perhaps the surviving family's small way of expressing their appreciation for what I did for them, but I take the gesture of friendship to heart, and will always remember it forever.

35

Being Investigated by the FBI in America

AFTER LEAVING UPenn, I took a job as a researcher in a New York-based consulting firm called Consad. Its founder was a former government employee who was familiar with how the government operated. He had decided to specialize in government-commissioned research and start this firm.

I worked at this company for five years, researching the effect of urban air pollution on economic development. This groundbreaking project would become very influential.

By 1970, the US had already become conscious of the necessity of environmental protection, but the Environmental Protection Agency did not exist yet. Air pollution problems still fell under the purview of the US Department of Interior. But the types of air pollution faced by each state were different, and so were their levels of severity. For example, in an industrial city like Pittsburgh, black smoke billowed out of its many steel factories, enveloping the city with black air. The University of Pittsburgh's stone spire was covered in soot. Los Angeles was the first American city with expressways which were overcrowded with cars. It was also a basin, which meant that the polluted air from the cars could not disperse easily.

The US government wanted to know what effect an investment in environmental regulation — as well as what effect a quick or slow implementation of regulatory policies — would have on economic development. For example, Pittsburgh was bound to produce a lot of pollution. If pollution were to be reduced, steel companies would inevitably incur greater costs. As a result, would the steel industry shrink, or the price of steel rise? To take another example, if the government imposed a requirement on the auto-industry to install fixtures in each car that would curb pollution, what impact would this have on the car industry given that this would necessarily give rise to increased prices, and decreased sales? If, because of these controls, companies moved their factories to Florida, would this result in an increase in both the population of Florida and the income of the average Floridian? Taking into account all these possibilities, I constructed a mathematical model using a computer to run my calculations and analyzed the effect of implementing air pollution controls on seventy US cities. This report was the US's first study of the correlation between air pollution control and economic development, and it received widespread attention. It was even published in an academic journal in the UK. A few years later, at an environmental conference in Japan, a US government representative brought along this very paper. Seeing me sitting in the audience, he pointed at me and said "This study was conducted by Professor Lo over there."

Of even greater influence was another study I conducted. This time it was on Puerto Rico. Puerto Rico was not a US colonial territory, nor a dependent. It is an unincorporated territory and is free to govern itself. Like Guam, its people did not have the power to vote for the US president, but they did have the right to elect their own senator. The US government at one point decided to develop Puerto Rico, but how were they going to do it? Puerto Rico has over seventy municipalities. Should the money be spent on roads or generators (or on any of the other nine public amenities)? Should it be spent in the capital or on the most backward places? What economic benefit would each strategy bring? What was, in fact, the best combination of investment? Finding the answer was my assignment.

Puerto Rico was situated in the Caribbean and its distance from New York was roughly about the distance between Taipei and Hokkaido. For a period of time, I flew back and forth between New York and Puerto Rico. Each time, I would stay for about two weeks. The report I compiled at the end was not bad at all. More than ten years later, a geographer would tell me to my face that this report that I did was revolutionary. When the President of an Australian university — also a geographer — met me for the first time, he brought my report along with him.

I very much liked my work. Although, like any other researcher, I was dealing with data, I wasn't holed up in a lab or in an office. I could get to know a foreign city very intimately, and discover how big the world was, all the while applying my knowledge in economics. Based on my objective findings, a government could make rational decisions and pursue strategies for the betterment of its people instead of acting on gut instinct, like a blind person crossing a river, without any sense of direction.

In 1973, one day shortly after New Year's Day, I was offered a dream job by a Polish man. He introduced himself as an employee of the United Nations (UN) over the telephone. The UN wanted to set up a branch of the UN Center for Regional Development (UNCRD) in Nagoya and needed an expert there. He said he read my report and knew I was fluent in Japanese. These two things combined made me the ideal person for the job. But, just as everything was fitting into place, an obstacle appeared. "What do you mean you have no nationality?" He asked in shock and dismay.

To be eligible to work for the UN, like in any other company perhaps, one must submit the relevant documents to the Human Resources department to prove your identity. Moreover, as an organization constituted by citizens of its different member countries, each employee must be a citizen of a member country. Unfortunately at that time, I was without any nationality.

In February 1964, after participating in a protest related to the 228 Incident, I was blacklisted by the Kuomintang Party. I knew my passport would be confiscated the moment I showed up at the embassy. So, rather than go through that drama, I simply let my passport expire when it was up for renewal and became a nationless person.

I had gotten my Master's within my first year of coming to the States. This made me eligible for Permanent Resident (PR) status. If all went well, after five years, I could even become a US citizen. However, in my ten years in the US, I never applied and was indifferent to my alien status. Now that this dream job with the UN dangled before me, I rushed to send in my application for US citizenship.

One day, a neighbor asked, "I hear that you are going to work in a very special field?" It turned out that the FBI had conducted an investigation on me so that I could get security clearance. They had asked my neighbors what kind of person I was.

Not long after, I got my US citizenship. Immediately after that, the UN sent me my passport, based on my new status as an American citizen, especially designated for UN employees. Within a month, I went from being a nationless person to a holder of two passports. Ironically, I had become American only to leave the US. Within days, I flew to Nagoya, Japan, and started work at my dream job at the UNCRD.

36

An MRT Pass for Global Travel
(The United Nations Laissez-Passer)

THE UNITED NATIONS WAS NOT OF COURSE ANOTHER "NATION." It was founded by many member countries. When I first joined the United Nations in 1973, there were 135 member countries. Now there are 193.

Simply put, the UN has two functions: one, to host conferences whereby each member country can send a representative and express his or her government's stance; second, to study the problems of each member country, and thus bring about betterment for the world. Its headquarters is based in Manhattan, New York City. If you walk to the end of East 42nd Street you will see rows and rows of its member countries' flags. There are two big buildings corresponding to each of its two functions: the round one for holding conferences, the tall and blockish one for its executive offices. Apart from these, scattered all over the world are research and aid organizations, for example UNESCO in Paris, the World Labor Organization in Geneva, and the organization that Taiwan ought to be familiar with: the WHO, i.e. the World Health Organization, also in Geneva.

Employees of the UN are scattered all over the world. At present, there are more than 40,000 of them, belonging to more or less four bands. At the topmost S band is the Secretary-General. After that you have the D band, for the various Heads of Departments (split into D1 and D2). This is followed by the specialists, categorized under the P band (further split into 7 subcategories from P1 to P7). Lastly, the "normal" employee is categorized under the "G" band — which is split into even more subcategories. When I first joined, I was assigned to the status P3. By the time I left my position at the United Nations University as a Chief Academic Officer and a Deputy Director of the Institute of Advanced Study, I was promoted to D1.

Each UN official has his own blue-colored travel document called a United Nations Laissez-Passer (UNLP), which opens the door to global travel. But only those from a certain category get to use the special customs clearance lane designated for diplomats at airports.

This UN officer's passport let Lo Fu-chen travel freely around the world as an economic consultant to different countries except his own motherland, Taiwan, owing to his strong stance against the autocratic ruling KMT party.

In my 33 years at the UN, I always got to use these courtesy lanes, as if my UNLP were an MRT train pass.

My work at the UN allowed me special concessions too. To its representatives abroad, the Taiwanese government would issue specially designated license plates, with the kanji "使" — shorthand for the ambassadorial representative. For the Japanese government, that kanji is "外" for ambassadors, and "領" for consuls. Apart from this, Japan has a category for cars that Taiwan does not have — there was a license plate for international organizations with the kanji "代" and a license number in white numbers over a blue background. At a Japanese gas station, I paid ten percent less than other customers because of my status.

If I bought a foreign car, I would be exempted from tax. In the 1980s, when I was stationed in Malaysia, I bought an imported Mercedes Benz for two thirds its market price and without tax as well. My Malay boss was very jealous so, four or five years later, when I left Malaysia, I sold him the car.

From 1973 to 2000, over a period of twenty plus years, I worked in three organizations belonging to the UN. The first, the United Nations Center for Regional Development, was based in Nagoya, Japan; the second, the Asia-Pacific Finance and Development Center, that was a subsidiary of UNESCAP, in Kuala Lumpur, Malaysia. My third workplace was at the United Nations University in Tokyo. At each of my three jobs, it was never sitting in an office. I would be shuttling between different countries. Members from one UN

The UN headquarters located in Manhattan, New York City has 2 main buildings. The tall skyscraper is the administrative building, and the arc-lined building is for conferences and meetings.

branch could be attached to another UN branch for special projects. For example, I could be dispatched by the World Bank to Korea, or dispatched by the UNDP to Iran. All these made me an even more frenzied traveler. In all, I have gone to over 40 countries in 5 continents because of my positions with the UN.

One night, before I would leave my home in the US for India, I said to my youngest son, David, then a sixth-grader, in words so he could understand, "Father will be going to India. The people there need me to teach them some things." My son frowned, "That's weird. Why would people want to pay you to travel so far, just so that you can tell them things? Don't they have anyone there?" Had my son been a little older, in university perhaps, I would have said I was a traveling economic advisor instead.

Actually, Taiwan has in the past sought the UN's advice. Former Finance Minister, Li Kwoh-ting[1], in his book *My Taiwan Experience*, alluded to the assistance in Taipei's urban development extended by the UNDP. Astrid Monson (1913-2006), an American advisor, was received by President Chiang Kai-shek and his wife when she came to Taiwan. In another case, Professor Li Bi studied Kaohsiung's Export Processing Zone Administration for three months and made a total of seven suggestions at the end of his study.

However, after 1971, when Taiwan left the United Nations, its economic advisors were never dispatched to Taiwanese soil again, because the UN only serves its member countries.

---

[1] Li Kwoh-ting (January 28, 1910 ~ May 31, 2001) was best known as the "Father of Taiwan's Economic Miracles." He had been Taiwan's Economics Minister (1965-1969) and Finance Minister (1969-1976). The "Science Technology Development Projects" he initiated help transformed Taiwan's economy from an agrarian-based system into one of the world's leading producers of information and telecommunication technology.

37

A Traveling Economic Advisor

The UN CHOSE NAGOYA AS ITS BASE FOR ITS REGIONAL DEVELOPMENT Center because in the 1960s, Japan had proven outstanding in its own regional development.

Postwar, leaving the countryside to make a living in the city was the subject of many Japanese songs and like in the Taiwanese pop song "Mother, Please Take Care Too" (〈媽媽請你也保重〉) that was a hit in 1961. Take a look at its lyrics:

> I have arrived in the capital of another place
> Although lonely, I work hard from day to night
> Mother, please take care too,
> Try not to catch a cold in harsh winter...

These lyrics might as well apply to the Japanese youths who came to work in the city from the rural Northeast region. One day, they were at their graduation ceremony and next they were on board a Tokyo-bound train to find work. Arriving in Tokyo, they would get off at Ueno Station. In a few of these songs, seeing the clock at Ueno triggers memories of leaving their hometown for the city.

While the population surged in Tokyo, so too did Japanese exports at an unprecedented rate. The then prime minister, Ikeda Hayato, hired the economist Ōkita Saburo as his Director General of Economic Planning to formulate a strategy to increase the national income. Ikeda asked, how should one go about doubling the national income? Ōkita simply explained that if the national income were to double, then the industrial base must quadruple. Within seven years, Japan managed to double its national income, but income inequality also rose. Ikeda then came up with a base development plan, targeting the government's investments at twenty different centers spread across Japan, thereby, stimulating economic growth in the surrounding regions.

At the UNCRD, our task was to apply Japan's success formula to other Asian countries through strategic implementation. To understand what strategies would be required, I toured each country in turn, and submitted my recommendations for each country.

In 1974, I flew to the Philippines for my first mission. The government wanted to develop the Bicol region — situated 400 kilometers away from Manila. If this proved successful, they could replicate the model in other provinces.

During the car ride from the airport to my hotel, I experienced a great shock. Every time we stopped at a traffic light, kids would run up to my car. Some were begging for money while others were hawking goods. There were teenaged girls carrying smaller kids on their backs, selling cigarettes (not in packets, mind you, but in threes). There were children selling two cobs of sweet corn that they were holding in each hand. It was a pitifully small business model, if there ever was one. I saw these hawkers going up to a bus. There they found buyers, but they only sold one cigarette or one cob each time. I felt great injustice seeing these scenes. In London, Marxism had been born out of societal injustice as epitomized by such scenes. Out of

Marxism, Communism was born.

In 1974, strong Communist elements still existed in the Philippines. These Communists proudly raised their red flags, worshipped Mao Ze-dong and adopted guerilla tactics against the Marcos government. However, what they were against was landownership. Unequal distribution of land was a severe problem in the Philippines. Back then, the current president Benigno Aquino's family had 60,000 tenants renting the land on their sugarcane plantations. As for the Bicol region where I was headed, comprising 6 provinces, 80% of the land belonged to the two province mayors who also happened to be brothers.

Bicol was the poorest region in the Philippines and it also had the largest population of Communists, which made it a dangerous place. To minimize our chances of being attacked, we displayed the UN flag prominently on our jeep.

After a bumpy ride, I finally arrived at my destination. They had arranged for me to stay at a hotel. The provincial mayor welcomed me there with a meal. He decided that he would also stay there as well. In the morning, I decided to take in the scenery by going to the rooftop but I found a gunman there instead. He turned out to be one of the mayor's many bodyguards, hired to foil assassination attempts by the Communists. It was just like how it used to be in old Chinese villages.

Talking with the provincial mayor, I would be in for a greater shock. He told me that there was an island in the middle of the province that would be ravaged by typhoons a few dozen times a year. Each time it was hit by a typhoon, the central government would send aid money. Because the land was mostly his, most of the aid money would go directly into his pocket. He seemed to care only about his own interests. For example, I told him that the UN had agricultural experts who could help him determine which land would be most suited to grow coffee and which would be most suited to grow rice. We could teach him how to develop roads, how best to connect provinces, how land prices would inevitably increase when prosperity visited the region, how to pick a center for these six provinces that lay in a basin, and how, after this center was established, the prices of the surrounding land would increase and by how much. After giving him the whole presentation, the mayor only asked, "What do you want to grow here? This land is mine!"

This provincial mayor was just a tyrant. It was said that to maintain his power, he even closed down the airports to keep out the officials who were sent by the central government to prevent vote-rigging.

In contrast to the proud government officials and landowners, the farmers that I saw in the Philippines were humbly barefoot. The men were not unlike some indigenous tribe members in Taiwan. They had dangled mountain knives at their hips. The women covered their faces with veils. All of them were devout Catholics. There would be one especially elegant old church in all the small villages. Farmers would rise early in the morning to pray at that church before starting their work in the fields. Spain had colonized the Philippines for more than three hundred years, and the villages were still stuck in a certain feudal past established by the Spanish. Supposedly, back then, every girl's virginity belonged to the Spanish landowner. Now that ownership had transferred back to the Filipinos, commoners continued to be exploited in the same manner.

Soon after, Manila developed, and people from the provinces started to attend the university there. It was there they first encountered leftist teachings. Inspired by what they learned, they went home to instigate revolution amongst the poor. They reasoned that only through revolution, would these tyrant landlords be overthrown. But revolution had only brought about war.

My personal experience in the Philippines left me with the deep conviction that economic development was all about giving a leg up to the poor. Different countries were in different stages of economic progress. It was deeply meaningful to me that I could take what I learned from a first-world country to directly help a third-world country.

I went to the Philippines a few times, each time spending about two to three weeks. Other than observing for myself the situation and listening to local officials, I also collected materials that I needed for my research. In total, it added up to more than 200 books. Back in Nagoya, I assembled a team of over 20 regional development experts from Southeast Asia to work on my Bicol recommendation report. I returned to Bicol where I explained clearly how my recommendations

During Lo's first Asian mission in 1974, he helped the Philippines plan and develop the BICOL area, and also helped in training their own district develop experts.

In 1975, Lo and Malaysian scholar, Kamal Salih, jointly presented their theory at UNCRD. UNCRD's flag can be seen hanging in the background.

Always brainstorming with scholars and experts of different color, races, and nationalities, Lo (2nd from right) says, "I take pleasure from it. My youth hasn't been wasted." This is taken at London University, during the African Mega-city Symposium.

should be carried out. The officials, in turn, told me where they anticipated problems in implementing the proposal. After tweaking the report to take into account what they said, I submitted my final recommendations to the government of the Philippines.

These experts in regional development had not been taken out of the UN's pool of human resources. They were specially invited by me for the training course that I put together. Among them were economists, social workers, medical professionals, agricultural officers, engineers etc. I had to train them to get the most out of their individual expertise, adapt to one another and work as a team because regional development is about reaching a collective goal.

I used the case of the Philippines as practice for my first training course. Its government sent ten people over for the course — taking the opportunity to groom its own regional development specialists.

Training these corps of elite officials from different countries was not a matter of classroom instruction. Instead it was a matter of gathering "real-world" data and using this data to carry out an analysis. Once the problem was identified, these students would then brainstorm strategies to speed up economic productivity, and execute these strategies in the "real-world." To be able to pass on what I learned, and not just theorize in the confines of a lab — I was truly making a difference, not just to any one country but to the entire world.

After this training course was met with great success in the Philippines, we took it to Indonesia, and then to Pakistan and to Thailand. It's been 39 years since the course was first started by me in 1974, and I'm happy to know that it is still going strong, spurring Asian countries to reach greater heights.

38

You Know that You're Near a University if You Smell Tear Gas

In my tour of Asia as an economist advisor, my visits to South Korea proved to be most eventful.

In the 1970s, following instructions from my supervisors, I made a few trips to the Asian country. My earliest visit was in 1975. That first time, I was shocked to discover that rice belonged to a list of rationed items. I found this out when I went to a sushi restaurant and ordered sushi. When my order came, I realized that tucked under the slice of raw fish was not the white rice that I was accustomed to. It was a clump of barley and wheat and other mixed grains. "What was this about?" I asked the restaurant owner. He said that the government only allowed the population to eat rice on Wednesdays. Most of the rice had been set aside for export, so that the country could build up its foreign currency reserves. South Korea had been very poor in the 1960s but by the 1970s, its per capita income had risen to $1600 from $250. Evidently much of this was due to the successful development of its heavy industry, but its people must also be credited for cooperating with its austerity measures.

At that time, I was looking to set up another branch of the Center for Regional Development in Asia. I decided on Ulsan, an industrial zone in Southeast Korea. Seoul was originally the industrial hub. But just as Japan had done, Korea was now relocating its industrial zone, specifically to Ulsan. In fact, the famous Hyundai Corporation set up its very first shipyards here. As evidence of Ulsan's great success, it had grown, in a very short time, from a small harbor of 40,000 people into an industrial city of 1,000,000 people.

Joining the research team with me were Professors Kim An-je and Song Byung-nak of Seoul National University. We were all around the same age, 40 years old, and we became good friends. I always enjoyed talking with Kim An-je. Like me, he went to the US for further studies. He said that while he was in the US, he helped to change his kids' diapers. Back in Korea, he was not even allowed to step into the kitchen. If word got out that he helped out with the cooking, he would become a laughing stock. He also said with great humor that Korea's great misfortune in history was to have been sandwiched between two elephants (by this, he referred of course to China and Japan). Whether they were fighting or making love, Korea would always bear the brunt of their activity and became their playground.

In the second half of 1979, I returned once again to Korea, in the midst of a bloody coup. President Park Chung-hee had just been assassinated by one of his men.

Park Chung-hee, also the father of today's president Park Geun-hye, had ruled over South Korea for 18 years via a combination of military strength and great intelligence. On Friday October 26th, 1979, he had, out of habit, gathered three trusted friends to have fun in the company of beautiful women. These three were Cha Ji-chul (his chief imperial bodyguard), Kim Jae-kyu (the director of Central Intelligence) and Kim Gye-won (his Secretary-General). Shortly after their karaoke session started, Kim Jae-kyu took out a gun and shot Park's bodyguard, followed by Park himself, and then made a phone call to the Army Chief of Staff, Jeong Seung-hwa, to persuade him to join his coup. Instead, Jeong arrested Kim Jae-kyu on charges of treason. Just as it seemed that power would fall to Jeong, on December 12th, Chun Doo-hwan, a commander under Jeong, arrested Jeong on charges of corruption and put him in jail. During this tumultuous period, the government changed hands not once but three times when I happened to be in South Korea.

As the political drama played out in front of their eyes, South Koreans watched with their mouths wide open, but their anger was festering inside. Their wrath culminated in the famous Gwangju Incident of May 1980. Around this time, I had been sent by The World Bank to advise on South Korea's Five Year Economic Plan. I hadn't been in Seoul for more than a few days when the Gwangju Incident erupted. University students organized an anti-government protest in the southern city of Gwangju. In reaction, the government gave instructions for the military to arrest protesters. The police even pierced steel wires into the protesters' palms and tied them together, so it was easier to drag them away. When the news of their cruelty reached the North, students in Seoul took to the streets and pitted themselves against the police. The roads were covered with tanks, whose engines never turned off for one moment. Some of these tanks were stationed by subway entrances, so that nobody could enter or leave the subway. The South Korean government assigned me a special car. If I got out of the car and smelt a whiff of tear gas, I would know that I was near a university. The smell of tear gas is very hard to describe. It's not like gas that you use in your kitchen, but you can recognize it by its effect. It's bound to choke you.

From my vantage point as an economist, I could see the reasons for the Gwangju revolt. Since ancient times, the Korean Peninsula has been divided up into three areas, Goguryeo in the North, Silla in the Southeast, and Baekje in the Southwest. South Korea from 1961 to 1979 was ruled by the tyrant Park Chung-hee, who was from Silla. During this time, Silla was selected especially for development. More than 80 percent of the industry took place in Silla, and expressways linked Silla to Seoul. On the other hand, Baekje continued to be underdeveloped. For example, no expressway was thought as necessary to connect Baekje to Seoul. Clearly, there had been prejudice in Park's economic strategy.

In 1971, Kim Dae-jung challenged Park Chung-hee for the Presidential throne, only to lose by a narrow margin. After the election was over, Park sent his men to arrest Kim on charges of treason, on account that he posed a threat to national peace. Kim was from Baekje. It was easy to see why people from Baekje felt so oppressed. I remember reading a modern Korean poem that claimed that Baekje people are as helpless as Okinawans.

After the Gwangju Incident, Chun Doo-hwan did not appear in public for a week. When finally he made an appearance, he announced the appointment of 120 people as members of his new government's preparatory committee. One third of these were from the military, the second third comprised of government officials, and the last third were university professors. My two Korean friends (including Kim An-je) were summoned. Kim An-je was very nervous about this offer. If this new government were to collapse, he would surely be stoned to death. On the other hand, if he did not accept this new position, he would get into the government's black list. He came to discuss his situation with me. With a look of panic on his face, he asked, "What can I do?" I walked him through the different options. Yes, he was right about the latter. If he did not accept the invitation, trouble would indeed come after him. However, if he accepted the government post and produced successful results that all could see, surely no one would have reason to attack him.

He ended up taking the offer.

39

Half Tables at a Wedding Banquet in an Iron-Curtain Country

AT THE CENTER FOR REGIONAL DEVELOPMENT IN NAGOYA, a constant stream of professionals passed through our doors to take part in our courses. One day, we welcomed a Chinese woman who worked at the State Council of the People's Republic of China. In those years, it was always a little surreal for a Taiwanese to encounter a Mainlander abroad. China and Taiwan had already cut off relations for more than thirty years. Military control in Taiwan was very strict. On the streets and in the media, you would never see a Communist flag. Being caught with Communist propaganda meant big trouble. You would likely be sent to prison on a remote island. However, whatever political tension existed between Taiwan and China did not seem to apply in Nagoya. I was an economist employed by the UN. China had not yet had its first regional development scholar. According to the terms of my contract with the UN, I was to advise all its member countries, China included. It sufficed that this person from China and I shared a common goal, which was to bring about greater economic development in China. There was no need to bring politics into the picture.

Among friends, I've always liked to speak my mind. I think it's a pleasurable thing to be able to do so. I've never kept anything from friends. So, this Chinese woman easily came to know that I was not only Taiwanese in origin but also fiercely pro-independence. I would joke by calling her "a female bandit [1] cadre." She didn't seem to mind.

---

[1] The Kuomintang Party and the Chinese communists used to call each other "bandits."

It was through her that I made the acquaintance of her boss, Zhang Yen-ning (張彥寧), vice chairman of Council for Economic Planning and Development (CEPD), who visited me at my home when he visited the US. Zhang was originally from Shenyang. A specialist in the chemical industry, he had once been the Vice Chief Engineer at the Ministry of the Petroleum Industry. The former Premier Zhu Rong-ji (朱鎔基) had also been vice chairman of CEPD, but compared to him, Zhang was more qualified.

In 1980, before I left the UNCRD, Zhang arranged for me to visit China.

When Lo visited Wangfujing, one of Beijing's most popular shopping streets in 1980, the streetscape was dull and people dressed in nothing but gray or blue.

Ever since 1949, China had adopted a closed-door policy towards foreigners. A year after the Cultural Revolution ended in 1977, Deng Xiao-ping decided that China would throw its doors open once more to outsiders. I went at the beginning of this new policy, and saw for myself many of the strange customs and habits behind the Iron Curtain.

For example, in the Beijing map that I bought, I couldn't find the airport anywhere. At Wangfujing [2], I was immediately surrounded by passers-by, who gawked at the camera I was holding. At Beijing's Xiyuan Hotel, the hotel staff asked me if I had any food coupons on me.

There were not many restaurants in Beijing, so we often couldn't get a whole table for the four of us who had come on this trip together. In most cases, we made do with "half-tables." One day, as fate would have it, we shared a table with a pair of newly-weds. The bride was dressed in red. Their half of the table was the site of their wedding dinner party. There were guests in attendance too, except that they were all standing behind where the bride and the bridegroom sat, salivating at the meal placed before the new couple.

Of course, the Beijing of today, thirty years later, has been reborn. But, in the 1990s, when I revisited Beijing, much had already changed. A few Western colleagues and I were seated in a Liulichang

2 Wangfujing literarily means "prince's mansion well." In the Qing Dynasty, ten aristocratic estates and prince residences were built here. There is also a well famous for the quality of its water. Wangfujing is one of Beijing's most popular shopping streets now.

restaurant by the name of Kong Shan Tang when a young man walked in. The moment he saw our group, he walked over and said to me disapprovingly, "You brought Westerners to eat here?" He meant to say that it would be a loss of face for the Chinese, to expose foreigners to such bad food. I didn't hold this against him or get angry, but merely stated (a) I am not from China (b) this is what we would eat in the States.

In the 1980s, when I first flew into China, the itinerary my hosts had planned for me mainly centered on Beijing. But, at my request, they chartered a small plane for me so I could tour the South as well. It was a trip that would be full of curiosities. In Jiangsu, they arranged for me to visit a commune. Now, in Taiwan, one's address is broken down first by the country, the town or village, then finally the neighborhood. From the 1950s to the 1980s, the most basic unit of a Chinese residence was a commune. This communal system was still in place when I first visited.

The thing that struck me as strangest about a commune was the hospital. After walking through the entrance, the patient had to first choose whether he wanted to see a Western doctor or a Chinese one. It was entirely up to him to decide. If the former, he would turn right. If the latter, he would turn left.

In 1978, after the Communist Party embraced Deng Xiao-ping's "open-door policy," they chose to implement it first in Guangzhou. No other region opened up, certainly not Beijing, which was far up north. But, it seemed that nearby Suzhou did get affected. In Suzhou,

I was invited one day to watch a theatre performance by a Shanghai troupe. Everyone seated in the audience that day wore Mao suits. We were in a somber sea of gray. When the female performer appeared on stage, the entire house went "Whoa!" I was puzzled about why they were so excited. Her performance had not even begun. But perhaps it was the very red of her cheongsam that thrilled them so. The Chinese must not have seen such a bright color for a long, long time.

40

Sounding the "Midnight Bell" at Hanshan Temple

ARRIVING IN SUZHOU, I specifically asked to see Hanshan Temple, made famous by Tang poet Zhang Ji's (張繼) "A Night Mooring by Maple Bridge." (〈楓橋夜泊〉) According to Mother, Father loved this poem most. She would recite it to me in Taiwanese, and I knew it well by heart:

> The crows crying, the moon lost in the frost-sky,
> (月落烏啼霜滿天)
> Asleep I feel sad with the maples in fishing light.
> (江楓漁火對愁眠)
> Outside Gusu, Hanshan Temple stands upright,
> (姑蘇城外寒山寺)
> Her bell tone reaching my boat at midnight.
> (夜半鐘聲到客船)

Whenever I recited it out loud, I would think of Father, who had passed away before I had reached my first birthday. We had not lived together. Anything related to him at all I pursued with great interest.

So, I eagerly took in the scenery of Hanshan Temple now before my eyes, even noting the height and curvature of the stone bridge that enabled boats to pass underneath. Suddenly, I understood that it was from a boat traveling through one of these canals that the bells in the poem were being heard.

At that time, tourism had not opened up in the region. The guide that took me to Hanshan Temple told them that I had been sent by the UN; that was how I got to sound the bell. It was during the afternoon at the time, not midnight like in the poem, but I was nevertheless utterly thrilled.

What happened next in Hangzhou was even more moving. When I first arrived, it was already late at night. All of Hangzhou was unlit. I had checked into Xileng Hotel (now Shangri-La Hotel) which was right next to the lake. It was pitch black outside my window. So, at five in the morning, before the sun had lit up the entire sky, I rushed to the rooftop to take in the view of the magnificent West Lake.

Walking around the lake afterwards, I was overcome by a rush of thoughts and sentiments. At that time, the West Lake had just been opened to the public for the first time. Foreign visitors were far and few between and the water was still crystal clear, as it must have been a thousand years ago. Walking on Su and Bai causeways, I had the feeling of traveling back in time. Poets Su Shi [1] and Bai Ju-yi [2] seemed to be walking right next to me.

After seeing West Lake with my own eyes, I could finally understand why those who came from the Yellow River could rule Jiangnan. [3] Beyond Shanhai Pass in the North, Han people became

---

1 Su Shi (1037-1101), also called Su Tong-po, was a writer, poet, calligrapher and statesman of the Song Dynasty.

2 Bai Ju-yi (772-846) was a Chinese poet of the Tang Dynasty. He was one of the most prolific of all Chinese poets, but is best known for his short occasional verses written in simple language.

3 Jiangnan, literally means "south of the river," which refers to the South of Yantze River. Due to good weather and rich soil, Jiangnan has represented prosperity since ancient times.

the minority. For example, Hans make up less than 40% of the population in Rehe. The Great Wall was built to prevent outsiders from coming in. Those who remained inside these walls, including those who built their lives up around the Yellow River, forged deeper bonds. Those in the South on the other hand, lived carefree existences, surviving on bananas plucked from the trees. If I had lived in ancient times, I would definitely prefer the carefree Jiangnan existence over the constant strife and struggle of Beijing officialdom, where one could get beaten up any time.

The different fantasies that West Lake evoked evaporated the instant I stepped back onto the streets of Hangzhou. Surrounded by soldiers from the People's Liberation Army and seeing the clothes hanging out to dry on poles between buildings brought me abruptly back to 1980s China.

I had to make many official stops during this trip. The Chinese government at that time had great respect for UN officials. In Shanghai, they arranged for me to stay at the Presidential Suite on the top floor of Jin Jiang Hotel. It was where President Nixon stayed in 1972, when he came to sign the joint U.S.-China Communiqué. With three bedrooms and a living room, the size of the suite was probably 200 square meters.

Among the stops, Peking University left the deepest impression on me. I spoke with the professors from its Economics Department. Dressed in Mao suits, they lived and breathed Marxist Economics. The defense industry constituted whatever heavy industry China had at that time. Washing machines were still being made in munitions factories. As a matter of fact, the Chinese had no notion yet of the "service industry". When someone asked me, "How do you think China's economy should be developed?" I replied simply, "China should concentrate on the production of consumer goods — goods that will have a demand." This strategy should be a matter of common sense to any economist. I think it would have been the standard advice offered by any foreign expert to post Iron-Curtain China.

41

Testifying at the US Congressional Hearing

SIX YEARS LATER, I would be dispatched again by the UN to Beijing; the welcome would be even stronger than the last. But truth be told, I had done something three years before that had made them fuming mad.

It all happened when I went to testify at the US congressional hearing. Claiborne Pell, the Chairman of the Senate Committee on Foreign Relations, had served the Senate for a very long time, and he knew a lot about Taiwan. In November 1983, he convened a public hearing, specifically inviting "witnesses" to the Senate to testify, and to explore the question of Taiwan's political future while allowing other senators to understand the issue. I was one of the three to testify. I represented the overseas Taiwanese organizations. The other two were William A. Brown, Secretary of State for American Pacific Affairs, representing the US State Department, and John F. Copper, Chair of the Heritage Foundation's Asia Center, representing the Kuomintang.

In the week after I received this invitation, I spent night and day reading all the books I could find about Taiwan, including Wu Cho-liu's (吳濁流) *The Orphan of Asia* [1]. In my lifetime, I worked especially hard twice. The first time was when I was writing my Ph.D. thesis and the second was this time that I spent preparing to take the stand at the US Senate. I wrote an essay in Chinese of about 10,000

---

1 Taiwanese writer Wu Cho-liu's 1946 novel *The Orphan of Asia* showed the swings and confusion surrounding the national identity of the Taiwanese people under Japanese rule.

words, which I then translated into English by myself. Then, I got an American to smooth out what I had translated. On November 9th, 1983, I wore a grey suit, sat on the witness stand sandwiched between the other two witnesses. We sat much higher up than the committee members in front of us, while a group of reporters crowded behind us.

Each witness spoke for 15 minutes, and then proceeded to field questions from the committee. Pell, the chair of the committee, asked me when my ancestors first arrived in Taiwan. I replied, 1736. Then, as though we were just having a friendly chat, he said, "Oh, then my ancestors arrived in America later than your ancestors arrived in Taiwan." I replied, "You Americans are very fortunate to have a nation to call your own, but we never got a chance in four hundred years." Most importantly, I said that the US government's stand on Taiwan's legal status was not clear. I proceeded to raise the question: *Would the American government ever entertain the possibility of an independent Taiwan?* The Senate submitted my question to the State Department. The answer they came back with was cause for joy. The State Department replied, "If Taiwan were to declare its independence and suffered military aggression because of it, the US, on the basis of its Taiwan Relations Act, would be obliged to intervene and protect it against all attacks." A few days later, on November 15th, the Senate Committee on Foreign Relations took a vote on the "Resolution on Taiwan's Future". Thirteen approved, one objected, and three abstained. Just like that, the resolution was passed. On this resolution, it is clearly written, "Taiwan's future should be settled peacefully, free of coercing, and in a manner acceptable to people on Taiwan." On November 18, the Ministry of Foreign Affairs of the Peoples' Republic of China (PRC) made a formal protest to the U.S. Department of State. It stated that "This action of the U.S. Senate Foreign Relations Committee constituted a deliberate infringement on China's sovereignty and an open interference in China's internal affairs." Five days later, on November 20th, the entire Senate would pass this resolution by 63 votes.

Wu Xue Qian, China's then Foreign Minister, registered his protest soon after, saying that such a resolution on Taiwan's future represented a "brazen intervention in China's internal affairs." Hu Yao Bang, general secretary of the CPC Central Committee, even threatened to cancel President Reagan's visit to China.

42

Meeting Zhao Zi-yang (趙紫陽) and Zhu Rong-ji (朱鎔基) at the Beijing Conference

By RIGHT, testifying in the US as I did, and straining Sino-American ties, I should have earned the hatred of the Communist Party. But because I was a UN official, I got to go to China again three years later. When Deng Xiao-ping resolved to opening China's doors to outsiders in 1978, he had ushered in a new era. For example, shortly after China's Iron Curtain lifted, an international conference was held at The Great Hall of the People in Beijing. That conference was organized by me.

It was my second time in Beijing. Although it was already 1986, there was still no such thing as vended newspapers. News was posted on bulletin boards. There was also no such thing as a bookshop. As matter of fact, there was no toilet paper, either. My guide could

Premier Zhao Zi-yang (3ʳᵈ from left) gave his opening speech.

Professor Edward Chen (1ˢᵗ on the right) from Hong Kong, who coined the term "Four Asian Tigers", was also present.

All Asian-Pacific countries were concerned about China's opening policy and the procedures China's going to take, thus eagerly sent in their high ranking officials and scholars to attend the conference.

not resist asking me to pass him toilet paper from my hotel for him to bring back to his family. But Beijing had undergone quite a few subtle changes. For example, in a cab, the driver might ask to buy my foreign exchange coupons. With these coupons, he would be able to walk into a "friendship store" [1] and exchange them for rare imported goods like Coca Cola.

Indeed, I was right about the effect that China's new liberal policy would have on Asia. I was also right about China wanting to announce its new policy to its neighbors. Though in 1978, China had decided in its Third Plenum of the 10th CPC Central Committee that it would pursue a new open door policy in 1979, by 1986 its doors were still closed to the outside world. Whatever was being prepared inside for the world to see, all of Asia wanted to know. To the Asia Pacific Development Center I proposed a grand and formal platform for Beijing to reveal its plans to its neighbors. The proposal was accepted. After deciding on the title, "The Asia-Pacific Economy Towards the year 2000," I would also oversee the planning of this conference as Head of Economic Cooperation Research at the Asia-Pacific Development Center.

But how to connect with the China that just opened its lid? And with who? Luckily, I found an ally in my ex-mentor, Professor Lawrence Klein. He connected me with his classmate, Pu Shan (浦

---

[1] The Chinese friendship stores are state owned and first appeared in the 1950's. The stores sold Western, imported items as well as high quality Chinese art and crafts exclusively to tourists, foreigners, diplomats, and government officials. But there are no such restrictions any more.

山), China's most outstanding economist at that time. He headed the Institute of World Economics and Politics at the Chinese Academy of Social Sciences. Pu Shan had received a Ph.D. in Economics from Harvard in 1949, only to return immediately to China, to apply what he had learned. He had even been Premier Zhou En-lai's English secretary at one point. According to Klein, Pu Shan had taken a theory of respected master-economist Joseph Alois Schumpeter and very creatively mathematized it. Had he continued to develop his talent in the West, he would have likely won a Nobel Prize.

Pu Shan told the powers-to-be about my proposal. Sure enough, as evidence of Pu Shan's influence, the Foreign Affairs department quickly got in touch with me, and the program was green-lighted. Although it was Pu Shan's Institute of World Economics and Politics that I spoke to, it was the Foreign Affairs Department who put everything together. Zhu Rong-ji, then Vice President of the China Council for the Promotion of International Trade, would decide whom China's Internal Affairs Department would nominate for the conference and, what sort of papers they would present at the conference. One year after the Beijing Conference, he would be promoted to Mayor of Shanghai, a role that won him respect and acclaim. Under his guidance, Pudong (a district of Shanghai) flourished. In 1998, he would become the Premier.

The day before the conference, Zhu Rong-ji invited the entire team of over ten people from the Asia-Pacific Development Center to Dong Lai Shun Restaurant for lamb shabu-shabu. During the

The day before the conference, Zhu Rong-ji (up, sitting in middle) invited the entire team of the Asia-Pacific Development Center to Dong Lai Shun Restaurant. The party was divided into 2 tables. Lo sat with China's top economist Pu Shan (below, sitting in middle).

meal, Zhu Rong-ji told us this would be the first time that Premier Zhao Zi-yang would make an appearance himself at the conference, to brief the world about Chinese policy. At that time of course, I did not know that Zhu Rong-ji would one day become the Premier himself. He came across as very down-to-earth and logical. There was nothing flamboyant or boastful about him, nor did he speak down to us.

It was up to me to decide who represented each Asian country for this conference. In all, 17 vice presidents and ministers took part. It was a very politically representative crowd. Among the academics in attendance were Professor Edward Chen (陳坤耀) from Hong Kong, who coined the term "Four Asian Tigers", and Professor Miyohei Shinohara from Hitotsubashi University in Japan, an expert on business cycles. I was especially thrilled that Shinohara could make it. Because Taiwan and China had severed ties, I was unable to invite anyone from Taiwan to attend. However, I did get Taiwan-born Professor Lin Tsung-piao (林聰標), chair of the Economics department at the Chinese University of Hong Kong, to fly to Beijing. Dormant for forty years, cross-straits relations would once again be revived in October 1987. When the Beijing Conference opened in 1986, Chiang Ching-kuo was still alive and his policy of "No Contact, No Discussion, and No Compromise" was still very much enforced. If any Taiwanese were caught traveling to Beijing, he would no doubt be sent to jail. So, when all the participants of the conference posed for a group photo, Lin Tsung-piao was very careful and took off his

In 1986, when there was still no cross-straits relations, Lo (front row, 1ˢᵗ on the right) went to China as a UN official, and organized an economic conference at Beijing's Great Hall of the People. All in all, government representatives from 15 countries and many Chinese high ranking figures took part in this conference. Included in the picture are: then Chinese Premier Zhao Ziyang (front row, 9ᵗʰ from

right), Vice Minister of Foreign Affairs Department, Qian Qichen (front row, 7th from right), Vice Director of Chinese Academy of Social Science, Huan Xiang (front row, 7th from left), and Zhu Rongji, then Vice President of the China Council for the Promotion of International Trade, Malaysia's Secretary-general to the president (front row, 4th from right), and Vice Premier of Thailand (front row, 8th from right).

glasses to avoid being recognized and getting into trouble with the Kuomintang government.

These international conferences organized by the UN facilitated multilateral dialogue. But sometimes they could touch a sensitive nerve. China and North Korea being long-time Communist allies, North Korea might protest if South Koreans were prominently seen. I was issued a "reminder" that if South Koreans were to come for this meeting, I should take special care to seat their representatives on the side.

Preparations would take half a year. On November 20th, the Beijing Conference officially opened. This date was memorable because it also happened to be the birthday of Sun Wen (aka Sun Yat-sen, founding father of the Republic of China). Elsewhere in the Great Hall of the People, a commemoration of the 120th year of his birthday was being hosted by the Secretary of the Communist Party, Hu Yao-bang. At the Beijing Conference, Premier Zhao Zi-yang gave his opening speech. "From now on, China will open its doors to Asia-Pacific countries and the rest of the world and encourage investments. We hope that in 30 to 50 years, our economic standards will be as good as that of any developed country." When Zhao Zi-yang spoke of China's economy as being part of the greater Asia-Pacific economy, we were all thrilled. This certainly represented a milestone in China's liberalization.

When the Beijing Conference concluded after four days, the consensus among all the participating scholars and officials was

Professor Miyohei Shinohara (middle) is an expert on business cycles. He recognized Lo's ability and invited him to hold another economic conference in Tokyo.

Thailand's Vice Premier Thanat Khoman also expressed his eagerness in inviting Lo to hold another Asian Pacific economic conference in Bangkok.

extremely positive. But they were also puzzled why had China ignored previous suggestions by outsiders, only to pay heed to a mere Head of Research at the United Nations? And not only did China agree to this conference, she sent her highest echelon of politicians. Shinohara wanted me to move immediately to Tokyo and hold another conference. Thailand's Vice President Thanat Khoman also expressed his eagerness for another edition and he hoped that it would take place in Bangkok.

Because of its huge success, the Asia-Pacific Development Center decided to make the Conference a regular affair every one and a half years. I would go on to organize the Tokyo Conference in May, 1988, the Bangkok Conference in November 1989, and the New Delhi Conference in May, 1991.

43

Lugging Back Jinhua Ham from from Thousands of Miles Away

THANAT KHOMAN HAD A PH.D. FROM THE UNIVERSITY OF PARIS. For over ten years, he had acted as Thailand's Foreign Minister and Vice Premier. He was an old hand at international politics. At dinners during the Beijing Conference, he carried himself with great ease. One time, he took out a pen from his suit pocket. We were all wondering what he would do with the pen. He asked the only woman at the table, my wife Chin-fun , "Would you like some chili?" and proceeded to slowly twist the cap of his pen as if he were handling a pepper grinder. As small flakes of the condiment fell out from the other end, he smiled. "I must always take this with me." He couldn't have a meal without spicing it up. Like the majority of Bangkok's Chinese population, Thanat Khoman's ancestors hailed from Chaozhou. After becoming Thai, they adopted Thai customs and made chili a part of their regular diet.

In my tour of the world, apart from being able to discuss regional development with the world's *crème de la crème*, I was lucky to be able to sample international foods too.

I admit to being a gourmet. Mother always liked to tell Chin-fun about how I loved going to wedding banquets in my younger days, chowing down chicken drumstick after chicken drumstick. Apparently, my love of food was evident even then.

I often tell my friends, if I hadn't gone overseas, I probably would have become a chef.

Not only did I like to eat but I also loved to cook. During my time at National Tainan First Senior High School, I had the means to eat at restaurants or at roadside stalls but I often ended up preparing my own meals. I once described myself in the third person and said, "This person's right hand holds a knife. The other holds a fork. Whenever he's not cooking, he's eating."

I remember reading a novel in senior high school. There's a scene in it involving two Jews at a "real" Parisian restaurant. One of them said to the other, "When war comes, the victims are always us Jews. If we are both alive after the war ends, let's come back to this restaurant." I understood this. During wartime, one's feelings are often torn between hope and despair, and sometimes these mixed feelings are projected onto the food placed right before you. While the characters in the book ate, I vicariously ate along with them too. Though I was still young then, I was capable of feeling their sorrow, and I even remembered well the name of the restaurant — Le Fouquet's.

When I first visited Paris in 1979, I made it a point to visit this restaurant, situated between the Champs-Elysees and Avenue George V. It was not difficult to find. You can walk from Arc de Triomphe to Le Fouquet's in two or three minutes.

Le Fouquet's opened in 1899. Situated at a street corner, the restaurant has borne silent witness to the rapid changes of the 1920s and the 1930s. Artists and writers, poor and rich alike, built up their lives in this city. Until recently, movie stars and international celebrities, at their heights of their successes or at their loneliest moments, could be seen at this restaurant. The signature red of their canopy is now an indispensable part of the Parisian landscape. The building that Le Fouquet's is part of has since been bought over by Japan's NEC. At one point, the restaurant seemed destined to close, but was bailed out by Parisians in the end.

One year, the World Bank sent me to Paris on a five-day work trip. I was given a daily stipend of $300. After the work was done, just before I was due to fly home, I was suddenly overcome by an urge to visit Le Fouquet's. At the restaurant, I ordered vintage champagne to go along with raw oysters. Holding my champagne glass as I looked out of the window at the busy street life, only then did I feel that my Parisian trip hadn't been for naught.

It was not until later, when I was boarding the plane and recalling my meal at Le Fouquet's, that I realized that I forgot to leave a tip. At that time, I was living in Japan where tipping was not customary. Oh well, I said to myself, this will give me a reason to return. The next year, I did go back, and when it came time to leave a tip, I told the waiter, "Last year I forgot to tip, so this year I'm leaving double." Everyone laughed.

The World Bank sent me to Thailand too. In the day I would visit the villages. To my surprise, Thai communists went to great lengths to display a photo of King Bhumibol Adulyadej on the lectern even as they deliver spiels about Communism. In a country where peace had reigned for a long time, the venerable King was prized as the source of stability. Even during the military coup in the 1970s, very few people were killed, leading some to describe the new military government as a mere changing of the guard.

The World Bank paid me two to three hundred dollars for my work each day. But there always seemed to be a hole in my pocket. Whenever I had money, I would end up spending it. At that time, sharks were not yet endangered, so I took the money that the World Bank gave to me and spent it on shark fin.

It wasn't enough to bring only shark fin back to Japan. To make shark fin soup one needs three kinds of meat: Jinhua ham, an old hen, and pork ribs. Although it was possible to find Jinhua ham [1] in Japan, it was difficult to find and very few shops sold an entire leg of ham. So, one time, coming back from China, I smuggled a whole leg of Jinhua ham, about two feet long, into my suitcase. (What I was willing to do for good food!) The best Jinhua ham can be found in Shaoxing. The pigs there are of a different breed than the rest and have smaller bodies. Another distinct characteristic is that their heads and buttocks are black [2]. Only the middle of their bodies and the four legs are white.

While I was studying at the University of Pennsylvania, Chin-fun and I would go to the Italian food market, where the crabs would sell for cheaper than even in Taiwan. You could buy 12 crabs for 3 bucks. We often brought a dozen or two back home. The time-consuming task of cleaning the crabs with a toothbrush fell to me. To steam

---

1 Jinhua ham is a type of dry-cured ham named after the city of Jinhua, where it is produced. This ham has a well over 1000-year history behind it. It was awarded first prize in the 1915 Panama International Merchandize Exhibition.

2 This special breed of pig is called "two ends black" (兩頭烏) because of this distinct characteristic.

them, it sufficed to crack open their backs, give them a good brush, and then close them back up. To fry them, it sufficed to cut them up into four pieces, throw them into a wok, and then add garlic, scallion, ginger and wine. The fragrance was sure to fill your nostrils. After adding egg to the wok, you would soon get the *pièce de résistance* dish "Crab with Egg White" — a sure hit with overseas students.

In my Chiayi childhood, my biological mother was a great chef, who would cook for me and I would learn from her. She made a first-rate sea cucumber. After buying a big dried sea cucumber, you have to soak it in water, where it doubles or even triples in size. Then you boil it for a little while, set it aside, and cut it up the next day. Sea cucumbers have innards that smell like dried squid — very fishy. After cleaning it out, you boil it again, but this time with scallion to rid it of its fishy smell. Then you proceed to soak it in water again. The repetitive process of boiling and soaking the sea cucumber takes about two days. Consider it ready when you have what is three to four times the dried original. At this point, stuff it with minced pork, scallion, ginger, mushroom, and shrimp. After that, thicken it with steam. Then and only then will it be ready for the dining table.

44

Lamb's Eyes for Dinner

ONCE I WAS SERVED LAMB'S EYES — AN IRÁNIAN DELICACY.

In October 1979, the Korean government underwent a coup. Earlier that year (Jan. 1979), the Shah of Iran, Mohammad Reza Pahlavi, was also overthrown by Islamic religious group leaders. He fled to the US as a result. During this era, many countries were still playing tug-of-war between tyranny and democracy. One could not yet resort to democratic means to resolve problems peacefully. In 1979, I was in Seoul during the Korean coup. Days before the Iranian upheaval, I also was in Iran to witness their people's discontent.

A year before that, around the months July and August, the United Nations Development Programme (UNDP) invited me to give a lecture in Iran. King Mohammad Reza Pahlavi was still in power then, and I saw for myself how the kingdom was already in decline.

400 km from Tehran was an ancient city called Hamadan, one of the original stops along the Silk Road. I decided to fly there. Among my companions were three other international lecturers. The first time the small plane tried to land it failed because the wind was too strong, so the plane climbed up again. My companions were visibly scared and looked at me. I joked, "Never mind, I'll give you an umbrella, if the plane plunges again, all you need to do is open the umbrella. You'll land safely."

The university we planned to visit had just opened. Most of its professors had returned after graduating from American universities,

During his nearly 30 years' service for UN, Lo traveled around the world and accumulated great experience and knowledge. He has lectured at the University of Tibet, and has seen the gun-manufacturing village in Afghanistan desert.

intent on serving their nation through education. Our team spent two days exploring the idea of regional development with Iranian professors and students. In return, the students gave us a tour of their villages. This was my first visit to the Muslim world and my first time experiencing how desert people live.

Everyone knows about the phenomenon of oases existing in the desert, but perhaps not many can explain it. Well, apparently, there are rivers underground that have been around for a few thousand years. After this was discovered, man dug wells so that they could draw water directly from these sources to nourish their livestock. In some places where the land is low, water can be channeled directly to the earth's surface, creating an oasis. Around such oases, people set up homes, grow potatoes and wheat. Over time, whole villages develop. Shepherds would then come to these villages to barter their lamb meat for wheat or potatoes, in this way establishing an economy. It was only when I got there that I discovered for myself that Iran is actually an agricultural state.

But the professors and the students at the university didn't seem to be very happy about their king. In the 1970s, when international oil prices shot up, the Iranian Shah became among the wealthiest men in the world. Instead of sharing his newfound wealth with his people, many of whom were struggling to stay alive, he indulged himself to the hilt. Later the Shah's sister started encouraging farmers to grow poppies. Come harvest time, it sufficed to crack open poppy fruits, extract their white juice, set the juice to dry and voila! Dark-colored opium strips were formed, much more valuable than the wheat or potatoes that they grew before. The farmers listened to her advice and transformed the best piece of land in the village into a poppy field. Soon after, military personnel were sent by the Shah to protect the harvest. After some farmers had grown affluent from the opium, salesmen also came peddling goods that the farmers were previously unable to afford. Before, the farmers were simple folk. But now, many farmers started bribing the soldiers and smuggling the opium that they themselves had grown. Today, half of the opium coming out of Iran is actually smuggled, and the order of the old days has never been restored.

On our journey back to Tehran, we decided to travel by jeep instead. Immediately after entering the city, we found ourselves in congested streets. Along the way, we saw many abandoned cars on the roadside, remnants of crashes. At the hotel, we could not help but notice mechanics and chauffeurs hailing from Southeast Asia. All of this was symptomatic of Iran's newfound wealth. The number of cars had increased tenfold from fifty thousand to five hundred thousand in the span of a year. Mechanics and other supporting staff, such as chauffeurs, were so heavy in demand that they had to be lured in from neighboring countries with high wages and offered hotel accommodation.

In my recommendation that I finally submitted to the United Nations Development Programme, I stressed the importance of managing and distributing water resources while Iran pushed for industrialization. The government would do well not to neglect its villages. After all, the majority of its people still lived in rural areas.

At the conclusion of our official business, our hosts took us to a restaurant. Restaurants are small in Iran. They're at most a hundred square meters without any private rooms. But Iranians are hospitable to a fault. Each time a guest finishes his drink, the watchful host fills it up without fail. Even cucumbers, considered a luxury fruit, are immediately served again once they have been eaten. So those of us who weren't exactly cucumber lovers learned to leave one or two pieces on our plates.

Shortly into the meal, the entire round table was overladen with dishes. In front of me, on a plate, lay a lamb's head staring at me — complete with teeth. The enthusiastic host urged me to take my fork and eat the most delicious eyes. According to our host, the lamb's head and eyes, considered a delicacy in Iranian cuisine, are reserved for their most important guests. As advisors from the UN and travelers from afar, we were first in line. I've always been a gourmet and an adventurous eater, but that day, staring eye-to-eye with the lamb in front of me, I got cold feet. I made like I was eating it but only took a small bite from an insignificant part.

Fast forward 20 to 30 years later, after I became Taiwan's top representative to Japan, I had a chat with Koo Chen-fu (辜振甫), the former chairman of the Straits Exchange Foundation and of Taiwan Cement. He told me the story of how he came to eat a lamb's eye, reminding me of my own narrow escape. Like me, he had been invited to dinner by his Iranian hosts. Urged not to pass over the tasty ocular treat, he ended up swallowing an entire hardened eyeball in one gulp. By the time his plane stopped over in Austria, the eyeball was stuck in his intestine. He had to be admitted into a hospital for an operation to take it out.

45

Eating Soft-Shell Turtle

Every TIME I EAT SOFT-SHELL TURTLE, I get a bit homesick.

During my childhood in Chiayi, soft-shell turtle was common fare. There were wild turtles in the river all the time, which a local hawker caught and sold. My mother was his frequent customer, so much so that on the more idle days, the hawker would even visit us at our home bearing a few choice turtles. "Want to eat soft-shell turtle today?" When I was young I would often hear my mother say, "Go for the big ones when buying chicken, but go for the small ones when buying soft-shell turtles." Smaller-sized turtles are truly more delicious.

For us in Chiayi, eating soft-shell turtles meant drinking turtle blood. It was good for bright eyes and for fending off myopia or presbyopia. When I lived in Japan after my wedding, Mother even prepared turtle blood in our Japanese home, scaring Chin-fun. Mother would ask me to bring her a chopstick, which she would use to gently poke the turtle's head. This would cause the turtle to think that it was under attack and bite the chopstick. Mother would seize that moment to swiftly chop off the turtle's head. The total amount of blood from one turtle comes up to about one wineglass, two wineglasses at most. Mother would add lukewarm sake to the glass. The resulting concoction tastes a bit like rice wine.

After being blacklisted by the Kuomintang in the 1960s, I could not return to Taiwan for a long time. Lucky for me, one could still eat soft-shell turtle in Japan. When Mother came to Japan for a visit, it was imperative to bring her to a restaurant to try turtle a la Japanese.

I took Mother to Kyoto, where there was a three-hundred-year-old restaurant called *Daiichi*. They prepared soft-shell turtle in four ways. First was the way mother liked it, the familiar turtle blood. Next came raw turtle liver, presented on a plate. This one stopped us in our tracks. None of us dared to pick it up. The third dish came in the form of a casserole brought to the table by the restaurant owner herself. For a moment, it seemed as if we were going to be treated to a colorful hotpot. However, when they took the lid off, we only saw clear soup with chunks of turtle meat. The turtle meat was cooked to taste like chicken and its texture was halfway between that of tendons and shark skin. Finally, the clear broth from this casserole was used to make porridge. With an egg thrown in, it was extremely tasty.

In 1986, I went to Hangzhou, China, and made it a point to try the lakeside restaurant "Louwailou" (樓外樓), famous for its fish and prawn dishes. When Chiang Kai-shek was still in Nanjing, he often organized dinner parties here. Later, Zhou En-lai also threw banquets here. Knowing that Louwailou served soft-shell turtle as well, I had specially commissioned them to cook a turtle stew (since it was not on the menu), and they did a fantastic job.

In the 1990s, upon my return to Taiwan, I discovered that quite a few restaurants have soft-shell turtle on their menu. I would most often go to the Tainan restaurant at Huaxi Street. The turtle there would take me back to my childhood days. At that time, one turtle would cost NT$600~800, cheaper than in Kyoto but more delicious.

Unfortunately, a scandal circulated afterwards about turtle meat containing parasites. All of a sudden, no one ordered turtle anymore, and restaurants took it off their menus.

46

Flying up Mount Everest on a Helicopter

OF COURSE, globe-trotting for my UN job, I couldn't possibly work twenty-four hours a day. Sometimes I indulged a bit.

The UNDP was looking for experts to advise Nepal. Thus, I was dispatched along with a Japanese hydraulic engineering expert to take a tour of the region.

Nepal is situated on a slope and its capital, Kathmandu, sits on the side of a very high mountain. Traveling to Nepal was different from traveling to other places. Usually, when you take a flight, your plane would climb up to the sky, where it would cruise for some time at high altitudes before coming down and landing somewhere flat. However, flying to Nepal feels like one is perpetually climbing and never really descending.

It's in this country that you find Mount Everest. Those who want to conquer this peak must spend several years training. For me, I paid my respects to the world's highest mountain by riding a helicopter up to the very top. After reaching the summit, I first looked down at the peak, all covered in snow, then the black mountain rock, followed by the green mass of forest, and lastly the grassy plains at the bottom. Houses dotted the stretch between the forest and grassy plain. Against this tremendous backdrop, the helicopter I was sitting in felt like a toy. I felt as if I'd entered a land of giants — perhaps what really lay before me was a chocolate cake at their dining table.

I'm told that these helicopter tours have to take place the first thing in the morning, at daybreak, because air currents later in the day are too unstable. Mountain climbers train for years to get to the

This is to certify that

MOUNT EVEREST
(SAGARMATHA)
had the privilege of greeting to-day

15ᵗʰ June 1978

Mr. Lo Fu Chen

Who took part in Daily "MOUNTAIN-FLIGHT"
ROYAL NEPAL AIRLINES

GENERAL MANAGER

Lo paid respects to Mount Everest by riding a helicopter up to the
very top at daybreak when air currents were most stable. Here's
his certificate of conquest. (Taken in the 70s)

top of Everest. I went up and down via helicopter and still received a certificate to show for my "conquest," and all before breakfast to boot!

In the 1980s when UN-Habitat was set up in Kenya, I was dispatched there as well. Taking advantage of the rare opportunity to set foot on African soil, I arranged to go on a safari as soon as work concluded.

Before World War II, when Kenya was still a British colony, safaris were all the rage. In fact, it was the choice pastime of the upper classes. As such, all hotels were lavishly done up. One might as well be in a hotel in London. When you walk out of your hotel, the first thing you saw was a moat surrounding it all the way around, protecting the guests inside from wild animals.

I joined a safari tour. The chauffeur seemed to know exactly where to find the animals and he gave us tips on how to observe them up close. This eye-opening tour revealed to me the fierce survival instincts innate to many animals. For example, when a lioness has already decided on its target, and is simply waiting for her opportunity to attack, she is entirely focused on her task. She couldn't have been bothered even when a vehicle several times her size appeared beside her, noisy engine or not.

Contrary to prior belief, I discovered that zebras aren't weak animals, especially in groups. A few hundred zebras assembled together don't fear a lion's attack. It's only when a lone zebra has been left behind by the group that it gets eaten.

The guide warned us that the most terrifying animal of them all wasn't the leopard, the wolf, the tiger or the jackal, but in fact the buffalo. You would be unwise to get too close to it with a camera. Should the buffalo lose its temper, and rush toward you — good luck, for it will give everything it's got to take you down.

Hippopotami stay underwater all day. Their bodies are massive and unwieldy. You'd be forgiven for thinking that they're lazy. The truth couldn't be further. They do what they do to survive. Being in the sun is bad for their skin. They stay underwater to keep their moisture. During the night is when they become active. They gallop at great speeds, sometimes at fifty kilometers an hour. In one night, they can cover up to a few hundred kilometers — easily the distance between Taipei and Kaohsiung.

The most striking thing about being in Africa is the lack of development around you. With only the setting sun and stars as companions, your transient retreat from worldly cares might as well be a living dream that you wake up to each lucid morning. In East Africa, there are just as many large cities as tribes and the largest among them, Nairobi, has several skyscrapers. When you're in the city, you are constantly reminded of the twenty-first century. But when you get out of it, you don't even have to go beyond twenty kilometers — it's as if you've traveled back in time to two thousand years ago, like a character in a magical fantasy.

For their colorful attire and exuberant dances, the tall and skinny people of East Africa's Maasai tribe are often the favorite subjects of camera-toting tourists who like to get off the bus just to take photos of them. At first, the Maasai tribe and the tourists on our safari got along just fine. Soon, it transpired that a white man inside the bus was covertly taking photos of them, breaking the rule of no free photo-taking. No sooner had I registered the situation, one of the Maasai tribe members had already picked up a rock and flung it at the offender inside the bus. This was how they meted out justice, unlike us who leave it up to the police or to courts of law.

47

Providing Economic Data for the G7 Summit

WORKING FOR THE UN, other than being able to sample delicious foods from all over the world, I also got to collaborate with world-class economists. It was truly exciting. It's a source of true happiness to be able to solve the world's economic problems with some of the greatest minds on Earth.

In my opinion, some of these international economists are ambitious to the point of Herculean. They even seem to bear the burden of the world's economic problems on their own shoulders. In 1991, when I was working as a senior academic officer at the United Nations University in Tokyo, my mentor and professor, Lawrence Klein called me out of the blue: "Hey, Fu-chen! G7 is holding a summit. Let's show them our research." Excited, I said, "OK!"

G7 comprised seven big industrial countries: the United States, the United Kingdom, France, Germany, Japan, Canada and Italy. Every year, representatives from these seven countries come together for a summit. G7's precursor was G6 (Canada became the 7th member in 1976). In 1997 Russia entered the club, making it what it is currently today: G8.

Klein wanted to study a few of the great economic questions facing the world. One such question goes like this: To cope with the East-West German reunification of 1990, West Germany must prepare US$200 billion to support East Germany. This sum will be taken out of the world's financial markets. What are the consequences of this sudden withdrawal on the world economy?

The answers to these sorts of questions could not be delivered via

Lo (left) and his UPenn teacher Lawrence Klein (right) have worked together on many projects, studying world economic changes. In the middle is Shishido Shuntaro, president of Japan International University.

For Lo, nothing can be more fulfilling than working, brainstorming and debating with world top economists about the world's major problems.

a mere two-way discussion. I was tasked to organize an international video conference.

Two weeks before the G7 summit, Klein flew to Tokyo. Together with seven to eight other economists, we stepped into a television studio in Roppongi for the conference call. We sat in a row before a rectangular conference table facing cameras. Klein moderated the discussion. I sat next to him.

In Paris, seven or eight other economists were similarly assembled in a room. There was a third location with more people at the United Nations Headquarters in New York, where there was also a big computer containing the econometric model that Klein had programmed, made out of countless of equations. You'd input a few key economic variables; then, after processing them for a few minutes, the computer would spit out the answers.

At the start of the meeting, representatives at the UN Headquarters, who had come prepared with statistical data, inputted them into the computer. A few minutes after the furious keyboard typing had subsided, the results came out. Then, the economists in the three locations examined the outcome and debated it real time. The conference call technology at that time was not as advanced as it is today. You could only do one-to-one video calls on the television screen, not multi-party calls. However, all involved could still hear the spoken discussion. After arriving at our conclusions, and summarizing our main points, we submitted our report to the G7.

The G7 Summit was a seven-country affair. It was not organized by the UN nor did this video conference occur as a result of our UN duties. Rather, it came naturally together because several passionate international economists decided to make it happen, out of our sheer desire to contribute to human knowledge. This video conference, facilitated by the UN University, also united the UN's different branches. It was superior to anything that could have been organized by one country. In the public eye, it was even more convincing.

I remember another occasion. In November 1996, President Bill Clinton arrived in Manila to attend the APEC conference. A few days before the summit, we coordinated another three-way video

In 2007, Lo and Nobel Economic Science Prize winner Joseph E. Stiglitz both received Waseda's "Accomplished Scholar" award.

conference call between Tokyo, New York and Paris. We made calculations based on the existing UN-LINK model and discussed the impact of lowering tariffs in the Asia-Pacific region, as well as how to accelerate its economic development. I remember our conclusion. Asia as a whole could sustain an economic growth of 6 to 7%, with China slowly moving towards 9%. Clinton's economic advisor then, Joseph E. Stiglitz, had been awarded the Nobel Prize in Economics. Nobel Prize winner Kenneth Arrow was his teacher. Arrow and Klein were as close as brothers. So, Klein went through Arrow to get Stiglitz to submit our findings to Clinton, and by extension, to the entire APEC conference members.

I wouldn't say that the economists in our group are at the very top of the world. But from where we stand, we're able to see (and, if we're lucky, influence) what goes on at the very top.

48

Drafting the Kyoto Protocol

THE UNITED NATIONS SERVES ITS MEMBER COUNTRIES. As an academic extension of the UN, the United Nations University (UNU) must occupy itself with the three big problems: survival, development and well-being. The content of my work was truly global.

We only have one Earth. Our resources are limited. We do not have enough food for everyone. Global warming is real and it has real consequences. These familiar warnings were first issued in the 1970s by an international think tank called the "Club of Rome."[1] In the 1980s, even more warnings were released. The Brundtland Commission assembled by Norway's former prime minister Gro Harlem Brundtland issued a report entitled "Our Common Future," in which the central tenets of sustainable development were established. "Man must find a new avenue of growth, whereby the standard of living can be raised without increasing our consumption of natural resources, so as to achieve sustainable development." The report emphasized that sustainable development means that the development of one generation must not affect the survival of the next.

Following, in 1992, the UN held its first ever UN Conference

---

1 The Club of Rome is a global think tank that deals with a variety of international political issues. Founded in 1968 at Accademia dei Lincei in Rome, Italy, the Club of Rome describes itself as "a group of world citizens, sharing a common concern for the future of humanity." It consists of current and former heads of state, UN bureaucrats, high-level politicians and government officials, diplomats, scientists, economists and business leaders from around the globe.

on Environment and Development in Rio de Janerio, Brazil. Over one hundred world leaders and government representatives took part in what was unofficially known as "The Earth Summit." It was the first time governments from all over the world sat at one table to discuss this problem. It was through this meeting that Agenda 21 was proposed. While Agenda 21 acknowledged the importance of sustainable development, no concrete solutions came out of it.

Representing UNU, I took part in the Rio de Janeiro conference and was inspired by it. Sustainable development and economic restructuring would become my main preoccupations during my many years at UNU. Countless scholars all over the world would also throw themselves passionately into these subjects. I would fly to Paris even more frequently because I would often be invited by the United Nations Educational Scientific and Cultural Organization (UNESCO) and Organization for Economic Cooperation and Development (OECD) to contribute to their research.

Joke Waller Hunter, who headed the Environmental Bureau of the OECD, was once the Netherlands' Minister of Environment. One day, she looked me up to suggest a collaboration. Members of the OECD were able to study each member country's environmental problems (mostly first-world countries like the US and those in Europe). On the other hand, those of non-OECD member countries like China, India, Indonesia, Brazil and Russia, were not yet being studied. To cover as much as 93% of the world's environmental problems, perhaps a team headed by me from UNU could start studying them. That was how I came to research China's sustainable development.

Apart from having its own departments of study, UNU had one advantage. We were partners with over 6,000 universities from all over the world. It was extremely easy to borrow human resources from these partners when undertaking large-scale international research. In 1996, I rallied resources from the Ministry of Science and Technology of the People's Republic of China, the Chinese Academy of Social Sciences, Peking University, and Japan's National Institute for Environmental Studies. Together we came up with China's "Green GDP" in 1993, using the new measure proposed in 1992's Earth Summit in Rio de Janeiro. In this new measure, Green GDP is calculated by deducting the costs of environmental destruction from the country's GDP. This was the first time that anyone had ever calculated China's Green GDP and the outcome was shocking.

In 1997, we went to China's Ministry of Science and Technology to give a presentation. The chair at that time was Song Jian (宋健). In the 1990s, China's economy was growing at unprecedented rates. GDP growth was as high as 10%, but, in 1993, this economic development had also depleted natural resources and created environmental pollution, costing the country as much as 8.9% of this GDP. In other words, the real Green GDP growth was only 1.1%. The government officer from the Ministry of Environment inquired, "How much money do we need to spend to salvage the situation?" We replied, "According to our experience in Japan, you need to invest only 1% of your GDP to reduce the costs on the environment by upwards of 8%."

In the 1990s, every country worked hard to understand and confront the problem of sustainable development. The UN would organize subsequent Earth Summits. In 1997, when the summit was into its third edition, all the countries involved finally decided that it was time to take action. 174 countries and the European Union signed the famous Kyoto Protocol and pledged to reduce coal emissions. Advanced industrial countries committed to keep the yearly rate of greenhouse gas emissions from 2008 to 2012 at 1990 levels in a bid to prevent the environment from worsening.

I attended this Kyoto conference as a representative from UNU. It was eye-opening. In all my decades working for the UN, it had always been the first-world countries leading the way for second-and third-world countries. In Kyoto, the situation was reversed. Third-world countries banded together to oppose the more advanced countries, forcing them to agree to their requests.

There were three types of participants at the Kyoto conference. Firstly, there were government representatives who held large-scale conferences at the Kyoto International Conference Halls. Secondly, there were representatives from non-governmental organizations who numbered the most. Lastly, there were the specialists. Because this was after all a significant conference organized by the UN, each branch sent their representatives to attend the conference. These participants held separate meetings at different hotels. At all these meetings, scientists from third-world countries were also very passionate. They would come bearing their objective findings and give effusive presentations. Inevitably, they would lay the blame on the so-called advanced countries. It was because of how these countries had depleted the Earth's natural resources for the past hundred years that we were now finding ourselves in our present woeful condition.

Outside the Kyoto conference halls was yet another spectacle that I had never seen in all my experience attending these international conferences. Representatives from NGOs gathered in large numbers to protest the actions of governments. They were waving flags and shouting and once again, most of these NGOs came from third-world countries.

Japan was the host of the Kyoto Conference. Drafting the Kyoto Protocol became the responsibility of its Ministry of Environment. During the meeting, I was invited by the Ministry to attend a small roundtable, and to weigh in on the terms of the Protocol. Of course, the terms would go on to be finalized by the representatives of all the participating countries attending the conference.

49

A "Taiwanese" Meets World Leaders from All Over

Pfrasticipating in the OB summit was another HIGH POINT IN MY career.

Fukuda Takeo (福田赳夫) was Japan's prime minister from 1976 to 1978. His counterpart in West Germany at the same time was Helmut Schmidt (who retired only in 1982). To use a Japanese phrase, the two of them were "同期の櫻" (cherry blossoms of the same period). They were very close because of their shared experience.

A year after Schmidt retired, he and Fukuda Takeo, still close friends, decided to organize a summit for former world leaders. It was hoped that this conference would provide a platform for these experienced politicians who now had nothing to lose, and who could therefore air their opinions fearlessly.

The organization's official name was The InterAction Council. But since people liked to call the retired the "old boys," which became OB when shortened, the annual conference was thus known as OB Summit. Of course, not all ex-presidents or prime ministers were automatically inducted into this Council. There could only be one representative from any country at any one time.

In 1995, hearing that Fukuda Takeo was very sick, the organizers decided to hold the OB Summit in Tokyo, as a way of sending him off. More than 70 former leaders attended this event, including former US president Carter, ex-Soviet Union president Gorbachev etc.

This meeting had nothing to do with the United Nations, but United Nations University's International Forum had the best amenities in all of Tokyo. One of its largest conference halls could seat up to a few hundred people. But more importantly, each seat came equipped with headsets that you could use to tune into different channels streaming live interpretations in different languages.

In the beginning, only the following languages were available at UN conferences: English, French, Russian and Spanish, selected because they were the official languages of many different countries. Since Japanese was used by only one country, the onus fell to the Japanese who came to these conferences to participate via one of the four languages.

Because the Soviet Union comprised eleven countries, it had eleven seats. Countries using Russian also included Vietnam. While I was in Vietnam, I had met several Vietnamese who had studied abroad in Russia. They represented a different kind of intellectuals from those who had studied abroad in France, their ex-colonizer. Chinese was later included, although it was only used by China. Arabic was also included. So currently six languages are available at UN conferences.

Japan's translators are among the world's best, with language specialists of all kinds, and further specialists within each different language. Take the two languages (Chinese and Japanese) I am most familiar with for example, I almost never heard any mistranslations.

Australia's former Prime Minister Malcolm Fraser was the chair of the designated organizing committee, comprising 13 members. Along with the wife of China's former Minister of Foreign Affairs and Vice Premier Huang Hua (黃華), He Li-liang (何理良), I was

INTERACTION COUNCIL

Report on the Conclusions and Recommendations
by a High-level Group on

THE CHALLENGE TO BALANCE
POPULATION INCREASE AND FOOD SUPPLY

Chaired by
Malcolm Fraser

10-11 April 1995
Tokyo, Japan

In addition to Mr. Fraser, Mr. Takeo **Fukuda** (Japan) from the InterAction Council and the following high-level experts participated in the meeting: Lee-Jay **Cho** (U. S. A.), **He** Liliang (China), Howard W. **Hjort** (U.S.A.), Hajimu **Irisawa** (Japan), Fu-Chen **Lo** (Taiwan), Robert S. **McNamara** (U.S. A.), Isamu **Miyazaki** (Japan), Gail D.**Ness** (U.S.A.), Ismail **Serageldin** (Egypt), Katsumi **Sezaki** (Japan), and Akihiko **Yoshida** (Japan).

Lo is among OB's 13 designated organizing committee members.
Taiwan appeared in parentheses after his name, unchanged and
caused no protests.

among these 13 who would help with the homework and prepare reports for the meetings.

In the run-up to the summit, when filling in my personal particulars for a required form, I decided on a whim to write "Taiwan." To my surprise, this was never changed. When the list of committee members was printed out, Taiwan appeared in parentheses after my name. After He Li-liang's name was China, of course. She was civil and respectful to a fault, and did not object to my use of "Taiwan" at any point.

On the world stage, Taiwan's visibility is scant. Therefore, like a child running around in a room full of adults, Taiwan inevitably

The conferences Lo takes part always decorated with flags of different countries except Taiwan.

desires to be seen and heard. That day, although I was miles away from home at an international event, the moment I saw the parenthetical containing my country's name, I broke into a smile.

The man of the occasion that day, Fukuda Takeo, was wheeled out by his son Fukuda Yasuo. He sat in the wheelchair, dressed in a most formal traditional Japanese kimono — black on top, gray below — appearing very solemn indeed. The moment he entered, the entire hall stood up, greeting him warmly with applause. Fukuda Takeo's doctor had given him specific instruction not to exceed five minutes for his speech, but he rallied his strength and spoke for twenty minutes. This was the first time I saw Fukuda Takeo in person, but it would also be the last. Two months later, he would pass away.

Fukuda Takeo may have been frail in constitution that day, but he was firm in his resolve to tell the world about the problem of an increasing world population combined with increasing food scarcity. After the meeting, based on the contents of Takeo Fukuda's speech, we committee members wrote up relevant reports.

At the conference that day, I saw with my own eyes other former world leaders too.

Pierre Trudeau, the former Prime Minister of Canada, was thin and tall. He was already 76 years of age, but nevertheless still good-looking. From the 1970s to the 1980s he had twice been elected prime minister, and had been romantically involved with the movie star Barbara Streisand. They often went on vacation together. But one day, it was suddenly announced that he had tied the knot with another woman twenty years younger — indeed, marriage and falling in love are two different things. Trudeau was a political figure with great character. There was always, for example, a rose pinned on his collar. He made it no exception on his trip to Tokyo — a brilliant red rose on his collar, exuding fragrance and charm.

Robert S. McNamara, America's Secretary of Defense during the Vietnam War, had also come. He not only attended the designated 13-people committee meeting, but was also one of the two speakers that day. I was no stranger to him. I had invited him to a conference I organized, "The Economic Impact of Reducing Armed Forces in the Post-Cold War Period," at the United Nations University. He was the chairman of the World Bank at that time.

One might say that McNamara is the most controversial figure in contemporary American history. Upon graduation from Harvard, he was off to a fast-tracked career. His talent shone such that it took him only 13 years to become the general manager of Ford Motors. At the age of 43, he was personally handpicked by President Kennedy to be Secretary of Defense. But fortune and misfortune come hand in hand. At his highest point, the seeds of his downfall would be sown. Most of McNamara's seven years as Secretary of Defense were spent embroiled in the Vietnam War. When America finally withdrew its troops in defeat, the blame was placed squarely on him.

Although the Vietnam War had concluded almost thirty years ago, on April 10, 1995, at the OB summit, around the time that McNamara's memoir was going to be released, McNamara steeled

The former Prime Minister of the Netherlands, Andreas van Agt, is a close friend of Lo and has visited Taiwan at Lo's invitation.

his eighty-year old body at the podium and apologized publicly for America's part in the Vietnam War. It was a great mistake, he said, to a room of applause. Admitting one's oversight is not easy. It requires great courage and wisdom.

At this conference, I also made the acquaintance of former Dutch Prime Minister Andreas van Agt. I would later invite him to the United Nations University's Higher Institute to be a Guest Lecturer. I also invited him to visit Taiwan in 2000.

Speaking of befriending world leaders, former Korean Prime

McNamara (photo 1, right) is the most controversial figure in contemporary American history. At the age of 43, he was appointed by President Kennedy as Secretary of Defense. But during his 7-years term, America was embroiled in Vietnam War and suffered defeat.

Minister Nam Duck-woo once worked in an office next to me. He was older than me by eleven years, and was as important to modern Korea as Yin Zhong-rong[1] and Li Kwoh-ting (李國鼎) were to modern Taiwan. It was Nam Duck-woo who led South Korea out of its post

---

1 Yin Zhong-rong (尹仲容, April 16, 1903 ~ January 24, 1963) had been Taiwan's Economics Minister and CEO of Central Trust. He was one of the few KMT officials who knew the importance of free trade. Under his leadership, Taiwan's economy stabilized and transformed from planned economy to market economy.

(Photo 3) Lo made the acquaintance of former Dutch Prime Minister Andreas van Agt at OB Summit.

war poverty and into the era of industrialization. When South Korea's per capita income reached US$1,000 in the 1970s, it was hailed as the "miracle on the Han river."

Nam Duck-woo had a Ph.D. in Economics from Oklahoma State University an American university. He came back to South Korea to teach. Soon, his ability was recognized by Park Chung-hee, who appointed him to the post of Finance Minister (1969-1974), and Deputy Prime Minister (974-1978). But after Park Chung-hee was assassinated in 1979 and Chun Doo-hwan took over, Nam Duck-woo was forced to step down.

After Nam Duck-woo left the government nucleus, he went as a visiting scholar to the East-West Center at the University of Hawaii. It was said to be the vacation paradise of failed politicians. World leaders who lost their power were often invited to the Center to "recharge." I myself have never experienced the loneliness from being at the top. For me it was merely a change of jobs. In 1981, I left my position in Nagoya to be a senior researcher at the East-West Center's Population Research Institute, and also taught part-time at its Economics and Geography Departments. Nam Duck-woo's and my office were separated by only a thin wall. Each month, we would alternate our lectures. I would speak about the Asian economy and he would talk about the Korean economy. In my day-to-day interactions with him, I discovered that he was not only an expert in economics, but also a leader with great charm.

One day, he knocked on my door to say goodbye. He was going back to South Korea. I asked him, "What are you going back for?" He replied: "I'm going back to be the Prime Minister!" Taken back by the news but happy for him, I congratulated him warmly. I thought if there was one line that all failed politicians would like to trumpet, it would be bidding goodbye to the East-West Center with what he had just said.

50

Chiang Kai-shek Enlists Schumpeter as Economic Advisor

IN ACADEMIC CIRCLES, the name Joseph A. Schumpeter doesn't require any explanation. His theory of business cycles and his account of capitalism's creative destruction are widely influential. He was born in Czechoslovakia in 1883 and he died in 1950. In the 1930s, he became a US citizen and went to teach at Harvard. He precedes us by a few generations. However, when I was in my 40s, I made the acquaintance of his last student, also at the University of Hawaii.

This last student of Schumpeter was Benjamin Higgins whom I called him Ben. Ben was a professor at Australia National University. But in 1981, he came to the University of Hawaii as a visiting scholar. One night, after dinner, he shared with me a little story about Chiang Kai-shek. Since Taiwan was still under martial law, the anecdote seemed even more mysterious. So I perked up my ears even more, and gave seventy-year-old Higgins all my attention.

Before the war, Ben had been an assistant of Schumpeter's at Harvard. One day, in 1940, a student of Schumpeter's by the name of David Kung stopped by to give Ben a present. He was puzzled by the generous act. *"I am only the professor's assistant, not your professor, why give me a present?"* he asked the student. David Kung said, Chairman Chiang Kai-shek [1] would like to invite Schumpeter to China and be Chiang's economic advisor but finds it

---

[1] Chiang Kai-shek was at that time Chairman of the National Military Council of the Nationalist Government of ROC, a position he held from 1928 to 1948. He was also Chairman of the KMT party, a position he held from 1938 to 1975.

difficult to ask the question. Could Ben possibly ask him?

This David Kung (whose Chinese name was 孔令侃, Kung Ling-kan) turned out to be the eldest son of Soong Ei-ling (宋靄齡), who was the older sister of Chiang Kai-shek's wife, Chiang Soong Mei-ling. Kung had attended university in Shanghai, and upon graduation, started working at the Central Trust of China's Financial Bureau. In 1937, when Japan invaded Shanghai, Kung retreated with the Central Trust of China to Hong Kong. Kung was still a young 21 years of age. Two years later, he received his letter of acceptance from Harvard, and it was there that he met the master Schumpeter.

Ben ended up conveying Kung's request. Schumpeter had never been to China himself. At that time, he happened to be embroiled in a quarrel with the Neo-Keynesians at Harvard. Rather unhappy with where he was, he decided to accept Chiang's invitation. His salary was negotiated in terms of gold. He agreed to leave in January of the following year, after the semester ended. Who would have expected that that year on December 7th, Japan would bomb Pearl Harbor and the US would declare war on Japan? As a result, his departure was postponed indefinitely.

Schumpeter had once given a lecture in Japan in the 1930s. Based on his experience there, he was moved to predict that "This garden-like country will be destroyed once." Indeed, three to four years after the bombing of Pearl Harbor, Japan tasted the bitter fruit of failure and finally surrendered.

After exchanging stories, new friends inevitably draw closer.

Lo invited Benjamin Higgins (left) and Honjō Kazuhiko to his home. After couple of drinks, both became tipsy. Higgins even did a dance waving a handkerchief over his head.

When Higgins shared his stories about Kung and Schumpeter, we became good friends.

Later, when I was taking up my post at Nagoya's Regional Development Center, Ben visited the center for half a year. He didn't know a word of Japanese. I showed him and his wife around quite a bit. Before he left Japan, he autographed a book as a present to me. His exact words to thank me for looking after him, on behalf of him and his wife, were: "To Fu-chen our fairy godfather" — a very mischievous phrase indeed.

One time, I even arranged for Ben and other international economists to experience Japanese rural life. Armed with a case of red wine, I herded everyone onto a bus that would take us to Gifu-ken in the mountains, where we were welcomed by the local village chief (who happened to be a friend of my brother-in-law). Cutting through the mountain village was a crystal-clear river. With the help of the village head, we caught over one hundred "ayu" (sweetfish), which we cooked around a charcoal fire. Stick after stick of skewered ayu was planted in a circle on the ground, where the flames roasted them from the center. The village head also demonstrated his deft skills of splitting up bamboo and turning them into conduits of water. With chilled water running, he placed the cooked "somen" (fine noodles) down the bamboo pipes. This was what was called "nagashi somen". All of us used our chopsticks to pick them up from the other end. This elicited great delight and wonder among the foreign economists. We toasted with the red wine at the end of the meal. So happy were Ben and his new Australian wife that they took off their clothes, and dived bare-naked into the river.

In their classrooms and research offices, economists acted as professors and scholars. Outside the classrooms, everyone led different lifestyles. Ben, for example, bought a large property in Australia. Behind his house lay a hundred hectares of land which he used to breed a few sheep that wandered about and multiplied. He let them be. He was happy to spend his whole day just looking at his sheep, and not seeing anyone. However, I felt that these professors liked to make new friends that they treated like their own family members and with whom they derived whole-hearted pleasure. No, these were not just intellectuals.

51

When His Fiancée Called Off the Engagement, He Tore Down the House

I KNOW AN INDONESIAN ECONOMIST BY THE NAME OF IWAN AZIS, another straightforward, salt-of-the-earth kind of guy.

Iwan Azis currently works at the Asian Development Bank. This is the international organization that keeps changing the country designation of Taiwan's Central Bank to Taipei, China which does much to invoke the ire of its CEO Perng Fai-nan (彭淮南), who makes noise about it every year without fail. One year, I was in Indonesia for a conference organized by the World Bank. I first met Iwan touring the University of Indonesia. He was only a research assistant then but his brilliance was plain for all to see. Afterwards, he would become a civil servant at Indonesia's Council for Economic Planning and Development. At my invitation, he came to Nagoya for a training course I organized at the Regional Development Center.

Iwan was born to a wealthy family. His father owned Indonesia's largest English newspaper, and collected antiques as a hobby. In order to store these antiques, he bought three bungalows — that's how wealthy he was. Before coming to Nagoya, Iwan got engaged in Indonesia, and built a new home. He was just getting ready to move into it and embrace his new life.

Who would have expected that during his four months of training in Japan, his love life would be turned upside down? His fiancée fell in love with someone else and broke off the engagement. Iwan didn't want to set his eyes ever again on that new house, so he ordered it to be torn down. Now that he was no longer getting married, Iwan decided that he would get a Ph.D. in the US. He asked me whether he should pick Harvard or Cornell. I told him that although Harvard's reputation is of course the best, Cornell had a better research department in the field of regional development. In my opinion, Cornell was better. Iwan heeded my advice and went to Cornell. Two years later, after getting his doctorate, Iwan mailed a copy of his thesis to my home, and solemnly declared: "I'm done!" He treated me as though I was his brother.

Iwan returned to his country to teach at the University of Indonesia, the best university in Indonesia, similar to how National

Lo and Iwan Aziz (1ˢᵗ on the right) visited the Mausoleum of the First Qin Emperor together.

Taiwan University is the best university in Taiwan. There, he buried himself in research. For a long time, I received no news of marriage from him. I thought perhaps he was too scarred.

One year, I organized a conference in Pakistan, and extended an invitation for him to come and present his economic model for Indonesia. Accompanying Iwan was a female assistant. Not only was she very pretty, but she also seemed smart and very capable. I cut to the chase the instant I had a private moment with Iwan. "What are you waiting for?" As if rudely awoken, he immediately proposed to his assistant upon their return, and tied the knot soon after. Iwan was very grateful to me, saying that I had brought him to his senses with that question.

One time, while teaching at the University of Indonesia, Iwan got invited to Taiwan on official business. The organizers arranged for him to take a trip to Ulai to see an aboriginal dance. "Why did they ask me to come and see my own country's dance?" He later complained, half joking but also half serious. Indeed he had a point. Some of Taiwan's aboriginal tribes and those of Southeast Asia belonged to the same family; even their languages were similar [1]. To give an example, both the people from Taiwan's Pinuyumayan tribe and the Indonesians have the same word for eating: "makan."

---

1 Both belong to the Austronesian language family, a language family that dispersed throughout the islands of Southeast Asia, Madagascar and the Pacific, with a few members on continental Asia. It is one of the best-established ancient language family that is spoken by 385 million people.

52

My Malay Muslim Brother

IN THE 1980s, when I was in my forties, I had a group of friends all like Iwan. We all taught or researched regional science and often worked on projects together and were more or less the same age. My wife liked to remark how each time we got together, we always seemed to be laughing. This was probably the truth. Since we were all in the same field, nothing held us from speaking freely and passionately. We enjoyed one another's company. I jokingly called our group "the mafia." Having never grown up with any brothers, I felt as if they were my own brothers. These friends of mine all had one thing in common. They had all gone to study in the US, and had returned after getting their degrees. They were full of ideals and passionate to serve their own countries. Of these, I was closest to Kamal Salih and really felt that he was a kindred spirit.

Kamal Salih was a Malay from Malaysia. He was born on Penang Island. Malays, like Taiwanese aboriginals, don't use surnames. They derive their "last names" from their fathers' first names. Therefore, Kamal Salih really meant Kamal, son of Salih. Kamal Salih named his son Samuel, hence the complete name of his son is Samuel Kamal, son of Kamal. When Malays trace their ancestry, they are really playing a game of overlapping (接龍, a Chinese language game whereby one person picks up the last syllable of a word said by the previous person and uses it to begin a new word, and so on and so forth).

Kamal had grown up poor, but he was very intelligent and did well in his studies. Under British rule, the Malays were not especially

Economics, like medicine, has many branches. Lo specialized in regional science when he was in his 40s. He had a group of like-minded, close friends whom he jokingly called "Maffia." Kamal Salih sits in the front row, 2nd from left.

encouraged to study hard in order to improve their political and financial standing. Malays were also by and large simple folk. Happy just to walk the streets, they were easily contented and not especially eager to seek knowledge. Kamal was among the earliest generation of higher-educated Malays. After graduating from university, he went to Australia for his Master's degree. He would finally get his Ph.D. from the University of Pennsylvania, in the same department as I. I was his senior by three years, so we didn't cross paths then.

After the war, the US was the most coveted place for academia, and as such attracted the best from all over the world. I went over in the 1960s, and the first scholars from Southeast Asia arrived about five or six years after me. Kamal was from the very earliest group of overseas students from Southeast Asia. Within two years of his return to Malaysia, he was appointed to Vice Dean of Universiti Sains Malaysia. Prior to his appointment, only English professors were appointed deans. (The British had colonized Malaysia in 1786). At that time, and this was not only for Malaysians, but also for Taiwanese, Thais, and Koreans — as soon as you proved yourself by getting a Ph.D., you were immediately deployed to the frontlines of the country's development, and assigned the most important roles.

The first time I met Kamal after his studies in the States, he had just returned to Malaysia for a year, and was not yet appointed to Vice Dean. I found him extremely quick-thinking. He'd studied in English from an early age, and his verbal and writing skills were on par with any American's. In 1978, we co-authored a book entitled "Growth Pole Strategy and Regional Development Policy: Asian Experiences and Alternative Approaches" which got picked up and used as textbooks by schools such as Harvard and M.I.T. It was proof that our academic caliber was world-class. You could say it was my very first calling card, entering the world of International Economics.

Chen Hsiao-hung (陳小紅), current Vice Chair of the Council for Economic Planning and Development of Taiwan, had once taken a class I taught at University of Hawaii's East West Center. Once,

Chang Ching-yu (張京育), former Bureau Chief of the Government Information Office, accompanied her to Japan for a cultural exchange. Introducing me to him, Chen made sure to bring up the fact that my books were used by nearly one thousand universities in the US.

Twenty years after the publication of our book, I received a letter from a university in South Africa, requesting my author photograph. They wanted to frame it and hang it in their Hall of Famous People because our book was apparently the book that most students had read. Kamal and I had gone through much together. He treated me like a brother and always had the following phrase at the tip of his tongue: "Fu-chen, whatever you say, I always agree with you." Although he

Lo and Kamal Salih went around West Lake (China) on bicycles.

was a Muslim, we were accepting of each other's cultural differences. Muslims don't eat pork, and so by right our eating habits should have clashed. But at the same time, in search of gourmet cuisine, Kamal would be quick to add: "Just don't tell there's pork inside."

In the 1990s, Kamal married his second wife. According to Muslim custom, a man could marry up to four wives. Malays exist too in Indonesia. In fact former president Sukarno, also a Malay Muslim, married three wives. The last of whom was Japanese. She'd often be invited on Japanese talk shows. Madame Dewi (Dewi Sukarno) is apparently still very popular on the media circuit.

Malay women have to abide by very strict rules. At year-end, a woman has to sit down on the floor before her husband, hold his hand, and then say to him, "This year if I have committed any wrongdoing, please forgive me." At this point, should the husband bring up divorce just once, it won't matter much, but if he says it twice, the problem becomes serious; mention it three times and the divorce is irrevocable. Nowadays, because of growing feminist influences, not every woman does it anymore, but this is an actual traditional Muslim custom. It probably sounds to you as if Malay women are not respected. But from my own experience, most men only marry one wife. Men with two wives are few and far in between. After all, not all men have the objective management skills that this arrangement would surely require.

53

A Japanese Celebrity Comes to Taiwan, Happy About Not Having to Fear Assassination

I WOULD SAY THAT JAPAN HAS FOUR REPRESENTATIVE ECONOMISTS: Kyoto University's Fujita Masahisa, Hamada Kōitchi, who strongly supported former Prime Minister Abe Shinzō's Quantitative Easing Monetary Policy, Aoki Masahiko, Japan's frontrunner for the Nobel Prize for Economics, and Tokyo University's Uzawa Hirofumi. I've had interactions with all these four economists. Fujita Masahisa and I both came out of UPenn's Regional Science Department. He received his Ph.D. four years after me. Hamada Kōitchi was a student in a class that I sat in during my years at the University of Tokyo. Professor Ōishi told me to reach out to him if I had any questions. In Aoki Masahiko's memoir, he mentions the friendship I shared with Ikuda Kōji. In addition, we were economic consultants on the same project in faraway Africa. Uzawa Hirofumi was a visiting professor I hired at the UNU; as such, we were on good terms.

At the end of April 2000, just before stepping down from my position at the UNU, I thought I might invite two close friends to visit me in Taiwan. One of them was the former prime minister of the Netherlands, Andreas van Agt and the other was Uzawa Hirofumi.

In his younger days, Uzawa was a student of Mathematics. After graduating from the Mathematics Department at the University of Tokyo, he started to develop an interest in economics. Around that time, by coincidence, the 1972 Nobel Winner Kenneth Arrow was giving a lecture in Japan. Arrow was both a mathematician and an economist. This fact alone encouraged Uzawa to apply to Stanford,

Uzawa Hirofumi kept his beard really long, which made him look like a "non-conformist." He opposed the automobile as a matter of principle and refused to use cars as a daily transportation means.

where Arrow taught. Within his first or second year there, he completed his dissertation, and achieved great renown for it. He later became a world-class economist. Even though he never got his Ph.D., he was invited to become a professor at the University of Chicago.

Upon his return, teaching at the University of Tokyo, Professor Uzawa's reputation spread far and wide. Later, on the basis of a thesis submitted to Tohoku University, he was finally conferred a

Ph.D. Dramatically, he even overturned a theory he came up with in his younger days. The more mature Uzawa came to realize that Economics wasn't just about using existing resources to help already wealthy people to increase their wealth. It should concern itself with sustainable development. His view set him apart from mainstream economists and in fact ran counter to what they represented. In his memoirs, he wrote, "I've lived an entire half a century as an economist. An economy that seeks to contribute to human happiness — might it not in fact bring about unhappiness?" This sort of reflection not only inspires respect but also gives pause in contemplation.

Uzawa sported a very long beard. Looking at him, you'd no doubt think "non-conformist." He opposed the automobile as a matter of principle because of its costs to society. One time, he and professor Ōishi accepted an invitation to a courtroom. There, they debated opposite views. Ōishi supported capitalists. Uzawa was against them. When they left the courtroom that day, a taxi was called for them out of respect. Ōishi naturally got into it. Not a hypocrite, Uzawa stuck to his principles and turned down the well-intentioned gesture, hopping on a bus instead.

In the 1970s, the Japanese government took back land from the farmers in order to build Narita Airport. The farmers banded together in retaliation while students joined in to protest the government's actions. Uzawa added his voice to the dissenting chorus. For two years, members of the right wing wanted to assassinate him. He had to hire a bodyguard for protection. When I invited him to visit me in

Taiwan, he was very happy and half-joked that he'd accept just based upon the fact that he didn't have to fear assassination during the trip. He'd no longer need a bodyguard.

Before he came, I sent word of his impending visit to President Lee Teng-hui. President Lee and I had both cited Uzawa's theories in our own dissertations, but only I had read the work and met the author. President Lee looked forward to meeting him in person at last and to having a discussion. So we made an appointment at his presidential home in Chongqing South Road. Around that time, Chen Shui-bian had just been elected as president, defeating Lien Chan. Angry Kuomingtang supporters surrounded President Lee's home. Fortunately, on the day of our appointment, the situation had calmed down. Inside his home, I saw that everything was all packed up in boxes. Completely unaffected by his impending move, President Lee and Uzawa conversed freely about the history of mathematics and economic theory, enjoying themselves. I sat by their side, respectfully listening in. Uzawa's wife and President Lee's wife were both present, along with Chin-fun. Later Chin-fun said that this episode gave her first-hand insight into the extent of Lee Teng-hui's knowledge.

Professor Uzawa brought us a gift of fate with his visit. When Chin-fun and I accompanied Uzawa and his wife down south for a tour of Tainan, we were welcomed there by the vice mayor of Tainan city Yang Huang Mei-hsing (楊黃美幸). As a result of our conversation, we discovered that Mei-hsing and I were both on board the Hikawa Maru, the ship I returned to Taiwan on after the war. I was ten and

Mei-hsing was still a one-year-old toddler in baby clothes. Mrs. Uzawa also took Hikawa Maru to the US for her overseas education.

Even more coincidentally, on April 30th, when Yang Huang Mei-hsing insisted on sending us off at Tainan's airport, she happened to buy a copy of the China Times. On the front page, the headliner read: "Lo Fu-chen Appointed to Top Japanese Representative Post." Both the professors and their wives whole heartily congratulated me.

54

My Appointment
Intensifies the
Awkwardness between the
President and His Premier

TO BE HONEST, when everyone congratulated me on my new ambassadorial role, I had not seen it coming myself. Before this, the only hint I got was when Legislative Yuan committee member Lee Ying yuan (李應元) of the Democratic People's Party telephoned me, asking, "If we were to appoint you as our top representative to Japan, would you be willing to give up your US citizenship?" This was hardly conclusive evidence for any appointment, of course. Although I had said, *"Yes, I would be willing to give up my American status"*, I hadn't in fact thought too much by the question. It had passed me by like a gentle breeze. I had lived outside of Taiwan for almost forty years after all. There was talk of many other candidates for the post, candidates with more connections, as well as deeper ones, to the Taiwanese government.

President Chen Shui-bian and I had no existing relationship. We had only met once before. In 1983, as a Taipei's Municipal Council member, he had visited the US. In a Chiang Ching-kuo-ruled Taiwan, a supporter for Taiwanese Independence was as much of a *persona non grata* as a Chinese commie. To come into contact with either was an act of rebellion for which you could be punished. Even friends and family would avoid you for it. I thought, since Chen Shui-bian had dared to look me up, I should introduce him to American congressman Stephen J. Solarz from the Democratic Party. In the 1980s, Taiwan began to see mounting challenges and actions taken against the dictatorship. As the chair of the Asia-Pacific group in Congress, Solarz was not an unfamiliar name to the Taiwanese. He had once opposed selling arms to Taiwan and forced the Kuomintang to investigate the Kaohsiung Incident [1] and the Chen Wen-chen (陳文成) Incident [2]. He had organized many hearings, and openly criticized Taiwan's military rule.

What might have given me an indication of my appointment was perhaps former President Lee's simple words to me just before I left his presidential home with Uzawa that day. He asked, "Have you received the notification? We're going to send you to Japan to be our top representative." He added, "We haven't announced your appointment only because the newly appointed Chair of the Executive Yuan, Tang Fei, is not in favor of it." I had never sought any official appointment in my life and didn't really understand what he had just said.

In May, after the news was announced, I went to see president-elect Chen Shui-bian to hear it from the horse's mouth. When Tang Fei nominated Chen Chien-jen (程建人) as his top representative to the US, Chen Shui-bian had let him have his man. However, Chen

---

1 The Kaohsiung Incident occurred in Kaohsiung, Taiwan on Dec. 10, 1979. At that time, Taiwan was still a one-party state. The opposition leaders held a demonstration commemorating Human Rights Day in an effort to promote and demand democracy in Taiwan. They ended up being arrested and sentenced to jail. The event had the effect of galvanizing the Taiwanese community into political actions and is regarded as one of the events that eventually led to democracy in Taiwan.

2 In the summer of 1981, Dr. Chen Wen-chen, a math professor at Carnegie Mellon University, brought his wife and son back to Taiwan for family reunion. On July 1, he was taken away by secret police for interrogation. The next day, his dead body was found on NTU campus. Although this case remained unsolved, many believed he was murdered by the KMT government.

Lo Fu-chen retired from UN in 2000. On the same year, he was appointed by the newly elected President, Chen Shui-bian, to be Taiwan's top representative to Japan.

Shui-bian wanted me as his top representative to Japan. Will Tang Fei interfere? This injustice aggravated President Chen to no end. In Chen Shui-bian's view, Defense and Foreign Affairs are departments that fall under the purview of the President. Revisiting the political landscape of that time, Chen Shui-bian had been democratically elected by the people of Taiwan. The Democratic People's Party had triumphed on its own efforts. As president, Chen had the power to form his own government. That said, the Kuomintang had been in power for more than half a century and still occupied an absolute majority in the parliament. Although Chen was now in power, he was still well aware of the political reality. Concessions must be made. Appointing Kuomintang's former Chief of General Staff Tang Fei as his premier was one such unavoidable concession. But who would expect that my appointment as top representative to Japan would intensify their inherent friction? This standoff between Chen Shui-bian and Tang Fei on the matter of foreign affairs gave me not much room to maneuver. I ended up staying in a Taipei hotel for more than a month. I hadn't counted on being appointed to be the top representative to Japan, so after leaving my position at UNU, I had packed up all my furniture and belongings in Tokyo — there were more than 150 boxes all in all — and stored them in a moving company's storage facility in Japan, until the time came to ship them to Taiwan. I was already looking forward to enjoying my retirement in Taiwan. I rented an apartment in Taipei and paid the first three months' rent as a deposit. If this new appointment really came through, I would have to go back to Tokyo. Like small birds at the tip of a tree branch bracing for a typhoon, Chin-fun and I were stranded. It did not make sense to go back to Tokyo just yet, nor was it to move into our Taipei apartment. That's why we checked into Ren-Ai Road's Howard Hotel, to calmly await the outcome.

55

The Japanese Princess Was Forbidden to Watch Television During Her Childhood

I'M NOT SURE WHO RECOMMENDED ME FOR THE POSITION AS THE TOP representative to Japan, nor do I understand what their reasons were for doing so. Chen Shui-bian did everything he could to oppose Tang Fei, insisting that I accept the appointment. I can't say for sure if he did it only to pit himself against Tang Fei, or because he really trusted my experience and ability. However, it's true that I had accumulated quite a bit of cachet among the Japanese and was quite plugged into Japanese society.

I had known Princess Kiko, the wife of Prince Akishino-no-miya, the second son of the present Japanese emperor Akihito, as a child. Her father, Kawashima Tatsuhiko, was my junior at UPenn. Also a Regional Science Ph.D. candidate, he lived on campus with his family. Kiko was two or three years old at that time. Kawashima later went to Vienna to do research. During his two years there, he invited me to give a lecture there. I was working for the UN at the time of the invitation. So I met Kiko again, who was in primary school.

I still remember that she and her younger brother were both quiet and obedient children. Kawashima was very strict with his children. There was no television in their house. The children were not allowed to watch TV. After they returned to their Tokyo home, where there was a television set, they were only permitted to turn it on for at most one hour each day.

Perhaps because Kawashima was a professor at Gakushuin University, Kiko also attended university there. That was where she met Prince Akishino-no-miya. I was told that Kiko wasn't the sociable type, but because she liked Prince Akishino-no-miya very much, she would join whichever extra-curricular club he joined. After their impending marriage was announced, a reporter asked Kiko, "When was the first time the two of you talked?" She answered, "One day, when he accompanied me across the road. That was the first time."

When I taught at UNU, I visited Kawashima's home on the campus of Gakushuin University. A few years ago, when we caught up over a meal, Mrs. Kawashima reminisced about how they lived back then. Their living room was frightfully small, only 6 tatami mats (less than 10 square meters). The dining room was only seven and a half square meters, just big enough for four and a half tatami mats. The royal family was going to visit them to present their betrothal gifts, accordingly to custom. In preparation for their visit, they emptied the dining room and combined both the living and dining spaces together, freeing up 17 square meters for their guests.

When news of Princess Kiko marrying into the royal family spread, the former dean of UPenn happened to be in Japan to receive an honor for his contributions to US-Japanese relations. UPenn's alumni association in Japan organized a gathering at the International House of Japan in Roppongi to welcome him. The building was originally a fief lord's residence, dated from the Edo-period and changed ownership many times. It had even been the residence of royalty at one point. (The mother of the present Japanese emperor Akihito had been born there.) Now it is used by the International House of Japan. Open only to members, its courtyard is elegant and peaceful, without the commercial air of the typical hotel. Whenever I visit Tokyo, I always like to visit there.

On the day of the welcome gathering, Kawashima brought Kiko along with him. As the newly announced member of the royalty-to-be, she was already a celebrated figure in the news. Everyone was delighted to see her walk into the room. When Kiko stood up to give a speech, I saw many in the room still seated. However, Kawashima stood very respectfully by her side listening to her. Kiko was no longer just his daughter, but a princess-to-be.

Once I had gone via my friend Chen Heng-chao (陳恆昭) to invite the Crown Prince to attend an academic conference at UNU. Chen Heng-chao's brother Chen Hsien-ting (陳顯庭) was my senior by three years at Tainan First High School. Both Chen brothers were good friends of mine and attended Harvard, where they were taught by the famous Harvard professor Lai Hsiao-he (賴孝和) (Edwin O. Reischauer). A former US ambassador to Japan, Reischauer took very good care of his students. It was through his recommendation that Chen Heng-chao got his teaching position at Cambridge. The Crown Prince would be one of his students there. Because of their shared Harvard background, Chen Heng-chao also knew Crown Princess Masako's father, Owada Hisashi, the former Japanese ambassador to the US. Chen Heng-chao had married the daughter of Taiwanese pearl magnate Cheng Wang, who lived in Japan and spoke Japanese. According to him, he visited the Royal Palace at least once a month to have a meal with the Crown Prince and the Princess.

In my 24 years working for the UN, I had served in three organizations. Two out of three of these were in Japanese cities: Nagoya and Tokyo. My working life in Japan spanned over 17 years in all. During this time, I've had contact not only with royalty but also with countless other important figures in Japanese society.

Honjo Kazuhiko, who headed the United Nation's Centre for Regional Development (UNCRD) in Nagoya, was my direct supervisor. His background is also worth mentioning here. His brother's father-in-law Tōgō Shigenori was Japan's Minister of Foreign Affairs in the post-war period. Tōgō had married a German woman,

Japan's Prince Akishino-no-miya's wife, Kiko, comes from a scholastic family. Her father, Kawashima Tatsuhiko (sanding, 2nd from right), was Lo's junior at UPenn.

Honjo Kazuhiko (3rd from right) was Lo's direct superviser at United Nation's Centre for Regional Development. Honjo has a younger brother who was Japan's ambassador to the US in the 1970s.

and the two of them had only one daughter. Honjo Kazuhito's younger brother married into the Tōgō family and changed his name to Tōgō Fumihito so that the family name could be carried on. In Japan, foreign diplomats traditionally pass on their roles to the next generation. Tōgō Fumihiko would become the Japanese ambassador to the US in the 1970s, and his son, Tōgō Kazuhiko, would become the Japanese ambassador to the Netherlands.

Honjo Kazuhito graduated from the University of Tokyo's Architecture Department. In 1955, he took a position in a company entitled "Japanese Housing for the Public." It was newly set up to build apartments for young salary men who could not afford the high cost of housing. The Japanese would come to call it "public housing." At first, Honjo decided that the model of this public housing would be "2DK," i.e. that each two-bedroom apartment would comprise a dining room and a kitchen. But "2DK" would soon evolve to include a third bedroom and a living room and become "3LDK", which would become the basic model for modern housing in post-war Japan. Many of Taiwan's old four-story or five-story apartment buildings are based on the same model.

Americans often make fun of the Japanese "matchbox" housing. Honjo's wife would also gently poked fun at him, "Masa, it's all because of your 2DK design that modern Japanese now live in such tiny homes!" In actuality, everyone was poor after the war, and many people were moving to the cities. Enough housing had to be constructed, and they also had to be affordable for the poor. As such, there were compelling socio-economic reasons for this "2DK" model of housing that had been Honjo's brainchild.

Honjo was a member of the Japanese elite that I got to know in my late thirties and early forties. In my fifties and sixties, I got to know another — Nagai Michio, founder of UNU. Nagai, who had a Ph.D. in Social Studies Education from the Ohio State University, was once the Minister of Education. He also was the first minister unaffiliated with any party and did not come from a family with a political background. He was respected by everyone. Under his watch as the Minister of Education, Nagai set up UNU. On its campus there is an office especially reserved for him.

Taiwan was once Japan's colonial outpost, so I thought the Nagai family would be partial towards Taiwan. It turned out that Nagai's father Nagai Ryutaro had studied in the UK, and had once been the Minister in charge of colonial territories. He was also Tokyo University's first professor to teach colonial policies. Nagai was succeeded by Nitobe Inazo, who was in turn succeeded by Yanaihara Tadao. Yanaihara authored a book entitled "Taiwan under Japanese Imperialism" (《帝國主義下の台灣》), in which he criticized the Japanese government. Yanaihara taught Chang Han-yu, my professor at National Taiwan University, so you could say I was his "grand-disciple".

I outlined this genealogy to Nagai, and thus our connection. Moved, he said that when he first met me, he had taken a liking to me immediately. Later on, he would invite me to lecture in many places.

56

Becoming Tokyo's Only
Foreign Consultant

Such a human genealogy differs greatly FROM THAT OF Kuomintang's connections, which has a basis in history. When Japan surrendered at the close of the Second World War, Chiang Kai-shek sought neither revenge nor compensation. The Japanese were deeply grateful for this. From the end of the war until the 1970s, Kuomintang's relationship to Japan was largely in the hands of those close to Chiang Kai-shek, Ho Ying-chin and Chang Chun [1]. Getting to know Japanese political figures was their goal. Ma Shu-li (馬樹禮), Taiwan's top representative to Japan during the Chiang Ching-kuo era, was trusted to represent Chiang Ching-kuo and to rub shoulders with the high officials in Japan. He himself had no motivation to network and to infiltrate the various ranks of Japanese society, nor did he possess the understanding to do so. Only during Lee Teng-hui's presidency, Koo Chen-fu, former CEO of Taiwan Cement, was able to penetrate the Japanese financial world.

My connections to Japanese academic and cultural circles are stronger. Take for example, Takahashi Junjirō, the longtime board member of the most prestigious private institution, Keio University. He's a good friend with whom we share "the relationship of a fish". In my late twenties and early thirties, when I was studying at UPenn, Takahashi had been my classmate. We weren't exactly thriving financially back then. To help make ends meet, we took house

---

1 Chiang Kai-shek, Ho Ying-chin (何應欽), and Chang Chun (張群) all attended the Imperial Japanese Army Academy in the 1900s, where they befriended each other.

painting jobs together. When he was studying for his Master's, Chin-fun helped him type his dissertation. One day, he presented a fish to us as a token of his gratitude. Though informal, this gesture signified a deep and unchanging friendship that held strong even after we left the US, whether we were in Japan or in Taiwan.

Among the various specializations within the field of Economics, I had chosen to tackle the problems of large urban cities. During my time at UNU, Tokyo's city council had also hired me as a consultant. Big cities aren't just plagued by traffic problems. Other problems include inequality of wealth distribution, economic development, cultural promotion and preservation etc. Consultants came from various disciplines. One of the consultants who was on board at the same time as me was the lyricist Akuyū. Younger than me by two years, Akuyū is comparable to Taiwan's Fang Wenshan. Both of them became famous for their lyrics.

I remember a discussion about the waste management issue, which left a deep impression on me in two ways. Tokyo buries its waste in Tokyo Bay. You can play golf there, but you can't smoke because waste produces marsh gas, which is highly flammable. Also, waste can actually be converted into cement. Although the cost of doing this is more expensive than typical cement, it's cheaper than incinerating it altogether.

It was only when I showed up for the meeting that I found out that I was the only foreign consultant attached to this project, perhaps because of my ability to speak fluent Japanese.

Tokyo's governor at that time was Suzuki Shunichi. He was ex-colleagues with a good friend of mine, Martin Meyerson, the president of UPenn (1970 to 1981). Their relationship was two-fold. They were friends with each other, but they also learned from one another. After the war, in 1959, Suzuki became Tokyo's vice-governor and assisted Governor Azuma Ryotarō in organizing the Tokyo Olympics. He proved so capable that people wondered if he was the actual governor. Starting in 1979, Suzuki would be elected governor for four consecutive four-year terms. So the spirits of Tokyo and Suzuki Shunichi are closely infused.

In order for the city to rise from the ashes of war, Post-war Tokyo invited two American professors to advise their development. One of these two was Meyerson, a Harvard professor of Urban Planning. That was how he and Suzuki Shunichi came to collaborate together, and how they cultivated a deep friendship. In Japan who you know is a valuable capital. Often, the more networked person is considered the better worker. The Japanese are very sensitive and aware about class and social background. They have to be, because class and social background determine the language you use with the other party. Meeting someone new, a Japanese must accurately judge the other party's standing, indicated by (a) which university he graduated from (b) his birthplace and (c) his current position. Only then would he be able to proceed with the conversation, using language appropriate to the other party's social standing.

57

Giving the Deputy Secretary General of the United Nations A Secret Tour of Taiwan

BEFORE I BECAME TAIWAN'S TOP REPRESENTATIVE TO JAPAN, as an official of the United Nations, I wasn't supposed to do anything for Taiwan by right. But I was always concerned about what was going on in Taiwan, and my desire to help Taiwan never completely left me. It was always at the back of my mind. Eight years before I became Taiwan's top representative to Japan, I secretly did a great favor for Taiwan. I boldly brought the Deputy Secretary General of the United Nations to Taiwan.

In March of 1992, I received an invitation, by a professor from the Regional Science Department at Cornell to attend an international

While working at UN University, Lo arranged for the Deputy Secretary General of the United Nations, Heitor Gurgulino de Souza, and his wife to visit Taiwan.

conference on Applied Regional Science at Academia Sinica in Taiwan. But the political blacklist compiled during Taiwan's rule under the two Chiangs was still in effect. Chin-fun and I were still on this blacklist, which meant we were not allowed to go back to Taiwan. Chiang Ching-kuo had passed away in 1988, and for a few years after that, those blacklisted tried to pit themselves against Kuomintang's anti-democracy by returning to Taiwan and "crashing the gate" — but all in vain. As for me, I used this invitation letter to apply for a new passport at the Taipei Representative Office in Japan. But before submitting my application, I first let the NHK television station know that as a chief academic officer from the United Nations University, I was no longer permitted to return to my country of birth by the people who controlled Taiwan. So when Chin-fun and I presented ourselves at the Taipei Representative Office in Japan, we were closely shadowed by NHK reporters and their cameramen.

This strategy worked. As I anticipated, the Kuomintang feared having their dirty laundry aired in public. The then top representative to Japan Lin Chin-ching (林金莖) immediately issued me a new passport. Curiously, on the Taiwanese visa itself, these words were stamped: "Allowed to Enter Taiwan." As holders of our own country's passport, returning to our countries, why did we need to be checked and be given the clearance to do so? We were not foreigners who have overstayed their welcomes and thus exiled. We shouldn't have to check with anyone whether we were permitted or not permitted to return to our own country.

My homecoming was finally taking place after being away from Taiwan for thirty-one years. Setting foot on my country's soil again, I observed noticeable changes to the natural environment. In the air above Guanyin Mountain, for example, hung a gray cloud of ash and the water in Tamshui River was no longer clear. Returning to Tokyo, I immediately submitted a recommendation to my Rector to set up an Environmental Institute in Taipei. The United Nations University had over ten research institutes scattered all over the world. For example, there is the World Institute for Development Economics Research in Finland, and the Maastricht Economic Research Institute of Innovation and Technology in the Netherlands.

The Rector approved my recommendation, so I asked Huang Kun-hu [1] if I could trouble him to act as intermediary. Huang forwarded my letter to President Lee Teng-hui. Lee asked how much this Environmental Institute would cost. I said that the host country of the Institute would have to contribute roughly US$40,000,000 and cover its annual administrative budget. Lee did not take long to come back with a "yes." Since UNU's research center is an academic unit, I suggested that the party responsible for overseeing this project might be the Ministry of Education. Lee then privately dispatched a professor to meet me in Tokyo and to iron out the details of our collaboration.

---

1 Huang Kun-hu (黃崑虎) is a Taiwanese entrepreneur who had been a stout supporter of Lee Teng-hui. He also served as chairman of "Taiwan Friends Association," and had been national policy advisor to President Chen Shui-bian.

What follows is the main act of the play. In the second half of August of 1993, Chin-fun and I accompanied Rector Heitor Gurgulino de Souza and his wife to Taiwan. Because I was on an official visit, I used my UN Laisser-Passez to go through customs. At that point, I was thinking that since 1971 when Taiwan was forced out of the United Nations, and all its ties with the United Nations severed, Taiwan has probably not seen this special UNLP for over twenty years.

During our three days in Taiwan, our schedules were fully packed. Accompanying de Souza on his visit to Lee's home, I saw how happy President Lee was. Not for a single moment did he stop smiling. The significance of de Souza's visit was not lost on us. After Taiwan had backed out of the UN, Taiwan had not welcomed such a high-ranking UN officer (de Souza was just one rank below the Secretary-General). Lee even told de Souza: "Next time you visit, I'll bring you to Hualien. It's even better there." He added that he had already assigned the Chair of the Executive Yuan, Lien Chan, to be in charge of the Environmental Institute. Stopping by the Executive Yuan, we were met by Lien Chan himself, who welcomed us warmly with his eloquent words. "You have the ideas, we have the muscle!" he said, flexing his muscles literally. In short, he meant to say: *you are in good hands; Taiwan will not disappoint.*

Afterwards, we met with the Minister of Education and Minister of Foreign Affairs as well as made stops at the Industrial Technology Research Institute, and of course the National Palace Museum with

In 1992, the political blacklist was finally abolished. Lo Fu-chen and wife finally came back to Taiwan where they have left for over 30 years.

A year ago, Lo was still on Taiwan's political blacklist. A year later, he had brought the Deputy Secretary General of the United Nations and wife (on the back) to Taiwan. The photo shows them visiting Premier Lien Chan at the Executive Yuan.

its countless cultural treasures. Everything was going smoothly. But unbeknownst to us then, a storm was already brewing.

By our third day in Taiwan, the news of the Rector of the United Nations University's tour of Taiwan leaked to the Chinese papers in New York because of full-blown coverage by the Taiwanese media. The Chinese representative at the UN immediately submitted a protest to the UN's Secretary General, requesting that we leave Taiwan immediately. Sent from the UN Headquarters in New York, the Secretary General's telegraph reached the Tokyo office soon after. Tokyo then called us in Taipei in a desperate bid to reach the Rector and convey the Secretary General's order to leave Taiwan within twenty-four hours.

Though the order was urgent, to be honest, we didn't feel very pressed, perhaps because our Headquarters was so far away. The Rector's son had long heard about the superior quality of Taiwan's bicycles, so I even accompanied him to buy his son a bicycle before we left.

Upon our return to Tokyo, we found the set of twenty faux antiques in five big boxes that the Director of the National Palace Museum, Chin Hsiao Yi, had sent us. I opened them and decided to exhibit them at the Representative Office. The quietly displayed antiques seemed to endlessly reverberate with the daring notes of our recently concluded secret tour.

After the news of the tour was widely known, all plans for the Environmental Institute were put on hold indefinitely. But, perpetually optimistic, I told the Rector, "We are simply ahead of our time." I truly do believe it's only a matter of time before the UN flag will rise on the shore opposite Guanyin Mountain.

58

Yamanaka Sadanori's Silver Cane

PRESIDENT CHEN SHUI-BIAN AND CHAIR OF LEGISLATIVE YUAN Tang Fei's silent standoff had begun with the opening of the new government because of me. Nevertheless the new appointments had to be decided at some point. On May 28, I finally received the official letter of my appointment. During the long period of waiting, it was as if I had been cooking in a pot with a lid over it. My movements had been constrained. Now that the lid was finally taken off, I shot up with the steam, and in my newfound freedom, I could wave my arms and legs.

I reported first to the Minister of Foreign Affairs, and spent three days listening to reports that would bring me up to speed on all the required protocol. Then, without even sparing a day, I was flown to Tokyo to take up my position.

The reason for which we had to do it so quickly was because the Japanese Diet was about to undergo elections. It wouldn't be right to leave the top representative's position empty during important moments of major political change.

The Japanese government had not been stable for nearly two decades, but now a further element of chaos was suddenly being introduced. In April, Prime Minister Obuchi Keizō suffered a stroke and died. During his commemoration in mid-May, his successor, Mori Yoshirō, allegedly said these words that shocked the entire nation. "Japan is a Kingdom of God that has as its center the Emperor." With these words, he transported Japan back to the time before the Second World War, in willful defiance of the basic constitutional laws that put the country's people at its center. Mori's downfall was rapid. He was quickly forced to dissolve the Diet [1] and call another election. After receiving my briefings at the Ministry of Foreign Affairs, I immediately flew to Tokyo to take up my position because the Japanese Diet was scheduled to be dissolved on June 2nd, and campaigning for the new election would begin on June 25th. Once the campaigns kicked in, councilors and house representatives would all be busy canvassing for votes in their respective districts. It would be next to impossible to make my rounds and properly introduce myself.

Japan and Taiwan had broken off ties in 1972, after which it could no longer act as official allies. Should any matter arise, it was no longer possible to contact the other country's Minister of Foreign Affairs directly. Luckily Japan operated by the cabinet system, its ministers were virtually all Diet members. It was possible for Taiwan to go through other routes to establish communication channels with the upper echelons of Japanese politics. Comprising Japan's House of Representatives and House of Councilors were two hundred and fifty members willing to preserve friendly ties with Taiwan. They'd set up a "Japan-Taiwan (the Republic of China) Parliamentary Friendship Association."

As the Taiwanese representative to Japan, this Association was

[1] Japan's National Diet is composed of a lower house that is called the House of Representatives, which has 480 members, and an upper house called the House of Councilors that has 242 members. Both houses of the Diet are directly elected under a parallel voting system.

Lo and wife met current prime minister of Japan, Abe Shinzo, at the Emperor's carnival.

Since there is no diplomatic relations between Taiwan and Japan, Lo and his wife can neither join other diplomatic corps nor their spouses' group activities. Fortunately, Lo befriended a Japanese royal member, Prince Takamado-no-miya, whose wife is the honorary president of International Flower Arrangement Association. Through her, Mrs. Lo joined the association and was finally able to participate in social activities with other diplomats' spouses.

the most important window of opportunity into Japanese politics.

From the point of view of the Japanese Diet members of the Association, Taiwan's political upheaval must seem even greater. For decades, they had been used to working with the Kuomintang. Asked to switch to the Democratic Progressive Party all at once, they were understandably confused and uncomfortable.

The first person I called on was the leader of the Association, Yamanaka Sadanori. The first moment he set eyes on me, he cried, "I'm old! I'll finish this term and then I'll retire." Talking with the Japanese, you can't take their words at face value. Yamanaka was not in fact old. He hadn't reached 80 yet. At their first encounter with other people, the Japanese are always careful to a fault, preferring indirect to direct communication. With "I'm old!" Yamanaka was probably just trying to provoke a reaction to affirm the contrary.

At first, Yamanaka didn't even know how to pronounce President Chen Shui-bian's name, which signified how ignorant he was with Taiwan's new ruling party. He couldn't help murmuring that, "I don't know Chen Shui-bian. Even my son's older than he is." That was also a probing question.

After a long conversation, Yamanaka finally broached the key question he had wanted to ask. "Who sent you here? Was it President Lee Teng-hui, or President Chen Shui-bian?" I answered, "Both the same!" and further elaborated, "You see, President Lee and I both went through a Japanese education, having lived in Japan, while both Chen Shui-bian and Lee Teng-hui are Taiwanese leaders who are emphatic about democracy. Listening to my answer, Yamanaka immediately relaxed and the lines of his face visibly became gentler. In my conversation with him, I could feel his admiration vis-à-vis my qualities. When he spoke about Kuomintang and Lee Teng-hui, I was able to respond in fluent Japanese. After that, trust seemed to flow between us, and he made special arrangements to organize an Association meeting just for me. This way, I made the acquaintance of thirty to forty Diet members in one sitting, including Vice President of the Association, Hiranuma Takeo, Asō Tarō, and Ōgi Chikage. All were very important political figures who would go on to be elected to the Cabinet.

In traditional Chinese society, the family is more important than the individual. Members of the family must take orders from the head of the family. In return, they receive care and protection from the leader. The Japanese are "group animals." The individual must be subordinate to the group, and must only take actions that conform to the group's actions. One must not act independently of the group. Herein lies the key to understanding the essence of Japanese politics. Thus, when Yamanaka took me to make the acquaintance of the other Diet members, he intentionally requested for me to sit by his side, and for the rest to sit across from us. This was no doubt an indication of his admiration and support for me. And if he, as leader of the Association, treated me this way, the Diet members under him had better not show me any disrespect.

Before visiting Yamanaka, my colleagues at the Taipei

Representative Office told me that he was a tyrant in the Japan-ROC (Taiwan) Parliamentary Friendship Association. If that was the case, it was not altogether a bad thing to be backed by a tyrant. Thanks to Yamanaka's backing and influence, my four years as the top representative to Japan were rather smooth. For this, I am still very grateful to him.

Yamanaka was born in the southernmost part of Kyushu, on the island of Kagoshima. During the Japanese colonial period, Kagoshima saw the largest number of Japanese emigrating to Taiwan. In fact, Yamanaka had studied in Taipei's Second Teachers School (now National Taipei University of Education at Heping East Road), before going to teach in Kaohsiung's Siaogang district. In the early 1970s, he

Owing to diabetes caused foot problem, President of Japan-Taiwan (ROC) Parliamentary Friendship Association, Yamanaka Sadanori, had to walk with a stick.

was appointed to Satō Eisaku's cabinet as Minister of Trade. When the US returned Okinawa to Japan, an event that happened because of his involvement, he was immediately assigned to oversee the Okinawa Development Agency. With his qualifications and ability, he could have been President of the House (of Representatives), or a Prime Minister. However, one unfortunate inability stood in his way. As Prime Minister, he would have to receive edicts from the Emperor's hands and would have to walk backwards out of the room. One cannot turn his back on the Emperor to leave his presence. Yamanaka's legs were allegedly afflicted with diabetes neuropathy, which prevented him from walking backwards.

During a conversation, Yamanaka told me that from the Meiji Period, silver walking canes symbolized the gentleman and to be presented a silver cane by the Emperor was the best gift one could get. With this in mind, I went to the Mitsukoshi department store and specially ordered a silver walking cane as a gift to him. The handle was made out of silver and did not have any pattern or drawing on it. It was designed to be simple and sturdy.

In the spring of 2004, Yamanaka passed away. A family member revealed that when he was alive, he always used this walking cane at home. I was moved and asked if I could take it back as a memento. The Yamanaka family agreed, and presented me with the silver walking cane I had given him. When time comes and I have to use it, I will depend on this silver walking cane and use it to keep Yamanaka in my thoughts.

59

Being "Smuggled" into the American Embassy

AMONG THE INFLUENTIAL FIGURES IN JAPANESE POLITICS, former Prime Minister Hashimoto Ryutaro should not be overlooked. When I visited him in person, he was right in the midst of organizing an international conference. He said, rather brusquely, "Anything to do with the relationship between the Liberal Democratic Party and Taiwan, go to Shiina instead. You don't need to ask for me."

In case you don't know, Shiina's full name is Shiina Motō. He was a councilor at that time. Like a lot of other Japanese House members, Shiina came from a wealthy and influential family. The famous Gotō Shinpei, an influential figure in Taiwan's modernization, was Shiina Motō's great-uncle. Gotō had arrived in Taiwan at the turn of the 20th century to oversee the Civil Affairs Bureau under Governor Kodama Gentarō. He was given the authority to manage the colonial outpost through a detailed methodology. These were the preliminary steps he outlined: 1) Conduct a census 2) Gather all details about land ownership 3) Research Taiwanese customs and habits, etc. Today, he is widely credited for his fundamental role in Taiwan's modernization and shift away from agricultural society. When he returned to Japan, Gotō would become Tokyo's mayor.

Shiina Motō's father Shiina Etsusaburō, however, had a relationship with Taiwan different than Gotō. Shiina Etsusaburō was both the Minister of Foreign Affairs and the Vice Chair of the Liberal Democratic Party. Before Japan severed ties with Taiwan, he visited as a Japanese special envoy to meet with Chair of Executive

Yuan Chiang Ching-kuo. The moment he stepped out of the airport, he was surrounded by angry student protesters holding placards.

As for Shiina Motō, he had studied Physics in his younger days, and had even done a stint at the US's famous Argonne National Laboratory. Later, he abandoned that career to succeed his father's political career. His American background and impeccable English put him in good stead to understand and collaborate with Americans, and to improve Japanese-US ties.

During Lee Teng-hui's time, Taiwan initiated a special project implicating Taiwan, Japan and the US. Every year, representatives from these three countries met in Hawaii for three-way talks. Representing Taiwan was Lee Teng-hui; representing Japan was Councilor Shiina Motō and representing the US was Deputy Secretary of State Richard Armitage. The US and Japan both became Taiwan's most important partners while Shiina would become a significant figure in Taiwanese-Japanese diplomacy. Lee wanted to honor him with a medal, but Shiina respectfully turned it down. It wasn't until August 2003, in the fourth year of Chen Shui-bian's term, following the example of the US awarding Shiina with one of its highest honors, did he come to Taiwan to receive his honor. The honor that Shiina received in the States was the highest honor given out by the US State Department, the Secretary of State's Award for Distinguished Service, which the Japanese called "米國國務長官特別功勞賞". It was only awarded once to a foreign national prior to him. Evidently, the Americans thought most highly of Shiina's contributions. The award ceremony took place at the American embassy in Japan.

When I was working for UNU and was a US citizen, I would be invited to the US embassy for a celebratory dinner every Fourth of July. Now that I was the Taiwanese representative to Japan, however, I was no longer invited. Taiwan did not have diplomatic relations with either the US or Japan, after all. After the ties were severed, Taiwanese representatives to Japan were struck off the US embassy's invitation list. The Taipei representative office was situated in Tokyo's Shirokanedai in Minato-ward while the US embassy was located in Akasaka, also in Minato. Although only three kilometers separated the two physical offices, the political distance between the two had become infinitely insurmountable. Still, Shiina did not seem to register all this, and sent me an invitation to the gala dinner. I was thus "smuggled" into the US embassy, crossing a rift that had spanned several decades.

Among the hundred plus people present at the dinner was Ambassador Howard Baker who greeted me at the door. Baker had been the Senate Majority Leader, while Baker's wife had been a senator herself. But it was Richard Armitage, then Deputy Secretary of State, who occupied the center of the spotlight. It was he who was Shiina's political ally and close friend after all.

Armitage had a military background, which you could deduce from his muscular wrestler-like build. But his kindness — he had, for example, adopted ten orphans — also reminded you of Aladdin from *One Thousand and One Nights*. I did not shy from him at the US embassy. We shook hands very naturally. He knew who I was, and I knew who he was. We left it unspoken, smiling at the other.

60

Getting a Li Shih-chiao (李石樵) and a Grand Piano into the Taipei Representative Office

SPEAKING OF THE US EMBASSY, there was something about the building that was most attractive to Chin-fun and me in all the years we attended their Fourth of July celebrations. It was the fact that authentic paintings, borrowed from American galleries and museums, that graced its walls everywhere. It made the embassy a cultural exhibition center in and of itself, and projected the US ambassador's cultural refinement.

The first time Chin-fun and I stepped into the Taipei representative office, both of us came to the same conclusion that something had to be done about its appearance.

After the war, Taiwan's embassy was situated in Motoazabu in Minato-ward. It was converted from Gotō Shinpei's residence. After diplomatic ties between Taiwan and Japan were severed, the building was taken by the Chinese, and converted into their embassy. After negotiation, Japan allowed the Taiwanese to use a park land in Shirokanedai in Minato-ward and build a representative office there.

The Taipei Representative Office consisted of two buildings. The first was a five-story office building, and the second, a two-story residence for the Representative. These two buildings were connected. The first time I set foot into the residence, I couldn't help but feel a little sad. Not only did cheap prints hang on the walls, but they were also secured in place by disposable white plastic hooks. Supposedly, a former representative used the wall space to display the photographs of himself with other famous people as well as his own certificates. The Taipei Representative Office being Taiwan's official face to Japanese society. The way it was decorated surely reflected our taste as well as our culture.

If this had been the representative office in some other country, perhaps its present form might have been only just acceptable. However, this particular office resided in the world's most refined and most aesthetically sophisticated country.

Taiwan has a world-class museum at the National Palace Museum, housing countless precious calligraphies, paintings, sculptures and

Both Lo's father and grandfather are good at Chinese calligraphy, hence Lo's mom had asked him to practice calligraphy ever since he was young. Once he started working worldwide, this skill became a tool in making friends.

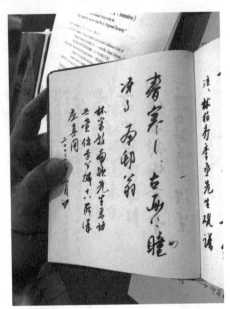

One of Lo's hobbies — writing poems at leisure time.

antiques. I decided to follow in the footsteps of the US embassy, and borrow some of these treasures from the National Palace Museum. However, I did some research beforehand. I asked a family member of a famous painter about the feasibility of such a plan. The frank response was "Working with the government is a great nuisance." So I was discouraged. Moreover, cutting through the red tape would represent a great expenditure of time that could utilized to address more pressing of matters. I might as well dip into my own pockets and use my own money. That's how I came to buy the work "Cow," by painter Hsieh Li-fa, for NT$600,000 (just under US$20,000).

As a matter of fact, I like calligraphy and collected antique scrolls from all over the world. In Kuala Lumpur, because of its significant Chinese population, there are many antique shops specializing in Chinese scrolls. One year, at one such antique shop by the name of Ji Zhen Zhuang (集珍莊), I bought a quadryptich by late Qing Dynasty calligraphy master Ho Shao-ji and hung the four massive scrolls in my Taipei Representative Office residence. Immediately, the room looked much better.

The famouse Taiwanese star, Judy Wong, who made it big in Japan, is also an outstanding lithograph artist. One of her works has Taiwan's scenery as its subject. Lo bought it to add sense of culture to the representative office.

Through Lo and wife's effort, the representative office looked like an art gallery, and the hall is constantly filled with visitors' piano improvisation.

The famous Taiwanese star Judy Ong, who made it big in Japan, had dual nationalities, Taiwanese and Japanese. Her lithographs have won several prizes, confirming her talent. One of her lithographs has as its subject the tea houses beside National Central University. It captures the essence of Taiwanese contemporary culture. So I used state funds of about ¥800,000 to ¥1,000,000 (currently about US$8,000 to US$10,000) to buy it for the Representative Office and hang it in the dining room where guests were welcomed.

For the first-floor living room, I bought and installed a grand piano, and next to it displayed a sculpture made by an overseas Taiwanese student in Kanazawa University.

Taiwan's pioneering painter Li Shih-chiao liked to paint roses, whether they were in gardens or in vases. He'd done many rose paintings. Through the JSL Auction Corporation, I bought one such painting, setting me back by more than NT$2,000,000 (US$84,000). This news of my purchase was later picked up by someone who had political reason to hurt me. He used it as evidence of my corruption. In politics, it's inevitable to come across political pests. One shouldn't let them get in the way of doing what is right. Li Shih-chiao's painting was bought with state funds through an auction. It is registered by the Minister of Foreign Affairs as public property and certainly not something I could take for myself. As a matter of fact, you could even consider it an investment. I learned that the value of the painting has doubled in recent years. From time to time, in politics, there will be attempts to damage other people's reputations. Those at the top must exercise good judgment, and learn to dismiss baseless accusations. Otherwise the entire political atmosphere will be cloudy, holding back civil servants from going about their own duties.

61

The Taiwanese Rep's American Ways

ALTHOUGH I WAS AN AMBASSADOR OF TAIWAN, I hadn't lived in Taiwan for more than forty years. This was exactly the reverse of the route taken by typical representatives to foreign lands. The former top representatives had been ex-Commanders-in-chief, Ministers, or Deputy Representatives, all of them from within Taiwan's political world. Only I had come from an international organization. I was like a solitary bird, whose wings had been carried by international winds, now perched on one of the branches in Taiwan's forests. And because this bird was not so familiar with Taiwanese government culture, it was using its voice to call attention to itself.

Like the time when talking with my subordinates at the Representative Office, I would say, "My door is always open." Anyone was welcome to come and talk with me. Because the majority of my subordinates were affiliated with the Kuomintang party, I liked to especially quote President Kennedy's inauguration speech in 1961, "Ask not what your country can do for you, ask what you can do for your country." By doing so, I was trying to encourage everyone working in foreign diplomacy to put the country first, instead of focusing on petty partisan politics. Later I discovered that I not only lacked the political DNA of the Kuomintang officials that allowed them to act pompously toward their subordinates, but I also turned to an American president for my words of encouragement to others.

I would also do something that past representatives had never done.

At the Representative office, the largest-scale event on the calendar had to be Taiwan's National Day dinner gala on October 10th. The number of guests often exceeded one thousand, out of which at least one hundred of them were Japanese Diet members.

At the Representative office, the largest-scale event on the calendar had to be Taiwan's National Day dinner gala on October 10th. And the reason for which it was so large-scaled was because it was meant to compete with China's national day celebration. Held nine days earlier, on October 1st, China's dinner gala usually hosted four to five hundred guests. Taiwan could not have a weaker showing. The number of guests often was more than a thousand, out of which at least one hundred of them were Japanese Diet members. The first National Day dinner gala under my stewardship saw more than one thousand five hundred attendees.

At my first dinner gala, as is customary for the host to give a speech, I spoke first in Mandarin, then switched to Japanese. The overall speech took up forty-five minutes, rather verbose. At my second year's dinner gala, I decided to change it up so that it was less drawn out. Among the guests were Dutch, Swiss, African and many other countries' ambassadors. I first spoke in Mandarin for three minutes, then in English for the next three minutes. In both of these introductions, I explained that since Japanese was the *lingua franca* of the majority of the guests today, I would be using Japanese to deliver my speech. In the end, everybody had a pleasant and relaxing evening. Even overseas-born Chinese gave me the thumbs up, saying that I was the first trilingual ambassador fully fluent in Chinese, English and Japanese, that they had seen in decades.

Now that the Democratic Progressive Party (DPP) had ascended to power, many DPP politicians seemed to have caught the Kuomintang's habit of paying courtesy visits to the presidential home. Not only would I make an unconvincing sycophant, I can't in fact bring myself to do it. What concerned me always was how to do my job well. Studying and working in the US, I had never needed to pay courtesy visits to my professor's homes and never needed to ask favors of my supervisors in private. All was aboveboard and fair. Chin-fun was like me. A few of the other officials' wives would show up at their husband's boss's residence to present gifts. She never did this sort of thing.

Lo organized a welcome party for his UPenn teacher, Nobel Laureate Lawrence Klein on his visit to Japan. The party took place at Lo's official residence as Taiwan's top representative to Japan. Also present were Japan's economic masters: Aoki Masahiko, Yoshitomi Masaru, and Fujita Masahisa et al.

From my university days, I had been in the US and worked in international organizations. Inevitably I picked up Western influences when it came to socializing. In the US, when invited to friends' homes, it was common for one to show up empty-handed. It was their custom. According to the law in the US, a government officer has to declare any accepted gifts that costs upwards of two hundred dollars.

On the other hand in Japan, it is centered around gift-giving. In my four years as Taiwan's top representative to Japan, I would already receive quite a few gifts on a daily basis. Around Obon (the Japanese Ghost Festival) and year-end, the two major holidays, the gifts would pile up even more. At the end of each month, I held a raffle for my colleagues at the office to distribute the gifts. I didn't keep a single thing for myself.

Our practices were so different from the representatives before us. My colleagues started to ask me and Chin-fun why we didn't take the gifts for ourselves. I thought to myself, "Where would I store all of them? I'm not a warehouse keeper." Chin-fun gave a more diplomatic answer. She smiled, and said, "Otherwise, what would I do?"

The Representative Office had one other custom. Every New Year, the wife of the Representative would give red packets to all the employees' children. The going rate was ¥3000 for a child in high school and ¥1000 for a child in primary school. Chin-fun never used state funds for her red packets in all of our four years. She told me, "My name is clearly written on these red packets. The money must come from me of course." And because it was her gifts to the children, even the menial task of writing the names of the children on the red packets she did not assign to any secretary. Rather, she hand wrote each name out herself, one character followed by another.

62

Lee Teng-hui Visits Japan, to Whose Credit?

M Y FOUR YEARS AS TOP REPRESENTATIVE TO
JAPAN SAW TAIWAN'S most significant breakthrough in foreign diplomacy. In April 2001, Lee Teng-hui was finally permitted to visit Japan.

I say "finally" because this visit was the cause of many years of conflict between the Chinese, the Japanese and the Taiwanese. Unlike Japan and Taiwan, Japan and China had diplomatic relationships.

The greatest diplomatic breakthrough during Lo's 4-year term as Taiwan's top representative to Japan is: former Taiwan president Lee Teng-hui (2nd from right) was finally permitted to visit Japan (in April 2001).

China naturally did not wish to allow Taiwanese presidents to visit a country with which they had a diplomatic relationship, especially if they were bearing the flag of "president." In the 1990s, what caused the greatest dissatisfaction among the Chinese about Japan were three things. First, in their account of the Sino-Japanese war in their secondary school teaching materials, they avoided the word "invaded" and used "went in and out (of China)" instead. Second, the Japanese Prime Minister still insisted on visiting Yasukuni Shrine, a shrine where Japan had buried those who had committed so-called "war crimes" in (the equivalent of Taiwan's Martyrs' Shrine). Third, Lee wanted to tour Japan, and Japan actually considered this possibility.

After Lee left his office as President, he became a civilian. By right, like any other civilian, he should enjoy unrestricted travel. However, China firmly denied his wish to travel to Japan. Within one year of my becoming top representative to Japan, Lee, on the pretext of seeking medical treatment, was allowed to set foot on Japanese soil.

Some Japanese politicians started to take credit for this significant diplomatic achievement. The then Japanese Foreign Minister Kōno Yōhei and Chief Cabinet Secretary Fukuda Yasuo had both thought that the time was not right yet for his visit. Etō Seishirō, Kōno's deputy, acted on his own to ask for permission, saying to Lee that he would take care of the matter. In the end, for his role in this diplomatic breakthrough, President Chen Shui-bian would present the Order of Brilliant Star with Grand Cordon to Etō Seishirō.

One evening, I was hosting a dinner at the Representative Office for the participants of the Japan-Taiwan Parliamentary Friendship Association. Chair Yamanaka Sadanori sat at the very center while his Vice Chair, Asō Tarō, sat to his side, followed by the rest in descending order of seniority. Etō of course sat at the end. When he spoke, Yamanaka came straight to the point, and said severely, "I'm told that recently somebody went to Taiwan to receive an honor, despite no one directly to my side receiving one!" Etō hung his head and said nothing, like a child being lectured by his father.

The Japanese government did not allow Lee Teng-hui to go to Kyoto. In Osaka, Lee went up the Osaka Castle, looked afar and said, "Kyoto is in that direction."

For Taiwan to confer an honor on Etō was a bit of a faux pas. It showed Taiwan's scant understanding of the protocol and hierarchy by which the Japanese political circle operated. The Japanese put the collective above the individual. If Etō explained that he hadn't coveted the honor, and that it was the Taiwanese who had eagerly imposed it on him, and that he couldn't bring himself to turn it down, the explanation would nonetheless be rejected. Even if the Taiwanese had thrust the honor on him, he could still have rejected it. In fact, that would have been the right thing to do.

The enormous influence of public opinion should also be credited in bringing about Lee's visit to Japan. The six major papers (Asahi, Yomiuri, Mainichi, Nikkei, Sankei and Tokyo) all unanimously supported Lee's visit. Once a month, I would have a meeting with the top representatives from each of these six major publications and bring them up to speed on Taiwan's latest developments and problems. But I wouldn't take credit for Lee's visit simply because I had held these meetings. Truth be told, whenever a difficult political mission has finally been accomplished, it is always the culmination of many parties' hard work.

I myself had privately participated in one of those "secret room" meetings so common in Japanese politics, and had convinced Fukuda to change his mind about Lee's visit. That day, only four of us were present. On the Japanese side, there was also Councilor Shiina Motō who accompanied Fukuda. From Taiwan was Peng Jung-tzu (彭榮次), whom everyone knew represented Lee. And then there was me.

The meeting was in a hotel room. Fukuda did not say he objected to Lee's visit, but he suggested that we take it slow. Seeing how cowardly Fukuda was, Shiina's tone hardened. He said that he could very well leak what Fukuda had just said to the media and let everyone see his true colors.

The then prime minister was Mori Yoshirō. Decidedly, the greatest credit goes to him. The previous Prime Minister Fukuda Takeo had assembled a team of politicians who made it their business to understand Taiwan and to foster better relations with Taiwan. When Mori took over, he inherited this team of politicians. Mori had a group of 90 politicians under his wing. His group was the largest faction in the Liberal Democratic Party (LDP). Even if he were to retire within a year of his stewardship as Prime Minister, he was still the undisputed leader of this faction. Prime ministers Abe, Fukuda, and Asō were only able to become Prime Minister because of his support.

As the newly appointed representative from Taiwan, I met with Mori. He only emphasized one thing, "Diplomatic ties between countries really boils down to ties between the present ruling parties of these countries." This statement put my mind to rest. The Kuomintang and the LDP had cultivated a relationship for decades. Yet, this would not stand in the way of the DPP-ruled Taiwanese government and the Japanese government's ties.

To foster relationships with busy political figures in Japan, I would first stop by their offices. Usually these visits lasted at most twenty minutes. If I had something important to discuss, I would ask, "When are you free to play golf?" At the start of golf, I would gently broach the matter for a bit, and then stop talking about it. The Japanese way of doing things is gentle and slow. Frankly and directly is not how they like it. It didn't make sense to hurry them for an answer. The matter would be contemplated during the round of golf. Then, when the round concluded, the answer would come. So, to make friends with Japanese politicians, invite them to play golf, even if it takes up time.

Japan's former Prime Minister Mori Yoshirō (middle) came to Taiwan and brought this 1936 Waseda rugby team flag as offering to his father's old teammate Ko Tzu-chang's altar.

My first round of golf as the representative in Japan was played with Mori. He invited the important Japanese Diet members, and during the round, he introduced me to everyone.

In private, Mori was a sentimental person. Before the war, his father, who belonged to Waseda University's rugby team, befriended an overseas Taiwanese student by the name of Ko Tzu-chang (柯子彰). Ko would later be known as the father of Taiwanese rugby. When Mori's father died, Ko traveled all the way to Mori's hometown Kanazawa to pay him respect. And when Ko passed away, Mori made a special trip to Taiwan to visit Ko's family. I went with him and saw him bringing an entire stack of old newspaper clippings with him as offerings to Ko's altar. They turned out to be newspaper articles from the 1930s, documenting Waseda's rugby team's period of glory.

Mori even told me that his father was very strict, so strict that he didn't dare to confide in him. During the war, his father once went to Siping, China where he took a bullet in the spine. He deliberately told his family to extract this bullet from his ashes upon his cremation. Indeed, his father hadn't lied. There really was a bullet. I jokingly told Mori not to tell China about this story. They may claim that the bullet belonged to them and asked him either to return it, or pay up.

63

A Handsome Guy
Regardless of Time Period

AT THE REPRESENTATIVE OFFICE, you would often see a man, more than ninety-years of age, with a head of white hair combed back, revealing a full face, red cheeks and a row of white teeth. A silk handkerchief poked out from the breast pocket of his suit. If he would oblige, I bet directors would hurry to cast him in their films.

This man's name is Peng Kai-dong (彭楷棟). Originally from Hsinchu, he became a Japanese citizen after the war, and befriended quite a few Taiwanese representatives. He often came to the Office to visit them. When I took office, he, as usual, wanted to meet the new guy in town. So, one day, Ms. Lin, my secretary, escorted him into my office. Who knew, the first time I set my eyes on him, I felt that I had known him for a very long time. He told me about the dramatic life story he had lived.

He was born in 1912. When he was only three months old, his fisherman father went out to sea but never returned. Later, when he was still a child, his mother remarried. He didn't make it to third grade. Before he was twenty, life dealt him yet another painful blow. His wife passed away.

When Peng was only ten years old, snooker was very popular in Taiwan. By chance, he got a job as a scorekeeper in a snooker hall. He fell in love with the game too. Before long, Peng followed a Japanese dentist back to Tokyo, where he learned how to play the game professionally. At first, he was very poor, often skipping meals to get by. He reminisced fondly of those years. He loved to eat every chance he got. He even bought a packet of sweet biscuits once and another packet of savory ones. With one packet in each hand, he alternated the sweet with the savory in his mouth.

Peng would finally become a big name in Tokyo and in 1932, he brought his glory back to Taiwan. Taiwan's biggest newspaper published a photo of him, captioned "The world snooker champion born on our very isle!" Everywhere he went, he was invited to demonstrate his amazing snooker skills.

In the 1930s, before his glory days had faded, Peng was out walking on Taipei's Honmachi Avenue (now Chongqing South Road) when he was spotted by a movie director, who cast him as the male lead in his movie "Looking Forward to Spring Breeze." (《望春風》) Peng's fame spread even more as a result, and because of it, he got to know important government officials. During the war in the 1940s, he would make a lot of money from his business in military supplies.

When Japan lost the war, Peng suffered defeat as well. Labeled a war criminal (of the lesser kind), he became *persona non grata* in Taiwan.

However, being in Japan gave him many ideas. He started to trade in gold, diamonds, and antiques. He even opened two luxury nightclubs in Ginza called "Golden Horse Carriage" and "Silver Horse Carriage" which were famous for a while. I found out from the older Japanese politicians that they had even gone there. So Peng had become rich again. But in 1952, he was caught trading American dollars, which was frowned upon by the Foreign Exchange Control, and locked up in jail, suffering another setback.

Scenarios that don't happen to the typical person always seemed to happen to Peng. In his lifetime, he would go through three sets of highs and lows. During that grim period in prison, he often thought of how his mother would ride with him in a small train around a sugar factory, and how they took a trip to Beigang to visit a Matsu (Chinese goddess of the sea) temple. To him, these were the sweetest memories of his life. Though far away in Beigang, Matsu's serious yet compassionate expression was very vivid in his mind. She consoled him endlessly and was the first to encourage him to start a collection of Buddha statues. Once again, he took one small step and another out of the valley into which he had fallen. Apart from buying Buddha statues, he also went to auctions in London and Paris, competing with international museums and collectors for world-class paintings by the likes of Renoir and Degas. He also bought Tokyo property. In the early 1980s, he was the 11th highest income taxpayer in all of Japan.

Among Peng's collections, his Buddha statues did the best. He donated his seven best to the Metropolitan Museum of Art in New York, and sold three to Tokyo National Museum. Even so, nearing his nineties, he started to contemplate the question of who he would bequeath his remaining treasures. At our first meeting, when he indicated his intention of donating some Buddha statues to Taiwan, I immediately seized the opportunity and made an appointment to view his collection. He brought me back to a five-story building in

Roppongi next to the Chinese embassy. At the entrance of his home was a large potiche vase that had a simple but elegant lotus bloomed within. Only Buddhas inhabited the five stories of this building, nothing else. As he gave me a tour of these Buddhas, he recounted stories of how he had collected them.

Buddhism originated in 6 B.C. century India. Its earliest sculptures were not of Buddha, but of pagodas which were objects of worship. Only when Buddhism spread to Afghanistan and Pakistan, in Gandhara and Mathura, did the first Buddha image surface. I told Peng about my own visit in the 1980s to Gandhara, a confluence of both Greek and Buddhist cultures. The famous Shakyamuni Buddha for example was evidently sculpted with Greek techniques. It was also flanked on both sides by sculptures of winged Greek angels. Buddhism then spread from Gandhara to the East, toward China, before reaching Korea and Japan. Meanwhile, another branch of Buddhism that had originated on the riverbanks of the Ganges spread towards Sri Lanka and Thailand, where one finds bodhisattvas with dancing forms. As I told him what I knew, Peng tugged my hand and exclaimed, "I really like you!" I realized that despite his long history of collecting Buddha statues and the high pedigree of the statues he collected, he had probably never been to the birth place of Buddhism itself. The fact that I had been there must have inspired his admiration.

Anyway, after that time, Peng seemed to fully trust me. He would tug my arm and say, "Every time I see you, you always set my mind at

Peng Kai-dong (2nd from left) first made his name as a snooker genius, then male lead in couple of movies. In his lifetime, he would go through three sets of highs and lows. In his old days, he put his trust in Lo and agreed to donate his precious Buddha statues collections to the Palace Museum in Taipei.

peace." In response, I would joke, "That's because I'm fatter!"

Later, I penned a very formal letter using calligraphy, inviting Tu Cheng-sheng (杜正勝), the head of the National Palace Museum, to Tokyo. Peng felt that we were both very honest, and decided to donate two hundred Buddha statues to the Palace Museum. During the signing of the contract between Tu and Peng, I was also present as a witness and added my signature to the contract. Now the bronze Buddha statues from Peng's collection are exhibited year-round in a hall named after him in the Museum.

Peng once told me, "Give me a little of your age!" To listen to it, one couldn't help but feel sad. At the brink of old age, anyone must feel pity about his days being numbered, about the fact that one's life, however glorious, must come to an end. However, in giving away a significant portion of his priceless collection to the National Palace Museum, Peng proved to be both wise albeit sentimental towards his country of birth. Though these Buddha statues wouldn't be passed on to his children and his grandchildren, they nonetheless allowed him to leave his mark forever on the world. So, I think he must have passed away [1] without any regret.

---

[1] Peng Kai-dong passed away on November 4, 2006, at the age of 94. In his will, he made another donation of 48 Buddha statues to the National Palace Museum.

64

In Which
Koo Chen-fu Says,
"Nevermore from Taiwan
will
There Emerge Such a
Person Again."

FORMER CHAIRMAN OF BOTH THE TAIWAN CEMENT CORPORATION and the Straits Exchange Foundation Koo Chen-fu is another person I met during my time as Representative to Japan that I greatly admire. A person with a wealth of political connections, Koo often selflessly introduced me to the person I needed for the benefit of Taiwan, and for that I'm very grateful to him.

Before I was the Representative to Japan, Koo and I had already met at an economic conference. However, because I've attended so many conferences, I can't say for certain which year we met. I only know that we met in Seoul. Koo delivered his speech in English. I was surprised that a Taiwanese of his age could speak such fluent English, so I went up to him and introduced myself. Usually unflappable, he couldn't help being shocked by my introduction, "Wow, a Taiwanese working for the United Nations?" I replied, "I've never been back to Taiwan." He didn't pursue the matter. Standing by his side was Liu Tai-ying, my junior by only one year at National Taiwan University who also studied Economics. He should have known who I was, but he didn't say anything.

A few years later, Koo, an amateur Peking opera singer, would perform Peking Opera at the Tokyo International Forum. I was very curious, so Chin-fun and I bought tickets for his show. We sat at the very back, watching his performance from afar. The next time we would meet again was after I became Taiwan's representative in Japan and we met face to face.

In April 2003, Koo received an honorary doctorate from Waseda

University. That day, Chin-fun and I went to his hotel to welcome him and his wife. We waited at first in the living room of his suite. The moment Koo stepped out to talk with us, Taiwanese came out of his mouth. I politely reminded him that his subordinates were also present in the room, would they be able to understand Taiwanese? He told me not to mind them. I found him both astute and sensitive in his judgment about human relations. He knew how to treat people of all backgrounds.

During this trip to receive his honorary doctorate, he was also invited to a special dinner party especially thrown for him by former Prime Minister Mori Yoshirō, at a famous *ryote*, Shimbashi Kanetanaka (新ばし金田中), located in Ginza. Of all the possible banquet venues, *ryoteis*, featuring *geisha* performances, is the finest. The *geishas* are in their fifties and sixties. Any *geisha* younger than them wouldn't be as good. As for the food served in the *ryotei*, it's been said they hardly fill you up. When you got back home, you'd still want to eat some ramen.

That evening, there weren't more than ten guests at dinner. Among the Taiwanese were Koo and me. Among the Japanese were two entrepreneurs and the rest were all political figures, Abe Shinzō, Fukuda Yasuo and Asō Tarō, who all eventually became Prime Ministers. The political and commercial figures present in the room were all from one generation after Koo's. Because the Japanese have a culture of respecting the elderly, everyone was polite to a fault to Koo. After the party was over, they came up to me one after another to praise Koo's stylish and refined manner of speaking.

Koo also had a very elegant approach to social matters. He told me afterwards that he would like to use the premises of the Representative Office to throw a "thank you" dinner party for Mori Yoshrō. The guests of honor would include: former Prime Ministers Kaifu Toshiki and Miyazawa Kiichi. Although the party would take place at the Representative Office, he would foot all the expenses related to it, and he would also send out the invitations himself.

We could talk about anything under the sky. The first time I

Koo Chen-fu has wealth of political connections in Japan. He often selflessly introduced Lo to the person he needed for the benefit of Taiwan.

treated him to dinner, he said, "Today's menu is first-rate." When he was twenty-two, the extremely talented Koo had done a wonderful oil painting of Mt. Guanyin. using purple and yellow colors. He presented me with a copy of this painting as a gift. In return, I wrote two poems to express my gratitude. According to his secretary, Koo turned to him after reading my poems and said, "Nevermore from Taiwan will there ever emerge such a person again."

On yet another day, I went to his office and discovered that he had a statue of Benjamin Franklin sitting on a wooden bench. Benjamin Franklin had been the founder of my alma mater, so I couldn't be more familiar with him. Mr. Koo told me that it was the souvenir given by UPenn when he received his honorary doctorate. Referring to my Ph.D, he then added, "Yours is the real deal. Mine is fake."

My time spent with Koo let me experience truly what is meant by the phrase "如沐春風" (a feeling of warmth entering the heart).

65

Being the Witness at Jason Wu's (吳季剛) Brother's Wedding

J APANESE UNIVERSITIES TYPICALLY HAVE A
DEPARTMENT FOR "Chinese Studies." "Taiwanese Studies" is
often be swept under this department, even if Taiwanese literature
itself might take up most of the course. In order to resolve this issue,
I decided to approach my alma mater Waseda to discuss setting up a
department for Taiwanese Studies. Waseda immediately assembled
a committee conducted by the President himself. External professors
and examiners were invited to weigh in too. It was affirmed by the
committee that Waseda did indeed possess the requisite conditions to

Through Lo's effort, his alma mater Waseda became the first
university in Japan to set up a department for Taiwanese Studies.

set up a department for Taiwanese Studies. The project moved along quickly. In October 2003, I personally inked the words "Department of Taiwanese Studies" in traditional calligraphy, which they turned into a plaque. Thus, the first department of Taiwanese Studies in all of Japan was born.

The first department chair Nishikawa Zyun (西川潤) was not only my classmate at Waseda, but his family had had a relationship with Taiwan for three generations. Nishikawa Zyun's grandfather Nishikawa Jun came to Taiwan before the war to look for opportunities. He would do well for himself, becoming the owner of a coal mine in Shuangxi, Taipei, as well as a Taipei Council member. Nishikawa Zyun's father, Nishikawa Mitsuru, in the post-colonial era, founded magazines dedicated to promoting local Taiwanese customs as well as literature. Among his own works were novels and poems, themed on Taiwanese culture. From his writings, you might pick out words like "媽祖" (Matsu), "台灣縱貫鐵道" (Taiwan's North-south Railway) and "秀姑巒" (Xiuguluan Mountain). In the post-colonial era, Nishikawa Mitsuru was quite a significant figure in Taiwanese literature.

Who would have expected that this Department of Taiwanese Studies would lead me to the family of US-based fashion designer Jason Wu?

After I stepped down from my post at the Representative Office, I moved back to Taipei to chair the Association of East Asian Relations. One day, a young Taiwanese man, after asking around quite a bit, found out about my connections to Waseda and came knocking on my door at the Association with the request that I write a recommendation letter for him. He was a complete stranger to me, and did not come via any intermediary. He graduated from John Hopkins University and was hoping to go to Waseda for his Master's. As I listened, I thought that even without a recommendation letter, he would probably get in by applying to Waseda directly, because John Hopkins was an excellent university. Nonetheless, I agreed to his request without much hesitation.

Four or five years later, just as this episode was going to disappear from my memory, I received a telephone call at my home. Chin-fun picked it up. The caller very politely apologized for disturbing us. She explained that she had gotten our telephone number from the wife of Ambassador Fang Chin-yen. Then she proceeded to introduce herself. "I'm Jason Wu's mother." For Barak Obama's presidential inauguration in 2008, Michelle Obama wore a dress that Jason Wu designed. It propelled the designer (who had just started out on his career) to international stardom. We, of course, knew who Jason Wu was, but since we had no connection whatsoever to the Wus, Chin-fun was still surprised by the call.

She then explained that five years ago, the overseas American student that I had recommended, Wu Chi-heng (吳季衡), was in fact Jason Wu's elder brother. Wu Chi-heng did get to Waseda in the end, and not only did he get his Master's, but he also found the love of his life there. She was his classmate Tung Hsiao-hui, a Japanese girl of Okinawan origin, whose grandfather was Taiwanese. Because of

Lo Fu-chen was invited by Jason Wu's parents to be the witness at his elder brother Wu Chi-heng's wedding.

these reasons, she hoped that I could be chief witness at Wu Chi-heng's wedding that was drawing near. I felt honored and moved to be asked. In fact, given the Wu family's celebrity status, Taiwanese political figures would be falling at their feet to perform this role. They could certainly have asked someone with connections that they might benefit from in the future. Instead, they picked who they saw as their benefactor, a retired old man, out of their simplicity.

Wu Chi-heng's parents were courteous to a fault. They first paid Chin-fun and me a visit at our home. Later, they invited me to sample the banquet dishes at the restaurant where the wedding dinner would be hosted. I found them earnest as well as honest folk.

On October 10th, 2010, Jason Wu returned to Taiwan to attend his brother's wedding at Grand Hyatt Taipei, only to be swarmed by reporters. Guests kept streaming in, filling the tables, and in the end, an additional banquet hall had to be opened to accommodate the number of guests. I saw many people rushing to take pictures with Jason Wu.

In 2012, Obama was reelected and once again at the inauguration, First Lady Michelle Obama picked another one of Jason Wu's creations to wear. Mother Wu gleefully told us, before the news had gone public, Jason had called home and said, "Mom, do you know whose dress the first lady picked to wear this time?" The answer was of course "Your son." We were thrilled and proud about his achievement as well. The children of Taiwan are indeed remarkable. It's also worth crediting their mothers. As a child, Jason Wu liked to create costumes for dolls. His mother took the leap of faith and moved with him overseas. She bought him his first sewing machine and just to allow him to actualize his potential. This was all because of his mother. I told her as much. I said her decision back then was "truly extraordinary."

66

Bringing Second Brother Up to Speed About My Life Abroad

LOOKING BACK ON MY WHOLE LIFE, I too had been recipient of an attentive mother's love. Mother dedicated her life to raise me, then selflessly let me go out into the world. She respected me and was kind to me. As an only son, I should have stayed behind to look after her when Sister married and moved to Japan. But,

Family picture with mother, sister Chao-rong, brother-in-law et al.

guided by the forces of fate, I had gotten only further and further away from her as years went by.

It wasn't that I was unaware of my Confucian duties. My leaving overseas to study after graduation was unintentionally kept me away, at first, but then I stayed away because I could no longer take being oppressed under military rule. Soon, I got blacklisted for my nonconformist views. Had I returned to do my duty by my mother, had I not been willing to turn my back on her, my own conscience and my soul, I would have been locked up in prison. So there was no choice for me but to continue drifting overseas.

Mother always held my well-being close to her heart and never once complained about my anti-Kuomintang actions overseas, nor did she ever once express any wish for Chin-fun and I to return to Taiwan to keep her company. It was not her way to burden me like that. She had a strong character. I'd never seen her cry a single tear in all my life. Occasionally, she would travel to Japan and the US to visit Sister and me, but for decades, she lived by herself in Chiayi. In October 1980, when she passed away, I received an emergency call from my old home in Chiayi. Not able to go back to take care of her funeral matters, I was numb with grief, and restless. I took the car out, and drove alone for hours on end, without any destination in mind. From Nagoya, I drove to Kyoto, made a detour to Lake Biwa and found myself in Nara, before arriving back in Nagoya. Back at home, I started to grind ink. I picked up a calligraphy brush and then slowly copied out a Heart Sutra, which I mailed to my Chiayi home the following day, with the request that someone help me burn it as an offering to my mother in Heaven. The year after mother's death, I was officially classified as a political dissident. In 1980, when I visited China as an official of the United Nations, the Overseas Community Affairs Council reported my trip to the Garrison Command Headquarters and identified me as a troublemaker. They rounded up the evidence of my 1960s involvement in the Washington protest against Japan's deportation of Liu Wen-ching and my 1970s role in chartering a plane to fly the banner bearing the words "Long Live Taiwanese Independence!" above the Williamsport stadium. I heard they even obtained a copy of my speech at the conference held at the University of Michigan in Ann Arbor.

Not only did they thoroughly investigate my background, they issued an order to freeze my assets in Chiayi. During this time, a cousin secretly helped me sell a piece of land, but the transaction wouldn't go through. The cousin then arranged for an under-the-table transaction with the buyer, and got half the money first this way.

Working for an international organization, I was respected all over the world for my expertise. I even had an entry in a Who's Who directory of famous people. To my homeland, however, I was only a dissident and a troublemaker in a dossier at a police station. Looking back now, I'm still quite speechless about the injustice.

How could I have committed treason against my own country when I was just a scholar fighting for a free and democratic Taiwan?

In fact, to realize my ambition, I spent a period of three years, between my jobs at Nagoya's United Nations Center for Regional Development and at Kuala Lumpur's Asia-Pacific Development Center, as publisher of a New York newspaper.

This was how it came about. One day, I received a call from Chang Tsan-hung, my ex-classmate at National Tainan First Senior High School and also the chair of the World United Formosans for Independence. He had raised US$120,000, he said, and he wanted to start a newspaper. I could write well, why not join him as publisher? Around this time, Wu Chi-fu's (吳基福) newspaper in San Francisco, The Far Eastern Times, had just closed down after two years and two million dollars. Starting a paper on only US$120,000 was perhaps a little too ambitious. Moreover, this money hadn't been donated by some wealthy patron. It had been collected from 2,000 patriotic overseas students, each forking out $60 they had scrimped and saved as a deposit for a year's supply of news.

These overseas drifters had pinned their hopes on a paper to expose the actual political, economic, and sociological realities facing Taiwan instead of the censored propaganda found in pro-Kuomintang publications. So I plunged right in, heady with idealism. My contract with the University of Hawaii had initially stipulated three years, but I resigned after a year to help make the paper a reality. I named it " 台灣公論報" (*Taiwan Tribune*). Taiwan Tribune would be printed in a small factory in Long Island City, New York. We rented an office housed in a large factory and bought two old typewriters on which we tapped out our articles word by word in the cramped space. Each tap was like a drumbeat, going tock tock all day.

Running Taiwan Tribune cost US$ 200,000 a year. After accounting for the subscribers' US$120,000, we still had a shortfall of $80,000. We continually needed to raise funds. I went for two years without any pay. During these two years I made plenty of withdrawals from my account, but no deposits into it. I was soon about to run dry. At the end of the second year, my eldest son Ted (Tse-hsin) was applying to college. That was when the reality of being unable to pay for his college education finally hit me. Dr. Chou Shih-ming (周炘明) stopped by to say he was willing to help out financially. I didn't want to neglect my own responsibilities as Ted's father, I turned down his kind offer. All throughout my own education, Mother had never once let me fret about school expenses. And now, my own son would have no way of paying for his college expenses. I fell into depression. In 1984, I once again packed my suitcases and headed for Malaysia to restart my economic career.

As publisher of Taiwan Tribune, I had once been sued. I had run an article alluding to the Dr. Kao Tzu-min as a dog (traitor). In retaliation, he spent US$200,000 to hire a lawyer and sued me for a sum of US$4.3 million. Seeing that the newspaper only took in US$100,000 a year, it was obvious that Kao's intention was to shut us down. Luckily, Chang Tsan-hung introduced me to former US Attorney General Ramsey Clark who defended me pro bono. Clark, who was trained as a human rights lawyer, argued that this was a case

During 1970s, WUFI core members would meet every week. They were just like brothers and sisters. Standing on the back (from right) are Lo Fu-chen, Tsai Trong-rong, Chen Lung-chi and Chou Shi-ming.

of a foreign power attacking the American civil right of free speech. In the end, we won the case.

Being able to dedicate oneself to one's ideals is a God-given blessing. I have no misgivings about my time running the newspaper. But looking at it objectively again, it was true that all was smooth sailing when I worked for other countries under the UN flag, whereas I had met only hardship when working for my own country. For decades, I was exiled. For decades, I couldn't pay my respects to my parents' graves. If my own relatives didn't come looking for me, I

Former US Attorney General Ramsey Clark (right) defended Lo Fu-chen pro bono. The day they won the case happened to be Clark's wedding anniversary. From then on, every year Lo would send Clark a bottle of wine on that day.

wouldn't look them up either for fear of causing them trouble. Even when my own blood brother, Fu-yueh, came to New York to give a sermon at a church, I didn't dare meet up with him, nor did he come to find me.

While still in high school, Fu-yueh had gained direct admission to Taipei Imperial University where he studied medicine to become a doctor. He had been my childhood idol. While he was at the university, he once wrote a letter back to Chiayi in which he mentioned that his classmates had gone out to drink and have fun. Dedicated to do well, he stayed behind on campus to study. When I left my hometown to study in Tainan, I brought this letter with me to remind me to work as hard as Second Brother.

For his Christian aspiration to serve the wider community, the middle-aged Fu-yueh also inspired respect. Not only did he set up " 福澤慈善基金會" (the Futzer Charity Foundation), he also founded a church under my biological father's name and created a hotline "生命 線" (life line) in Kaohsiung for people in dire circumstances to seek help. When a younger former Vice President Lu Hsiu-lien graduated from university, the first job she took was at this hotline in Kaoshiung founded by Fu-yueh.

After the blacklist was dissolved, I could go back to Taiwan at last and I paid a visit to Fu-yueh in Kaoshiung. By then he was already eighty years old, but his face was as serious as I still remembered it. We chatted casually. When he found out that I had worked for many years with the UN, he calmly said, "You've really made something

Lo Fu-chen has an international family. He and wife (front row, 2nd from right) reside in Taiwan. His first son Ted and family (front row, 1st, second, 3rd from left, and back row 1st on the left) live in Japan. His second son David and family (back row, 1st and 3rd from right, and front row right) live in the United States.

out of yourself!" Hearing this, I was extremely moved. Between my departure as a twenty-something student and my return at the brink of sixty, more than thirty years had elapsed, during which most of my elders had died. Among my family, nobody had known what I'd done beyond the fact that I had been blacklisted. At that moment, to be able to hear these words from Second Brother, I felt relieved. Now my many years in exile, spent traveling here and there, were known at last to my Taiwanese family.

Best of all, I was finally back in Taiwan.

All these decades, circling the globe again and again, I was unable to return to the country of my birth. While I was abroad, I saw the same moon as the one seen in Taiwan but yet it was not in a Taiwanese sky. For all that I have seen and experienced in my exciting career, I know my success and my reputation will eventually be forgotten. Perhaps it just matters that I'm back and that I can finally stand on my own soil now. And even if it just means I can enjoy a bowl of danzai noodles once more, why not? I am just happy to be back.

Chronicles of Lo Fu-chen

1935— May 8th: Born in Sakae-Machi, Chiayi, Tawian.

1936— January 1st: Adopted by Lo Cheng (Lo Chang-cheng according to family genealogy).

1941— March 17th: Biological elder brother Fu-hui died.

Went to Tokyo with Mother, and started attending Unoki kindergarten.

1942— Entered elementary school. Witnessed US's first air raid on Tokyo.

1944— As a third grader, retreated with school to Funabara Hotel, Izu Peninsula's hot spring resort to evade war-fire.

1945— April: Owing to US's heavy air raid on Tokyo on March 10, transferred to Saitama Prefecture as a fourth grader.

1946— February: Came back to Taiwan from Japan.

1948— Graduated from Chuei Yang Elementary School, Chiayi City.

1950— Biological father Lo Ya died at the age of 60.

1951— Graduated from Chiayi Junior High School.

1954—	Graduated from Tainan First High School.
1958—	Graduated from National Taiwan University's Economics Department.
	Performed military service as a naval reserve officer at Tsoying, Kaohsiung City.
1960—	April: Finished military service and left navy.
	Wrote an article to Free China (magazine) under the pen name "Guest of Nanshan Hut," criticizing Chiang Kai-shek's third term President as unconstitutional.
	June 19: Became sworn brother with 42 friends (including Huang Kun-hu, Chai Trong-rong et al.) at Guanzihling's Ching Ler Resort Hotel in Tainan Prefecture.
	August 3: Went to Japan and enrolled in Waseda University's Graduate School of Politics and Economics.
1962—	June 15: Married Ms. Mao Chin-fun, who was studying at Waseda's Graduate School of History.
1963—	Received Master's degree from Waseda University.
	August: Went to the US for further study at University of Pennsylvania.

| 1964— | Was elected as president of Taiwanese Association of Greater Philadelphia, and became a member of the United Formosa for Independent (UFI) against KMT Regime in Taiwan. |

September: Received Master's degree from UPenn.

| 1966— | July 4th: United Formosans in America for Independence (UFAI) was officially established under his initiation in Philadelphia, and he became a member of its central committee. |

October: First son, Ted (Tse-hsin), was born.

| 1968— | Received PhD of Regional Science from UPenn. |

Summer: Started working at Consad, a New York based consulting company, as a researcher.

October: Moved the whole family to Pittsburg owing to Consad's relocation.

| 1969— | March: Visited Dr. Edwin O. Reschauer (Harvard professor and ex-US ambassador to Japan) and described to him his Taiwan independence ideal. |

| 1970— | January: Consolidated Taiwan independent group in Japan, USA, Canada, Europe and Taiwan, World United Formosans for Independence (WUFI) was founded, and Lo became its central committee member. |

Second son, David, was born.

1971—	September: Student organizations that took part in the Protect-Diaoyu (Senkaku) Islands movement held a "national affairs discussion" conference at the Universtiy of Michigan at Ann Arbor. Lo was the only one representing Taiwan independence camp.
1972—	August: Went to Williamsport to root for Taiwan's Little League baseball team, got beaten up by Chinese naval divers and came back with broken glasses and an injured hand.
1973—	May: Went to Nagoya, Japan as UNCRD's chief of International Comparative Studies.
	Started ¥50,000 monthly donation to WUFI-Japan headquarters until 1980.
1974—	First encounter with the third world-visited the Philippines and initiated Combined Regional Development Training Course at UNCRD.
1975—	Co-authored a book with Kamal Salih entitled "Growth Pole Strategy and Regional Development Policy: Asian Experiences and Alternative Approaches" printed six editions by Pergamon Press, which got picked up and used as textbooks by Universities such as Harvard and M.I.T., and served as his calling card into the international academic field.
	Initiated Regional Development Training Course in Java, Indonesia.
	Employed by UNDP and went to India as economic advisor.

1976— Invited by Pakistan
government to organize a
regional development training
course. It was his first visit to
an Islamic country in south
Asia.

August 20th: Biological mother, Lo Chu Lian, passed away.

1977— Held regional development training course in Nakhon
Ratchasima, Thailand.

In addition to his regular job, took up volunteer work as
Amnesty International-Japan's board member, and helped
pass the Philippines political prisoner, Benigno Aquino Jr.'s
letters written in jail to AI's headquarters in London.

1978— Employed by UNDP to go to Iran as an Economic
consultant.

1980— November 19th: Was invited to visit China for half month.

May: Visited south Korea as the World Bank's consultant
and witnessed the Gwangju Incident.

October 10th: Adoptive mother Chen Chou (also known as
Chen Tseng-yen) passed away.

1981— January: Became senior researcher at the East-West Center's
Population Research Institute,
and also taught part-time at its
Economics and Geography
Departments.

July 31st: Became nominal
publisher of the newly initiated
Taiwan Tribune in New York.

1982—	February: Resigned from the East-West Center and became the full time publisher of Taiwan Tribune, in New York. Got listed in "Who's Who in World."
1983—	November 9th: Testified in Senate Committee on Foreign Relations concerning the Future of the People on Taiwan. On November 14th US senate passed <u>S. Resolution 74</u>.
1984—	September: Invited by Malaysia's Asian Pacific Develop Center (APDC) to be the chief of International Trade and Economic Cooperation Research.
	October 17th: Ex-councilman of Oversea Chinese Community Council, Dr. Kao Tzu-min, brought suit against *Taiwan Tribune* for libel. With help from former US Attorney General Ramsey Clark (who defended him *pro bono*), he won the case.
1986—	June 20th: Participated in the "International Conference of Newly Restored Democracies" in the Philippines and visited President Mrs. Aquino with Tsai Trong-rong.
	November 12th: Organized an international conference, "The Asian Pacific Economy Towards the Year 2000," at Beijing's Great Hall of the People. China's premier Zhao Zi-yang came to deliver the opening speech.
1988—	February: Collaborated with the director of Pakistan's Economic Development Research Institute and visited north Pakistan where East and West culture intersect, and ancient city Peshawar where Arabian world and south Asia culture mingled.
	May: Organized "Global Adjustments and the Future of Asian-Pacific Economy" conference at Tokyo, and collaborated with the renowned Japanese economist Shinohara Miyohei in compiling the English conference theses collection afterwards.

1989— November: Organized "The Future of Asian Pacific Economy: Contribution from Asian Economy and ASEAN" conference at Bankok.

1990— January: Appointed a new position as Senior Academic Officer and later as Deputy Director of UN University's Institute of Advanced Studies.

June: Went to China's Beijing University to give lectures.

Started monthly donation of ¥100,000 to WUFI-Japan headquarters until 2004.

1991— March: The fourth and last Asian Pacific Economic Forum he organized before his retirement from APDC was held in New Delhi.

1992— July 17th: Invited to attend an international conference on Applied Regional Science at Academia Sinica in Taiwan and came back to Taiwan after 31 years. The "political blacklist" was no longer a barrier at long last by President Lee Teng-hui.

1993— August: Arranged for UN's Under-Secretaries-General and Rector of UN University, Heitor Gurgulino de Souza, to secretly visit Taiwan and discussed the possibility of setting up an "UNU Environmental Institute" in Taiwan.

2000— April 30th: Retired from his UN position.

2001— May: Appointed as Taiwan's top representative to Japan (a position equivalent to ambassador, since Taiwan has no formal diplomatic relationship with Japan).

2004— April: Former Taiwan president Lee Teng-hui visited Japan for medical treatment in Okayama — a great diplomatic breakthrough between Taiwan and Japan.

2007— September: Served my 4-year term as top representative to Japan and came back to Taiwan to chair the Association of East Asian Relations, an organization under Ministry of Foreign Affairs.

September: Fully retired.

List of Lo Fu-chen's Major Academic Works[1]

Fu-chen Lo & Kamal Salih (ed.), *Growth Pole Strategy and Regional Development Policy: Asian Experiences and Alternative Approaches*, Pergamon Press, Oxford, 1978.

Fu-chen Lo, *Rural-Urban Relation and Regional Development*, Maruzen Asia, Singapore, 1981.

Fu-chen Lo, *Asian and Pacific Economy Towards the Year 2000*, APDC, Kuala Lumpur, 1987.

_____ & Shinohara Miyohei (ed.), *Global Adjustments and the Future of Asian-Pacific Economy*, PMC Publication, Tokyo, 1989.

_____ & Narongchai Akrasance (ed.), *The Future of Asia-Pacific Economies: Emerging Role of Asian NIEs & ASEAN*, Allied Publishers, New Delhi, 1992.

_____ , Lawrence R. Klein & Warwick J. McKibbin (ed.), *Arms Reduction: Economic Implications in the Post-Cold War Era*, UN University Press, Tokyo, 1994.

---

1 Lo Fu-chen's academic works are listed in http://www.worldcat.org/identities/lccn-n78-6628. From 1960 to 2011, his works all listed in 120 publications in 4 languages, as well available at 4709 libraries over the world.

_____, Ronald J. Fuchs, Ellen Brennan, Joseph Chamie & Juha I. Uitto (ed.), *Mega-City Growth and the Future*, UN University Press, Tokyo, 1994.

_____ & Lawrence R. Klein (ed.), *Modelling Global Change*, UN University Press, Tokyo, 1995.

_____ & Yue-man Yeung (ed.), *Emerging World Cities in Pacific Asia*, UN University Press, Tokyo, 1996.

_____ & Yue-man Yeung (ed.), *Globalization and the World of Large Cities*, UN University Press, Tokyo, 1998.

_____ & Yu-qing Xing (ed.), *China's Sustainable Development Framework: Summary Report*, Omega Publications, Tokyo, 1999.

_____, Tsuneyuk Morita & Shishido Shuntaro (ed.), *The Sustainable Future of the Global System I: Issues, Models and Prospects*, UNU Institute of Advanced Studies, Tokyo, 1999.

_____, Kazuo Matsushita & Hiroki Takagi (ed.), *The Sustainable Future of the Global System II*, UNU Institute of Advanced Studies & IGES Japan, Tokyo, 1999.

_____, Hiroyasu Tokuda & N.S. Cooray (ed.), *UN's Institute of Advanced Studies & UNESCO Research Institute*, Tokyo & Paris, 2000.

_____ & Peter J. Marcotullio (ed.), *Globalization and the Sustainability of Cities in the Asia Pacific Region*, UN University Press, Tokyo, 2001.